TABLE OF CONTENTS

TABLE OF CONTENTS CONTINUED

A Starter Guide to College for Clueless Students & Parents

For a State College or the Ivy League: Here's What You Need to Know

By Jake D. Seeger

Published by Starter Guides, LLC

Information Charts, Lists & Tables

☞ Chapter 1 ✍

General Topics

The Starter Guide covers the basics and has details on the full range of college topics, including some of the fine print.

A checklist is provided for each year of high school. Use the application checklist for each college and the other tracking forms.

It is a reference book for these many details for when you need them. Use some chapters now, and come back to other chapters later, even in a year or more. The next pages provide previews.

Students: Vital topics are covered to make better decisions for your future.

Parents: Find out what needs to be done. Make a plan. Give your student this book and say, "Check it out."

This book provides guidance and specific information for all parts of the college selection and application process.

What About a Community College First?

Or a State University?

Or a Private College?

How Do You Decide?

Let's get you through the basics, into detailed information, and point you in the right direction. Is a selective college affordable or realistic for you? Don't count it out yet. Can you get a great degree without huge debt? Sure, that's possible.

Here are some of the topics covered in this book:

- How to be college-ready
- Benefits of community colleges
- Selective admissions factors and expectations
- Activities and internships
- Practice and test prep for tests and things to do for tests
- Financial aid and cost comparisons
- Essays and interviews
- Timelines, deadlines, early applications and regular applications

After knowing more, students and parents can better review and discuss these factors to decide if college is indeed the best option, and if so, what type of college is best and together can make a plan.

Let's Get Started.

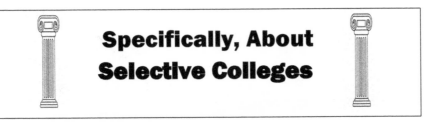

Specifically, About Selective Colleges

Could You Meet the Requirements, If You Really Tried?

Many bright students from working-class families could meet higher entrance requirements, but they don't know, so they don't get started early and thus end up ineligible.

Students, can you get As and Bs, if you really try? Can you take harder classes? If so, the top 50 to the top 100 colleges all have openings.

Did You Know
That the Ivy League is Affordable
For Working Class Families?

When a working-class student gets into a selective college, a lot of the cost may be paid for by the college (p. 239). For a very low-income household, such as when only one parent has income at $15 an hour, $30,000 annually, the average Ivy League net cost is about $7,000 a year *including room and board*, (p. 325).

At some generous private colleges, a family making $55,000 a year might pay $12,000 a year (including room and board), lower than costs at a flagship state college. Many selective colleges offer significant aid on a sliding scale to households with income on up to $125,000, or more, and typical assets (p. 239).

Do you think you could make it there, if you could just get in? This book helps you realistically examine your chances.

A Lot of People Pay Regular Price, But See What's Possible

Many of us end up paying regular prices for college. Even with aid, the costs can be substantial.

Still, a student should find out about scholarships and financial aid, based on his or her specific situation.

A hard-working student with potential should know what is possible. Find out. Don't be the one saying, "I didn't know."

Then, if one must pay regular price, so be it. A lot of people do so. No college guidebook will change that. Even without any aid, one can lower costs a lot with smart choices, such as using a community college or an in-state public college.

Still, getting good grades is not wasted effort. Students who worked hard in trying for scholarships, yet were turned down, are better prepared to finish a degree and excel in a career.

Let's not apologize for pointing out that serious work is required for any success, and that no result is guaranteed. You want guarantees? Sorry, but no.

If you don't try, you won't get there. That is guaranteed.

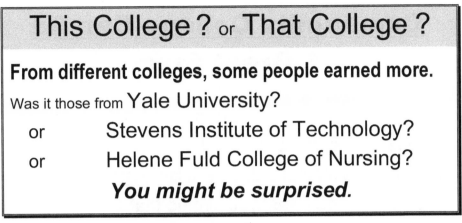

This College ? or That College ?

From different colleges, some people earned more.

Was it those from Yale University?

or   Stevens Institute of Technology?

or   Helene Fuld College of Nursing?

You might be surprised.

These figures are from College Scorecard.(See pages 46-47.)[1]

Stevens Institute of Technology (NJ) $ 87,300
is ahead of

Helene Fuld College of Nursing (NY) $ 85,600
is ahead of

Yale University $ 83,200

in an earnings survey of enrolled students who used federal loans or aid (pp. 41-47).

This shows that many regular colleges produce very good results for people, in case one doesn't get into Yale, which is, quite often, the case.

Here's Something: It's More the Student, Than the College

Credible research shows that ambitious individuals from regular colleges earn the exact same income as similar ambitious individuals from fancy colleges. Let's repeat that: The difference in income was zero between colleges. Evidence shows it is more the student, than the college[2] (p. 44). Just so you know.

Yes, try for different colleges, but don't worry to excess about *this* college over *that* college. Excel wherever you go.

Community College Can Be A Great Start

Did you know that you can start at the community college and end up with a bachelor's degree, and continue to a master's degree, a law degree, a medical degree or a PhD? Yes, you can do that.

If you can't afford a four-year college, start at a community college, some of which offer four-year degrees.

Still want to get out of your hometown? Great community colleges are in big cities, in the countryside, in the mountains or near the ocean (p. 104).

A community college can offer smaller class sizes, accessible professors, and an honors society for you to meet serious students. With careful planning, you can transfer the credits to a private or public four-year college.

Work, and pay as you go. If it takes longer, so what? A degree is still a degree. Less debt is less debt, too, isn't it? No debt is even better. Continue forward, even to a PhD.

If later you still want to try for a selective college, you'll need a great record, but you can apply as a transfer student for a bachelor's program. Santa Monica College students, for example, transfer to UCLA. Virginia Community College System students transfer to the University of Virginia (p. 97 and p. 101).

Low-Income Families:

Your State College May Help.

Here's one example: Students from families making around $30,000 annually (one parent at $15 an hour) or less might get extra financial aid from a state college, not just a private one.

Your community colleges and state colleges might have aid for low-income students. Some aid is based on low income alone. Some aid may be based on low income combined with high academics. Some aid is based on high academics alone, for which low-income students can compete equally with anyone else.

A community college combined with a regional college might cost a lot less than the main state colleges for the same degree. With federal Pell grants of up to $5,900 per year, low-income students might find this option more affordable, especially when living with family. Extra local aid, state aid or merit aid could lower costs further. But to find out, families have to apply.

Will parents or guardians fill out *all* the forms? Will students start early to get the best grades that they can? Find out what is possible (p. 111).

☞ **Chapter 2** ✍

A Story Tells a Lot

Facts are fine. Stories turn facts into life, so here are two students' stories. The starter guide begins on page 29.

Let's start with the true-life stories of two working-class high school students whose recent experiences led me to compile this book. The first student's story is about his path to college. I know this student and his family personally. I followed his progress and helped with the process many times. The account is from my observations and my interviews with the student and parents.

Another student from the same high school did not go to college. His story is on page 28.

Parents and students will learn from the stories.

The stories are both encouraging.

<u>One Student's Story</u>

Go to College?
Yeah, the University of Arizona
Or . . . ?

Freshman Year

Two working-class parents told their son, who was a bright student, that he could be successful, but they wouldn't pamper him or pressure him. They asked if he would prepare to apply to top colleges.

I'll refer to the student as John, not his real name, for his privacy. This story's details are factual.

His transcript with test scores is on page 326. Conversations quoted were observed by me or reported to me by the student or the parents.

In freshman year, John was highly skeptical that the type of advice in this book would make a difference for him.

He was in a working-class high school of about 750 students in a small town in Arizona (11,000 population), surrounded by cotton fields and dairy farms. The senior class had 166 students. Among these families, top colleges weren't brought up, except, it seemed, by John's parents. One parent said, "Face it, *our* kids don't go to Harvard."

The students, however, benefited from an upstanding new principal who added a wide range of advanced and IB classes, for the few who would take them. Mom and Dad asked John to take the hardest classes, to which he agreed, as easy schoolwork bored him.

He played freshman basketball. He played video games every night and all day long on non-school days. He read sports magazines, not books. He watched sports, and not much else.

His parents told him that if he studied more, the Ivy League was possible. John said, "That'll never happen. I'm going to Arizona," the

16

University of Arizona in Tucson, an hour and a half drive away

They agreed that Arizona was a great option. Even starting at the community college was smart. But what if one of the more selective colleges was an option? "That'll *never* happen," John said definitively.

Good Grades and Lots of Video Games

John prided himself on completing every homework assignment every day. Then he played hours and hours of video games.

He got As in three classes with the advanced designation and a 100 in regular algebra and a 98 in regular geometry. The one B was an 89 in Spanish, so he missed all As by one point. It was a great start.

The dad visited the teachers and the counselor to enlist them in this quest to an elite college. The teachers agreed to push John. The counselor, however, quickly settled on the local community college which gave free tuition to local students with good grades. Yes, free tuition for two years is rare and outstanding offer. With four years to go, however, the parents wanted John to prepare for the top colleges. What's the harm in trying? The counselor insisted on the local community college. "CAC: That's the ticket," he said. While they were thinking Cornell or Yale, he was dead set on Central Arizona Community College.

Dad and Mom both pressed John on his grades. Could he lay off the video games a few hours, at least, to work on Spanish? How about a 90 for an A, not another 89 for a B? Well, the kid definitely improved his video game skills but not his Spanish grade. He got an 83. He also dropped to an 87 in English, but the rest were As.

Sophomore Year

Activities and Mostly As

John kept up As in the advanced classes, and got another B in Spanish, an 88. Second semester, he got an A in Spanish, squeaking in at 90, his first report card with all As.

Mom and Dad did not have a complete college plan. John's only plan was to go to Arizona. John took no practice standardized tests. Nothing extra was lined up for sophomore summer.

John was on the varsity basketball team, which was one good activity. The parents prodded him for extra activities, so he signed up for science club. What about a regular class on campus at the University of Arizona? That would look good. They paid the $100 application fee for a non-degree student. One early-evening class fit his schedule. It was $1,200. But, after two car repairs and a house AC repair, the money for the UA course was gone. They skipped it.

Junior Year

Junior Year, October: The PSAT/NMSQT®ᴬ exam

This year, all John's courses had an advanced designation. He did well, getting a 96 in Physics and a 96 in Pre-Calculus, yet Spanish was a B again, an 86. Second semester was all As, with a 96 in Physics. Overall, his grades looked very good.

John took the PSAT/NMSQT®* exam after a miscue where he signed up and took the ACT® exam by mistake. The plan had been to concentrate on the SAT®ᴮ exam, by taking the PSAT/NMSQT®* exam as practice. John hadn't studied or practiced for either test. The ACT® exam score wasn't great. The PSAT/NMQST®* exam score wasn't great. The parents started to worry a bit.

Junior Year, January: A Good Internship

The father suggested an internship. John agreed. They went to the University of Arizona science buildings and visited the offices. John found an assistant professor who agreed to put him to work on Saturdays helping on a thermal conductivity research project. He measured reactions of different compounds to liquid nitrogen and

---

ᴬ*The PSAT/NMSQT® is a trademark registered by the College Board and the National Merit Scholarship Corporation, which are not involved with the production of, and do not endorse, this product.

ᴮ SAT® is a trademark registered by the College Board which is not involved in the production of, and does not endorse, this product.

recorded the results. He was a research intern with the University of Arizona Aerospace Engineering Laboratory.

The dad brought up Boys State, a respected program about government. After showing interest, John was selected.

Junior Year, March: Meeting College Staff

The family went to an information session for the University of Chicago. John explained to his parents what a complete, stupid waste of time it would be and tried repeatedly to talk them out of going, but they insisted. They had him wear a tie, which he also explained was stupid. John and the parents had an extended conversation with the college admissions officer. She said that John's grades in the harder classes were good enough, and that she thought the internship helped. The representative said it was possible for John to get in. Driving home, Mom and Dad were excited. John wasn't. He was highly skeptical he could get into such an elite college. "It's not happening," he said.

During a visit to Grandma's house in Los Angeles, John and the father visited UCLA and Occidental College. John really had not wanted to go, but his dad insisted. "It'll be fun." "Yeah, sure."

At UCLA, they spoke with a junior who was working at the admissions information desk. He said that the competition was strong. Many applicants had full research papers and lots of college credit. The junior said that some working-class kids do make it in, citing his own example. Dad and John walked among the students on campus, going into buildings, resting in study halls. They also walked around the Occidental campus, as the father wanted John to see a small college environment. John said he liked a large campus.

Another time, Grandma took John to a California Institute of Technology (CalTech) prospective student session, which John said consisted of 200 really nerdy kids, except, of course, him.

After interaction with people from higher-ranking colleges, John was still adamant most of the time that selective colleges were a pipe dream, but less so, the parents noticed. His resistance was less. He would use the word "maybe" once in a while.

His GPA was very good, ranking him third in his class of about 160 students. The two girls ahead of him, as he told the story, lived and died for As, which he said he refused to do.

Junior Year, Summer Break: Some Activities

At Boys State he met ambitious boys who talked about their activities and about different colleges. He met students who were aiming high, and providing competition. "I need more on my resume," he said.

He continued working at the university lab.

With prodding, John took a few practice standardized tests from a library book, timing himself, sitting at the kitchen table. In math, he cracked a 700 score, the elite college range. "See," mom told him, "you can do this." "It's not going to happen," John replied.

All summer, he practiced basketball every day for four hours as next season he would be the starting center. But mostly, he played video games and watched TV sports. For variety, he went to sleepovers, where they played video games and watched TV sports.

At this point, he was behind what many college advisers recommend, such as taking a standardized test at the end of junior or having practiced extensively on such tests.

Senior Year

Senior Year, September: A New Counselor and a Big Mistake

The mother visited John's new high school counselor and showed her John's high practice test scores. The counselor agreed that it was appropriate to advise John that a selective school was possible, as his grades and latest practice test scores were in the proper range, even for the Ivies. So, the parents hadn't been completely nuts after all.

For senior year, John selected the harder advanced classes.

The parents and John started files with checklists for each college.

Then they realized they had forgotten that selective schools require

SAT Subject Tests™.[C] At this late date, that would use up one of his chances to take the SAT test. Oops. He also should have taken the history test right after junior year when the material was fresh. He never liked history anyway. Oops.

Senior Year, October: The First SAT Test: Not So Great

His first official SAT test was October. John still insisted most of the time that a selective college was impossible. He worked on vocabulary practice only because his mom and dad kept checking the words on his app.

The Friday night before the test, the parents had to go to sleep early due to their varied work hours. Mom had worked her overnight shift as a nurse assistant and Dad had to get up at 4 am for a breakfast shift as a hotel waiter. Before going to bed, the father stressed to John *not to stay up late*. In the morning, he said, eat some breakfast and have a cola or some coffee to be alert. "Sure thing," John replied. In the morning, Mom took him to the test.

Later, the scores came in. Hitting 700 or better out of 800 possible in each section was the goal. He got a 640 reading, 620 math and 660 writing, below his ability. What had happened?

Well . . . He admitted that he had stayed up until 3:00 am playing video games. He didn't eat breakfast. He didn't have a coffee on the way over. He hadn't brought a jacket, so he was almost shivering in the cold testing room. In his mind, he was going to the University of Arizona with no scholarship possibilities, so the test didn't matter. He hadn't taken it seriously. He didn't give a rip.

An early-decision application would be due Nov. 1, but with John's lower scores, he might be turned down, so they skipped it.

Senior Year, November: More Tests? Really? Do I Have To?

John really did not want to take two subject tests, as he didn't need them for Arizona. Applying to other colleges was a stupid waste of time,

---

[C] SAT Subject Test™ is a trademark owned by the College Board, which is not involved in the production of, and does not endorse, this product.

he said. The parents insisted, "You *are* applying to other schools." He studied very little, griping the whole time. He got 660 on one test and 640 on the other, which are respectable scores, but 700 or higher is seen at the more elite colleges. At least the requirement was met.

Another SAT exam was ahead. The parents had him do vocabulary apps on his smartphone. "Be fastidious, not feckless," Dad joked. (This was a pre-2016 test, which included more obscure vocabulary words.)

They bought The Official SAT Study Guide™[D], insisting on some practice tests. As he went over wrong answers, John could see that getting more answers correct was possible. Doing all that schoolwork had prepared him better than he had expected. The test was not so impenetrable, after all. He saw that he could do better.

Midterm grades were all As. The team made the state playoffs.

Senior Year, December: More SAT Test Scores: Getting Better

The December SAT exam scores were 600 reading, 630 writing and 720 math. Wow, he had a score in one subject that cracked the 700 mark. Mom showed him on an Ivy League college website that a 720 score and his GPA were in the college's range of admitted students. He had to concede that it was a possibility.

He had one more test to go, the January SAT exam. (Some years no January tests are offered.)

A huge amount of time went to the applications. They had started filling out applications to 16 colleges. The fees had to be paid, about $50 for each college. The parents would pay for all of them, about $800, though it was a strain, since the father's income as a hotel waiter dropped a lot in the off-season, with no paycheck at all many weeks.

They hadn't planned well. "Let's use a credit card if we have to," the mother said. The family income was above the level for an automatic fee waiver.

Later, they visited the counselor to double check things. She asked about the fees to so many colleges. "It's a lot, but we think we should

---

[D] The Official SAT Study Guide™ is a trademark owned by the College Board, which is not involved in the production of, and does not endorse, this product.

pay. This is his one chance," Mom said. The counselor checked further and was told that the colleges do not want a fee to prevent any application that is not frivolous from being filed. As the counselor, she could attest to a hardship waiver, which was granted.

Senior Year, January 1: The Applications Are In!

John finished 11 applications, using a lot of the holiday break to finish. Applications went to:

University of Arizona	Arizona State University
Brown University	University of Chicago
Cornell University	Harvard College
University of Illinois (Engineering)	University of Pennsylvania
Stanford University	University of Virginia
Washington University of St. Louis	

Six other applications had been planned for, but had errors:

University of California at Irvine and
University of California at Los Angeles
(They forgot that the California state deadline was Nov. 1.)
CalTech (They forgot about a required science test.)
Massachusetts Institute of Technology
(They forgot about a required science test.)
Yale College (They missed the deadline by one day.)
Columbia University in the City of New York (No essay.)

He was done late the night of January 1. "That's it. I'm finished." Too tired to write another essay, he cancelled the Columbia application. "So much for New York City," he said.

His parents were proud of him for his efforts, regardless of what the outcome might be and they let him know it. The final SAT test John could submit to the colleges was on January 25th. He took more practice tests. He went over wrong answers.

Low scores so far		Best scores so far	
Math	620	Math	720
Reading	600	Reading	640
Writing	630	Writing	660

SAT exam scores are from 200 to 800 per section. Scores for those who are accepted at very elite colleges are mostly 700s, but many are in the 600s and a few 599s are taken (p.206).

Mom, Dad and the counselor advised John to take the last test very seriously.

This time, John was in full agreement.

Later, he said that after everything, including the huge process of sending in 11 applications, he had taken this last test very seriously. From practice, he had seen that correct answers were possible. His mindset had been to get every single question right.

His parents had been right all along, not just goofy optimists. He had been to some campuses and had met some admissions people. He had known he had an important opportunity before him.

The January scores were 740 in math, 710 in reading and 570 in writing. A 740 and a 710 were very good. He'd done well on his last test.

The final lineup of best scores, which most colleges use, was:

Math   740   Reading   710   Writing   660

John's scores and GPA were within the lower ranges of the selective schools he had applied to. For some colleges, he was in the midranges. He had some extra activities. It was still a long shot, as it is for about anyone, but he had given himself a chance.

Afterward, he told his dad, "Guess what was on one question? Feckless." They'll both remember that.

Mom and Dad had missed early test practice, tutoring, summer camps and application deadlines. John had been far from perfect, missing straight As, due to too much goofing off. At first, he didn't take the tests seriously, refusing to study extra at all. Regarding applications, he should have started sooner on just about everything.

They also, however, had done a lot of the basics correctly and had done a lot of extra things. John took advanced courses from his first semester of freshman year through senior year. Toward the end, Mom and Dad got practice tests and John did them. They visited campuses. They met people from top colleges.

The parents explained the difference between scholarships and student debt; between a $30,000 starting job and a $60,000 starting job.

John knew that he had a lot to gain by getting into a top college.

Interviews

John arranged two interviews. Brown did an alumni interview over the phone. The University of Chicago (UChicago) offered applicants an in-person interview with a senior UChicago student at the college.

After a Friday night playoff game, a one-possession loss to the eventual state champions, John took a budget flight to Chicago, staying at an uncle's house.

His team lost a state championship run, but on the bright side, he had an interview at one of the world's top universities.

In the interview, John thought that he and the UChicago senior had a decent rapport. He asked about the harder academics. He had seen a T-shirt, "UChicago, Where Fun Goes to Die." She said the work was difficult, but doable, if one were ready for it.

They filled out all the financial forms. Finally, everything that could be done, had been done. It was time to wait.

Senior Year, March: The Responses: Not So Good at First

The first college to reply was:
Harvard College	No

Then,
Brown University	No
University of Pennsylvania	No

> Three of the four Ivy League schools he applied to had said no. Oh, well, he had tried.

Then,
Washington University (St. Louis)	No
Stanford University	No

All the top colleges so far were no's. Things weren't looking so good.

But ... Then ...

University of Arizona	Yes

> It offered merit aid of $9,500 a year, most of the in-state tuition. Wow.

Arizona State University (ASU)	Yes

> ASU matched Arizona's scholarship. A great offer.

The relatives were called about ASU and Arizona, both in the top 100 worldwide in some rankings, with low in-state tuition and each with a good scholarship. It might be U of A after all, but with a scholarship!

Then,

> University of Virginia   Yes
>> One of the best U.S. public universities, and with a large financial aid offer.
>
> Cornell University   Yes
>> Cornell, of the vaunted Ivy League, said yes. Wow. The Ivy League. And with a lot of the costs covered. Wow.

All the relatives got another call. Then,

> University of Illinois (Engineering)   No
>> A very elite program said no.
>
> University of Illinois (Liberal Arts)   Yes
>> But, the math program said yes.
>
> University of Chicago   Yes
>> UChicago has had more Nobel Prize winners as students and professors than any other university in the world. It offered significant aid.

What Mattered Most?

What were the factors for the rejections and the acceptances? Though not perfect, his grades and scores were very good.

Maybe a bad phone interview nixed him at Brown and a good interview helped at UChicago. With no direct contact with Cornell or Virginia, they said yes, while others said no.

What mattered most? We just don't know.

See how the admissions process is? It's a jumbled-up set of factors. Even after you get in, you might not know what happened for sure.

The story shows that even with many miscues, disagreements, arguments, mistakes and rejections, a student and parents who do a lot of things right can receive some great offers.

I'll respect John's privacy by not indicating his choice, but he is working diligently and succeeding. Which is pretty good for a kid who had lived across from cotton fields in rural Arizona.

Who Had Believed It Was Possible Freshman Year?

And who had believed it was possible, freshman year in high school? Two hopeful parents did. They didn't give up and helped their child forward, despite mistakes along the way. The student had his ups and downs, but made a solid effort in total, and at the end especially.

The Exception? Perhaps

John's story may be an exception to a lot of other students' stories. Selective colleges can only accept some of the eligible applicants. Most colleges have limited scholarship funds. Some states are increasing aid, but a lot of U.S. students will pay regular prices at community colleges or state colleges. Private colleges may defray some costs, but significant costs remain for a lot of students. Yet, students have an ever-increasing array of options for education after high school, many of which are comparatively affordable, from trade programs at community colleges to regional colleges, to honors programs at regional and flagship state universities.

Now, please read another student's story on the next page.

Another Story:

The Student Who Did Not Go to College

Another student from our story's same high school took a different path. He deserves recognition for his accomplishments. This student, Chris, who was an acquaintance of John's, was a C student, at best. John told me about Chris because John was so impressed with how Chris handled himself.

Chris had a great work ethic, working for wages every day after school bagging groceries, while most other guys sat in front of video games. On weekends, he worked for his uncle, who owned a handyman service. Chris saved his earnings. He didn't buy new clothes, eat out or party. He bought a basic used car for cash. By graduation he had a pretty decent savings account, which he is building further with full-time work.

He isn't making payments on a new ride, but still driving his paid-for car. He may buy a modest house, but he sure won't rent an expensive place. He's building an investment fund. (It takes money to make money.) He is not going to college. He plans, with his uncle as a partner, to fix up working-class housing for resale and for rentals. "Chris will be rich one day," John predicted.

Not everyone has to go to college to gain financial stability and a good retirement.

Though it is far from the most important measure of a life lived well, let's ask who will end up with more wealth? It might be the kid who bagged the groceries over the kid who got into the elite college. Which will be just fine with both of them.

☞ Chapter 3 ✍

Career, Training & Education Options

Four Years of College is *Not* Your Only Option. There's More. There's Less.

Students, this isn't just about signing you up for a college, selecting a major, checking on some financial aid, and sending you off. There's a lot more to think over. Your educational and career decisions will be based on academic ability, personal potential, income, career goals, job markets, risk and many other things. This chapter mixes things together to present some scenarios. Some statistics are provided.

Standard Routes to Career Employment

About 43% of adults have one type of college degree.[3] Thus, about 6 out of 10 U.S. adults now go through life with no college degree. Routes to employment or business income include:

- Start at the entry level in a company or in a particular field and advance, with training on the job.
- Join a family or friend's business, or start a business.
- Get a one-year certificate or two-year degree from a community college or trade school, or a union apprenticeship and then work.
- Get a four-year college degree, (perhaps with transfer credits from a community college) and then start working.
- Join the military; as an enlisted person or with a bachelor's degree as an officer.
- Get a master's degree and start working.
- Get a PhD, medical degree or law degree and start working.

One can mix things around.

- One can work for a while, then attend college.

- A gap year program, which many colleges offer, allows students to be accepted to college, take a gap year, working, interning or traveling, and then start college.

- Get a two-year degree and work a while.

- Then get the four-year degree and work a while.

- Then get a master's degree, if it helps your career.

- Stretch it out. If you take a few years longer, to work and stay debt free, that is smart. As long as you don't give up, the degree will come. This option, however, should be compared to finishing in four years, which gets you into full-time work at a higher salary sooner. People successfully use either option.

- Understand what it will take to get a bachelor's degree. About one out of three students who start do not finish in six years.

Education is Open to All in the U.S.

Training and education of some type is open for anyone.

- Trade programs and union apprenticeships can lead to solid careers. Consider a lower-cost public program at the community college for the trades, or a union apprenticeship. Union apprenticeships pay you wages for parts of the program while you learn. You might have to wait to get in at some programs, or you may head to another region or state if more openings are elsewhere, but these programs are affordable. The accreditation for a public college is the same as for an expensive for-profit one. Sure, a for-profit college or training program has lenders ready with a loan; and will start you right away; and will promise a job, but watch out. They cost a lot of money, often triple the cost or more. And, how good is the job promise?

- Community college students can proceed to any career and degree. Community colleges have transfer agreements with four-year colleges, public and private.

◻ By working during college and using community colleges and in-state tuition at state schools on a pay-as-you-go basis, people can avoid any student loan debt, or inordinate amounts of it.

◻ Fancy colleges aren't required. Entrepreneurs and business leaders come from regular colleges. Steven Spielberg has been the most successful film director ever[4]. Did he go to film school at selective University of Southern California or UCLA? No. He took film classes at California State University at Long Beach.

Return on Investment: Does College Pay Off?

What is the return on the time and cost of a degree? Generally, it's a good investment. In general people with degrees have higher lifetime incomes. Still, for you as an individual it will depend on many variables. Plenty of people make bad decisions involving college. Read more:

Investing in College: A Guide for the Perplexed, by Malcom Getz, 2007, Harvard University Press, Cambridge, Massachusetts.

Mr. Getz has an economist's skills and practical advice. He has experience as a college professor as well.

Will College Pay Off? A Guide to the Most Important Financial Decision You'll Ever Make, by Peter Capelli, 2015, Public Affairs, New York.

Mr. Capelli warns about expecting an easy, big payoff from college. Some people have severe distress from debt and ineffective degrees. He guides us through factors that determine what pays off.

The Graduate Survival Guide: 5 Mistakes You Can't Afford to Make In College, by Anthony ONeal with Rachel Cruze, 2017, Ramsey Press, The Lampo Group, LLC, Brentwood, Tennessee.

This book walks you through getting a debt-free degree.

http://CollegeAffordability.urban.org

The Breaking Even section at the bottom shows when you make your money back on college, which by one estimate is at age 30.

A big problem is inordinate debt. Degrees make sense, but at $40,000 to $100,000 of debt? Or more? The degree isn't a problem; it's how to get it. You can get a degree without any debt, or inordinate debt. Go to a community college, then a state college and work as you go.

U.S. Starting Salaries After College

The government College Scorecard reports that the U.S. median annual earnings for all people who used a federal grant or loan who enrolled for any college, (two-year and four-year) ten years after enrollment was about <u>$35,000[5]</u>. Median means that half of U.S. college enrollees made more, and half made less.
<u>So, that's not a huge figure to work with after college to pay off loans. Know what you are getting into.</u>

Do not rush into a college decision, whether for a trade school or for a PhD, without knowing the benefits and risks. This book will not offer any analysis on the rate of return on the cost of a degree from a college or a trade school, but it will raise the alarm that you should look into it very thoroughly for your own situation. A lot depends on the major. Readers will have to do their own research and they should.

Large debts have serious consequences, especially if income is low. Smaller debts are more manageable, depending, again, on income, but also on your spending discipline.

Spending Habits Affect Loan Repayment and Retirement, Whether You Make $15 an Hour, or $40 an Hour

Spending habits are a key factor. People who spend all they make won't pay off loans quickly or build savings to invest for retirement. Think about college in the context of how you will live when working or running a business.

If you insist right away on the nicer ride, a lot of new clothes, the nicer living space to rent or buy, eating out a lot, trips here and there, and all pre-prepared food, you might look good on the surface, but you also might be broke. You'll either stay in debt, or just break even. If you miss a few month's paychecks, you'll have trouble. You won't have money to invest. (It takes money to make money.) At year's end, you will look at your W-2 and say "Where did all that go?" Back to work for you.

Those people you think you're impressing, your co-workers, your neighbors, the old crowd, your cousins, they don't care much anyway. Will they make one of your payments or give you $50? No.

Frugal People Are the Smart Ones

Those who track every dollar, budget in advance, live within their income, don't use debt (or use debt sparingly and pay it off), and save will make it in the long run, even on a lower income. Seek out budgeting help, which is free from www.FeedThePig.org (remember the piggy bank) which is a non-profit site from certified accountants. Among others, www.Mint.com from Intuit and www.EveryDollar.com have free budget apps and articles to read, although these are commercial sites selling other apps. Apple's Numbers, Google Docs and Microsoft's Excel, have various free budgeting spreadsheets. The website www.TheDebtMyth.com has articles on avoiding debt, getting debt free and a $5 (one-time fee) budgeting app.

At For-Profit Colleges, You, the Buyer, Should Beware

Do not trust the salespeople at the for-profit college with your signature on a $10,000, $20,000 or $40,000 loan until you triple check everything, including all other options. Of course, salespeople will tell you that their college is a sound investment with a red-carpet stroll to a job and point out every obstacle everywhere else. Their job depends on signing you up.

Does the salesperson at the For-Profit Air Conditioning College promise a job if you'll just hurry up and sign up for $20,000? First, you should visit ten air conditioning companies to find out if you might start as a laborer and be trained on the job. Could you be hired with a certificate from the community college for $3,000? Do you really need to pay $20,000 to For-Profit Air Conditioning College?

That goes for every profession from dentistry to computer coding, from nursing to welding, to a PhD in whatever. See if you can get job credentials at a lower price elsewhere, before you sign up anywhere.

(That also goes for the rep from the Liberal Arts College, peddling a $25,000 loan per year for a net-price $100,000 bachelor's degree, with a lot of assurances of the value of higher education. At that price, though? English 101 at the community college and Chem 301 at the state college cost a lot less.)

Parents and students can check salary averages for for-profit colleges on College Scorecard, which is a valid survey, as it comes from government data from actual earnings statements. This is an average among students with different degrees, so your average would depend on the degree, as nurses would make a lot more than nurse assistants from the same college. If sales staff claims that graduates average $52,000 and the College Scorecard average is $27,000, you had better sort that out. (Remember, the Scorecard - from the U.S. government - has W-2s and 1099s from 70% of students nationwide.)

Now, some of these for-profit colleges will help ambitious people find work. A person I know paid $45,000 for tuition and fees at a culinary college for an associate's and, being an ambitious guy, he was soon working in luxury hotels, though it wasn't at high salaries at first. Yes, he had a career, but at a price. Below is another story.

Is Every Single College Degree Worth It? It Depends

Here's a true story I personally know about. Two starting food chefs worked at a four-star resort. The entry-level positions paid only $24,000 a year, $12 an hour. This was in Tucson, Arizona in 2015, a lower-cost, and lower-wage, region.

Jack Went to College — Judy Did Not Go to College

My friend is one of the chefs. Let's call him Jack. He went to a two-year trade college costing $25,000 a year for a $50,000 total. He used $40,000 in student loans. Jack paid the other $10,000 in cash from part-time jobs. After starting work, he was still staring at the $40,000 debt, and his paychecks weren't very big.

Jack told me about the woman working right next to him every day. Let's call her Judy. She started in restaurants, learning on the job. While

Jack was in college earning zero, she had invested $200 a month in an individual retirement account (IRA) for a $5,000 total. Judy had the same job, but had spent zero on college and had no debt.

The Comparison

Jack and Judy were making the same money, doing the same job, standing right next to each other at work each day, but Jack was already financially behind Judy by $55,000.

$ 10,000	cash spent on trade school by Jack that could have gone to an investment for Jack
$ 40,000	student loan debt for Jack
+ $ 5,000	IRA stock market investment by Judy
= $ 55,000	financial difference between Jack and Judy

That's a huge difference! In only two years! Jack had not been gambling and drinking away all his money. Not at all. He's a solid citizen. Judy had not been some super entrepreneur, leaving Jack in her dust with a new restaurant startup. Not at all. Both had just been good employees. Let's compare their situations.

Jack is losing money to debt interest going forward and making significant payments to debt principal. Jack's payments to interest and debt will not come back to him again, ever. He can still invest in an IRA, or a 401k to get the basic employer match. He can get a mortgage on a modest house or condo, but he can't maximize such investments until his college debt is eliminated.

Judy is making money on investments going forward and will get both the interest and the principal back later. Being 100-percent debt free, she can not only get a full 401k employer match, but also invest more into stocks or other investments and still get a mortgage on a modest house or condo, all with no strain. Judy can save more for investments and pay off her house sooner, all while her standard retirement accounts grow. She could have a paid-for house at age 45. How's no rent or house payments for the rest of your life sound?

The interest will compound for years, to one person's benefit and to the other person's detriment. You can't argue with math.

Some colleges, universities and trade schools charge a whole lot of money. With credit guaranteed by Uncle Sam, under 2017 rules, in most cases the student or parent will be liable no matter what, even after a bankruptcy.

The Student Loan Lien: 'Til Death Do You Part?

People with moderate incomes have less room for error, so a college loan lien can be a huge, lasting financial problem. Other debts can be settled for much less, or eliminated with a bankruptcy, but the student loan lien cannot. Current rules mean that no one will negotiate down more than 10%. Once you are behind, penalties worsen. The compounding penalties and higher interest never stop. The balance can go from $30,000 to $70,000.

I know people in their 50s and 60s with student debt like that hanging over them. They worked honestly for a living, but they took these college decisions much too lightly. It was so easy to sign and head off to class. Then came setbacks: illness, injury, layoffs, divorces, or just much-lower-paying jobs than they expected.

With a federal lien, the lender is always there until you pay in full, or die. Founding father Benjamin Franklin said the only things that were certain were death and taxes. If a student loan had been available in 1776, Ben Franklin would have said the only things that were certain were death, taxes and a student loan lien.

But I Just Have to Go There; My Heart's Set on It

Students and parents, don't make a major decision based on your desires or dreams about how you always envisioned the upcoming first semester of college.

Yes, students, you can't wait to get off to college just like everyone else. And you want someplace good, just like so-and-so and so-and-so.

Yes, parents and guardians, you want to see your student off to a happy place, the ideal freshman experience at the ideal college.

What do you do? Just jump right in? If that isn't reasonable financially, have some maturity and tell yourselves no.

How Does Loan Creep Occur? Here's One Scenario

Young people are less prone to look ahead. (This is a scientific fact, as the planning and reasoning lobe of a young person's brain doesn't fully develop until the later 20s.)

For the loan on the first semester, it didn't look so bad, so you signed. One semester wasn't so intimidating. Then another. Then another. This is loan creep. Each semester, you felt compelled to go to the next. The loan is creeping up, higher and higher, on you.

Four or five years later, and you owe $40,000, or more. For the class of 2016 the average was $37,000 total in student debt.[6]

Let's see ..., at 4.45% on $40,000, the lender adds $1,800 interest each year. For $150 a month, the balance won't even go down, not one nickel. Get ready to pay, and pay and pay.

Here are repayment schedules on $40,000 at 4.45%:

Monthly Payment	Years to Pay	Total Interest	Total Out of Pocket
$ 414	10 years	$ 9,631	$ 49,631
$ 305	15 years	$ 14,896	$ 54,896
$ 252	20 years	$ 20,476	$ 60,476

Now, let's say your first job pays $20 an hour, $40,000 a year. It'll take some time to pay off that loan. But at first, it was only for one semester. And you *just had* to go for it, just like everyone else.

Instead of spending, excluding room and board, $50,000 to $60,000 on a bachelor's degree, as a general example, for $35,000 you could have gotten a bachelor's degree through the community college and regional college, leaving $20,000 to $30,000 to invest in a duplex, or a small house or condo to live in, or a stock fund, all good starting points. But all you have is debt. Lots of it. *Maybe you should have gone to a community college and then the regional state college.*

The college people will smile when you enroll. The lender will smile when you sign. Everyone will smile at your graduation. Will you smile as you pay and pay, and then pay some more?

Read "Degrees of Debt: Student loan borrowers, herded into default, face a relentless collector: the U.S.", from Reuters (7-25-2017) at: https://www.reuters.com/investigates/special-report/usa-studentloans.

Don't count on the lenders, servicers or federal agencies to explain your best options. You are on your own to find out what's best. One major loan servicer flat out said that lenders do not care if a college loan is a bad investment for you, the student. Think that over.

A Degree Is Good, If . . .

Statistically, earnings increase and unemployment rates are lower for people with degrees. You may hear the statistic that an average college graduate makes $1 million more over a lifetime than an average high school graduate.[7] That is valid information, but what about the variables? A business owner might have started as a laborer with no degree and now makes more than the average salary of PhD holders. Some people work their way up in a field with no degree. A social worker from Harvard may make less over a lifetime than an engineer from a state college.

Some People Choose to Make Less Money

Reed College is known as one of the hardest colleges in the U.S. to get an A at. Yet Reed has a lower salary average on College Scorecard than other similar academic powerhouses. Why? Maybe because many Reed graduates choose academia, social work, non-profits and government work, more so than go to Wall Street or Silicon Valley.

Some of the hardest-working, smartest graduates in the U.S. choose to make *less* money, focusing on the social impact of their careers, not on income. (One Reed student made a lot in Silicon Valley. Apple co-founder Steve Jobs went to Reed but he left after one semester. Maybe it's easier to make money selling stuff from Silicon Valley than to graduate with all As from Reed's exacting professors.)

Individual variations affect income, not degree level alone. Yes, for the averages, the higher the degree, the higher the income. That's valid information, if properly applied.

But do the statistics mean that getting any degree equals more money at any job? Not at all.

The $80,000 Degree

Is a degree in any major at a private college for $80,000 worth it, to later work from entry level to be an office manager at a retailer? I heard a woman tell that story. She said her choice of where she got her degree ended up being a very bad choice for her.

Degrees are viewed positively by businesses, and generally result in higher incomes, but at what price? A degree from the state college can provide such benefits, without the higher price.

As well, higher levels of education provide personal rewards and satisfaction, but, again, at what price?

Elite U. or State U.? Forget Your Ego, Earnings Can Be Similar

Those attending selective colleges in many cases do earn higher average salaries. The earnings differences, however, between regular colleges and selective colleges are not so much that students (and parents) need to be overly obsessive about getting into a selective college. As shown over the next pages, often, the pay is the same.

The ego boost of being accepted to an elite college is nice. Being turned down is a disappointment. Both are natural reactions, but don't elevate their importance. If you impress others for a few minutes, fine, but that's that. Those snooty people you would just love to show up? They won't pay $5 on the bill. Either way, why do you care what they think? You don't even like them.

A rejection is temporary and inconsequential. Excellent options at other colleges and in the world of work are ahead.

While others are so pleased to be off to the dorms at Expensive U., you can make the smarter choice to start at County Community College. You'll pay one quarter the price and can transfer to a state college (also at a lower price), to get the exact same degree.

Many who rushed off to Expensive U. graduate with large debts. The interest will eat their breakfast, lunch and dinner and their job may pay the exact same as your job, which was obtained with a state college degree. It happens. All the time.

Regarding Salary Averages

A janitor gets paid less than a scientist. Let's say that someone can't handle a scientist's job, but he can handle a janitor's job. Do we attribute the janitor's lower salary only to a lack of a degree ("If he'd only gotten a degree…") Not really.

No one kept the janitor from a degree, and he didn't neglect to get one out of laziness, but rather, he rationally concluded that a degree was above his ability. Yet, his janitor's salary can provide a successful family, social and spiritual life. He can build a good retirement. He would be placed in a category lower on a salary and educational table, as below, but it doesn't reflect a bad decision or an unsuccessful life. People do have different abilities, leading to different jobs and different salaries. That does not show in a table of statistics about degrees and salary averages.

Degree Level	Weekly Paycheck	Unemployment Rate
Less than high school diploma	$ 504	7.4%
High school diploma	$ 692	5.2%
Some college, no degree	$ 756	4.4%
Associate's degree	$ 819	3.6%
U.S. median of all workers	$ 885	4.0%
Bachelor's degree	$ 1,156	2.7%
Master's degree	$ 1,380	2.4%
Professional degree	$ 1,745	1.6%
Doctoral degree	$ 1,664	1.6%

Source: For 2016, U.S. Department of Labor Bureau of Labor Statistics [8]

Point No. 1)	**Salary Differences by College Do Exist, But Many Regular Colleges Are Right in the Mix with the Selective Colleges**

Earnings averages by colleges do show that Harvard, MIT and Stanford are among the highest. So, what else is new? Maritime colleges, technology colleges and medical colleges are up there too.

As expected, pharmacists, nurses, doctors, engineers, techies, and connected Ivy-League types, along with people who work on ships on the open seas, are all making some very good money.

What's maybe not so expected is that the statistics also show that many regular colleges, including public state colleges, are producing very good earnings averages. That's encouraging.

The point is, before you have a fit over selective colleges, realize this: Sure, the selective colleges are doing great. They are supposed to. But there is also a whole lot going on out there for U.S. students besides selective colleges. A whole lot more.

Regular Colleges Hold Their Own in Salary Averages

Check out the income averages on College Scorecard or CollegeResults.org. Nearly every college in the U.S. is listed. People are getting decent paychecks from a lot of regular colleges. Before you go into debt at Private U., look at the paycheck you can get after going to State U. for a lot less.

The U.S. government survey College Scorecard shows earnings averages for those people who used a federal loan or a federal Pell grant, which is 70% of U.S. students.[9] It shows earnings 10 years after enrolling. College Scorecard uses actual IRS income data from earnings statements, so the income data is valid. This salary information is available to the federal government because of a person's use of the federal programs. College Scorecard compiles the earnings information

41

by college, after removing names for privacy. What College Scorecard doesn't include are the nation's students who paid without using a federal loan or federal grant, nationally about 30 percent of students.

Thus, the Scorecard doesn't include students who paid their way without federal loans or grants by working during college. The Scorecard doesn't include earnings from students whose wealthier families paid the full price. Those people are probably making good incomes after college, as they graduate with no debt (although private loans could have been used), and family resources help them in the work world or in business.

This is true for regular colleges, along with the Ivies. Thus, every college's overall salary average is likely to be higher than what the College Scorecard reports, and more so for those colleges with the higher percentages of wealthy students.

College Scorecard has Harvard at $90,900 and Amherst at $59,700 in Nov., 2017, for example, but Harvard's and Amherst's overall income averages are probably higher because College Scorecard is not counting the earnings of the students from wealthier families. These are many of the students at Harvard and Amherst.

The College Scorecard Earnings Average Covers People from Average-Income Families

College Scorecard is a fair report of income for average folks, coming from their actual IRS income statements, not from a voluntary, hit-and-miss survey.

A few examples of college earnings comparisons are on page 43.

Yes, one college's earnings average is boosted by having a lot of students who become nurses and physician's assistants, for example.

And another college's average is lowered by having a lot of students who become social workers or by being in a region with lower wages.

I just want to show that the most exclusive colleges do not have a monopoly on graduates who earn good paychecks.

Earnings from high to median from a general selection of colleges are on pages 46 and 47.

Earnings Averages for
College Enrollees
(10 years after enrollment)

Some Colleges and Some Surprises

(See www.CollegeScorecard.ed.gov; click Find Schools; select the sort: Salary After Attending for a national ranking, or search by state or college name. The CollegeResults.org site uses the same information, with helpful search functions.

The College Scorecard shows average earnings for people who used a federal loan or grant, 10 years after enrolling in college, as explained on pages 41-42. Fall 2016 admissions rates and mid-range ACT scores (36 is the highest ACT score) are included for comparison, from College Navigator, Oct., 2017.)

From the College Scorecard survey, Oct. 2017, in average earnings:[10]

A	public University of Baltimore	$ 55,100

(49% admitted, mid-range ACT scores: 20-21)

beats out

	elite private Williams College	$ 54,100

(18% admitted, mid-range ACT scores: 31-34)

B	less-selective Drexel University	$ 66,600

(75% admitted, mid-range ACT scores: 25-30)

beats out

	Ivy League Brown University	$ 63,100

(9% admitted, mid-range ACT scores: 31-34)

C	Albany College of Pharmacy & Health Sciences	$ 122,600

(69% admitted, mid-range ACT scores: 23-27)

beats out

Harvard University	$ 90,900

(5% admitted, mid-range ACT scores: 32-35)

Point No. 2) It's More the Student, Than the College

Great Students Make Just as Much Money
After Going to a Good Regular College, Without Elite U.

Many students with high credentials and test scores who attended regular colleges *earned the same amount of money* as those with high credentials and test scores who attended the elite type of colleges. That's what a very reputable study, by Stacy Dale and Alan Krueger, through the National Bureau of Economic Research, found out. The college differential was zero. The student, not the college, was the primary factor.[11]

Let's repeat that: The college made zero difference in salary for similarly ambitious, high performing students.

Elite U. has a lot of students from wealthy families with good connections who will make high salaries. This one factor increases the salary average for Elite U. Another factor is that Elite U. is full of high achievers who end up with high earnings averages.

The same type of high achievers, however, thrive at other colleges, in jobs, and in business. Regular colleges are still great places for you high achievers to shine and later get the same higher earnings, even without having gone to Elite U.

The CEO Example

Here's one example: Decade after decade, at any given time, about half of top CEOs come out of regular colleges, not the super elite ones. So too, for the top managers from which CEOs are found. Across the corporate and business world, graduates from regular colleges often supervise the Ivy Leaguers.

Certainly, graduates from selective colleges often do well. They're supposed to. What's new? Still, in the workplace and in business, State U. graduates pass up Elite U. graduates all the time.

If You Don't Get Accepted, Performance Still Counts the Most

Let's suppose, that Elite U. turned you down. So, you're off to State U. Another student got into Elite U., but he turns out to be only pretty good, not a high performer.

Meanwhile, at State U., you get it done with a great record, diligent work and hustle. You join the honors college. You know the material inside and out. People, who know people, want to help you. One professor respects all the work you have done. He knows people at Greatest High Tech Company Ever, Inc. Who gets hired at Greatest, Inc.? You do and not Mr. Elite U. He'll do OK, but you'll do better.

Regional colleges, state colleges and smaller, less-selective, private colleges offer a path to success as well. What type of success might start at such colleges? How about being President of the United States of America? Students who became the U.S. President started out at Eureka College (IL), Texas State, Georgia Southwestern State and Whittier College (CA).

> Point No. 3) Selective Colleges May Increase Income for:
> (a) Students whose parents have
>   relatively little education,
> (b) Latinos and
> (c) African-Americans.

Selective colleges were shown, however, by Dale and Krueger, to increase earnings for top students whose parents had relatively little education, Latinos, and African-Americans. These top students did have higher incomes after attending selective colleges, than did similar top students who attended regular colleges.[12]

"One possible explanation for this pattern is that while most students who apply to selective colleges may be able to rely on their families and friends to provide job-networking opportunities, networking opportunities that become available from attending a selective college may be particularly valuable for black and Hispanic students, and for students from less educated families," they wrote.[13]

Average Earnings	College 10 years after enrollment	Enroll-ment	Admit Rate	25-75% ACT Scores	Public Univ.
$ 35,000	U.S. Median for 2- & 4-Year Colleges	n/a	n/a	17-24[14]	
$122,600	Albany College of Pharmacy (NY)	1,076	69%	23-27	
$112,700	MCPHS - Mass. College of Pharmacy	3,843	84%	21-27	
$ 94,200	MIT- Massachusetts Inst. of Tech.	4,524	8%	33-35	
$ 91,800	University of the Sciences (PA)	1,344	60%	23-28	
$ 91,400	Babson College (MA)	2,283	25%	27-31	
$ 90,900	Harvard University (MA)	9,915	5%	32-35	
$ 90,100	Georgetown University (DC)	7,453	17%	30-34	
$ 87,300	Stevens Institute of Technology (NJ)	3,115	39%	29-33	
$ 85,700	Stanford University (CA)	7,034	5%	31-35	
$ 85,600	Helene Fuld College of Nursing (NY)	459	Rolling	Optional	
$ 84,000	Maine Maritime Academy	1,014	76%	21-25	Public
$ 83,200	Yale University (CT)	5,472	6%	32-35	
$ 82,600	Worcester Polytechnic Institute (MA)	4,432	48%	Opt. 28-32	
$ 82,400	University of Pennsylvania	11,716	9%	32-35	
$ 82,100	Colorado School of Mines	4,610	40%	29-32	Public
$ 81,800	Carnegie Mellon University (PA)	6,283	22%	31-34	
$ 80,600	Bentley University (MA)	4,222	46%	25-30	
$ 80,500	Princeton University (NJ)	5,400	7%	32-35	
$ 78,600	Kettering University (MI)	1,904	72%	25-29	
$ 78,200	Columbia University (NY)	8,124	7%	32-35	
$ 77,900	Duke University (NC)	6,609	11%	31-34	
$ 77,900	Rensselaer Polytechnic Institute (NY)	6,265	44%	28-32	
$ 77,200	Lehigh University	5,080	26%	29-32	
$ 75,800	Georgia Institute of Technology	15,489	26%	30-34	Public
$ 73,900	Villanova University (PA)	6,999	44%	30-32	
$ 73,600	Cornell University (NY)	14,566	14%	31-34	
$ 72,300	Washington & Lee University (VA)	1,830	24%	30-33	
$ 70,000	Boston College (MA)	9,870	31%	30-33	
$ 70,000	Dartmouth College (NH)	4,310	11%	30-34	
$ 69,900	Case Western Reserve University (OH)	5,152	35%	30-34	
$ 69,800	Illinois Institute of Technology	2,944	57%	26-31	
$ 69,800	Fairfield University (CT)	4,032	61%	Opt. 25-28	
$ 69,800	Johns Hopkins University (MD)	6,042	13%	32-34	
$ 69,300	University of the Pacific (CA)	3,483	66%	23-30	
$ 67,500	Lafayette College (PA)	2,550	28%	27-31	
$ 67,400	Milwaukee School of Engineering	2,642	66%	25-30	
$ 67,100	Missouri Univ. of Science & Technology	6,906	79%	25-31	Public
$ 66,600	Drexel University (PA)	15,552	75%	25-30	
$ 65,900	New Jersey Institute of Technology	8,211	59%	23-29	Public

Average Earnings	College 10 years after enrollment	Enroll-ment	Admit Rate	25-75% ACT Scores	Public Univ.
$ 65,500	University of Chicago (IL)	6,001	8%	32-35	
$ 64,700	Michigan Technological University	5,589	76%	25-30	Public
$ 64,500	Vanderbilt University (TN)	6,871	11%	32-35	
$ 64,300	Rice University (TX)	3,893	15%	32-35	
$ 63,100	Brown University (RI)	6,926	9%	31-34	
$ 63,100	California Polytechnic State-San Luis Obispo	20,426	29%	26-31	Public
$ 62,800	Capella University (Online)	9,393	Open	N/A	
$ 61,800	University of California - Berkeley	29,310	17%	31-34	Public
$ 61,700	University of Maryland	28,472	48%	29-33	Public
$ 61,500	Emory University (GA)	6,861	25%	30-33	
$ 60,700	University of Virginia	16,331	30%	29-33	Public
$ 60,500	Virginia Tech	25,791	71%	24-29[15]	Public
$ 60,100	University of Michigan	28,983	29%	29-33	Public
$ 60,100	Wellesley College (MA)	2,482	29%	30-33	
$ 59,700	Amherst College (MA)	1,849	14%	31-34	
$ 59,600	New York University	26,135	32%	29-33	
$ 59,200	Binghamton University SUNY	13,632	41%	28-31	Public
$ 57,600	University of Illinois	33,932	60%	26-32	Public
$ 56,300	Haverford College (PA)	1,268	21%	31-34	
$ 55,800	University of Connecticut	19,324	49%	26-31	Public
$ 55,600	Middlebury College (VT)	2,523	16%	30-33	
$ 55,500	Texas A & M University	50,735	67%	24-30	Public
$ 55,100	University of Baltimore (MD)	3,222	49%	20-21	Public
$ 54,900	University of Texas	40,168	40%	26-32	Public
$ 54,100	Williams College (MA)	2,093	18%	31-34	
$ 52,500	Swarthmore College (PA)	1,543	13%	30-34	
$ 51,400	Vassar College (NY)	2,424	27%	30-33	
$ 50,200	University of Iowa	24,476	84%	23-28	Public
$ 47,600	Louisiana State University	26,118	76%	23-28	Public
$ 46,800	Howard University (DC)	5,899	30%	22-28	
$ 46,600	North Dakota State University	12,010	93%	21-26	Public
$ 45,600	Birmingham Southern College (AL)	1,293	48%	23-28	
$ 45,600	California State University - Chico	16,471	65%	19-24	Public
$ 44,900	Smith College (MA)	2,514	37%	Opt. 29-33	
$ 41,100	University of Mississippi	19,213	78%	22-29	Public
$ 39,900	Ohio University	23,585	75%	21-26	Public
$ 37,900	Reed College (OR)	1,410	31%	29-33	

Earnings averages are from the U.S. Dept. of Education, (11-20-2017), (collegescorecard.ed.gov; Find Schools; Sort: Salary After Attending). Enrollment, admit rates and scores are for fall 2016, as listed 11-20-2017 from the National Center for Education Statistics (nces.ed.gov/collegenavigator, enter name of school, click admissions tab). Salaries are 10 years after enrollment for enrollees using federal loans or aid (pp. 41, 42, 11). ACT test scores notation of "Opt." means scores are optional for that college, but are included for comparison.

Degrees Do Not Come with A Guarantee

A. The salary tables on pages 46-47 are to show higher earnings, on down to the national median of $35,000, which is the approximate median shown on College Scorecard for all two-year and four-year college enrollees.

B. People who attended public colleges with lower in-state tuition make similar money as people from private colleges at much higher cost. Look at all those examples of public colleges with good earnings. Don't these public colleges match up well with costlier private colleges, whose fancy reputations may not be so vital after all? And many, many more are shown in College Scorecard and CollegeResults.org, as this list was limited to just two pages.

Which Pays More? A Master's Degree, Welding Classes or Truck Driving School? It Depends

An adjunct professor with a master's degree may make less than an experienced welder or truck driver, maybe a lot less. The adjunct professor might have spent $70,000, or more, to finish a bachelor's and a master's degree. The welder might have spent $3,000 for a certificate degree at a community college. The truck driver might have spent $5,000 to finish a commercial driver's license course.

How Much Debt? How About None, By Paying as You Go?

Anyone can work a job to pay for classes as they go at an in-state rate to a public college, borrowing nothing. It's being done. It has been done. It's smart. It might take longer, but not that much longer, considering the bad consequences of high student debt.

People have comfortable retirements from salaries of $35,000 to $50,000 by saving and investing from their 20s on up, while avoiding debt. Keep that in mind, before you chase unrealistic, hoped-for riches of high earnings with too much college debt.

If a student is turned down for aid from four-year colleges, going to a community college is very smart.

☞ Chapter 4 ✍

College Admissions Basics

❖ <u>Grades:</u> Grades are vitally important in college admissions. Getting good grades forces students to know the material, which leads to good test scores and college readiness. Students should take the hardest courses for their ability. Don't shoot low, but if you take harder courses, don't overdo it. It's hard to judge sometimes. It's an age-old question. For selective colleges and scholarships, you want mostly As, a few Bs, and no Cs.

    ➤ If you have some hard classes already, an A in a regular course is better than adding another very hard course and getting a C. Then, some people say a B in a hard class is better than an A in a regular class, as it shows colleges that you will challenge yourself. Further, you might just get an A in the harder class, but that isn't possible if you skipped it to play it safe. Or you might start with a B, then get an A in the second semester of the hard class, which is a great result.

    ➤ Try one or more tough classes. If it is clear within the first two weeks that you made a mistake, transfer back to a regular class. If a regular class is much too easy the first week or so, then ask the teacher whether it will get harder. If not, consider transferring to something harder.

❖ <u>Tests:</u> Community colleges and some regional colleges may not require a standardized test. Students, if you know for certain that you are starting there, you might ignore the standardized tests. Don't, however, fail to see what a four-year college might offer you, just to skip a test. Students may take a standardized test throughout the year, even after high school graduation, if a college requires a test.

❖ <u>Tests:</u> Like it or not, standardized tests are part of the gateways, the funnels, that most colleges use for admissions and financial aid decisions. Yes, other factors are involved. For some colleges, the tests are optional. The Fair Test organization (www.fairtest.org) lists 950 colleges, including about half of the U.S.'s top 100 liberal arts colleges that do not require a test score for admissions. Still, some high schools grade easier than others. Thus, admissions officers wonder about grade inflation. They look to standardized test scores to see if students know the math and English. Students who pay attention in class and practice, can do fine on the tests.

❖ <u>Teachers:</u> Navigate teacher problems as soon as you recognize them. If you are stuck with a difficult teacher, then study extra on your own, rather than fall behind or get a horrible grade. Interact with teachers early about class requirements. The standard for math and English won't be lowered on senior-year tests because you had a problem with a teacher sophomore year.

❖ <u>Activities:</u> Selective college applicants should create a good record of accomplishment in some extra activities, not just busy work.

❖ <u>Applications:</u> Getting ready takes more time usually than does filling them out. Set up online accounts. Have the school registrar send transcripts. Order test results sent. Get recommendation letters sent. Download or send portfolios. With your essay done, one application can be completed in an hour, maybe more, maybe less. Financial forms can take an hour or more. Have W-2s, tax forms, retirement account totals and an approximate home value.

❖ <u>Essays:</u> I found 20 books on Amazon just about college essays before I quit counting. Ignore the impression that a very clever essay is important. That's an exaggeration. First, every other part of the application needs to shine. The essay confirms that one is a capable writer and thinker. Therefore, read up on essay tips, avoid boring pitfalls, tell about yourself, but don't agonize over it.

☞ **Chapter 5** ✍

Checklists for Each Year

Starting on the next page are general year-by-year checklists.

For each item, see detailed information in the rest of the book.

Yes, the details throughout the book are extensive. Take it one subject, one chapter, at a time. Use chapters as you need to, skipping over them at times, and coming back to them later.

The suggestions for the checklist are just that; suggestions.

Parents, guardians, and students: Don't get bent out of shape at any of these suggestions.

Yes, I recommend a fair amount to do for a student who is considering college, and even more for those who may try for a selective college.

For example: If you don't visit a campus early on, then so be it.

A visit could help motivate a student, but if you don't do it, the sun will still rise every morning and the colleges will still be there Jan. 1 of senior year when the applications are due.

The suggestions allow students and parents to see how much is available for them to do from 8th grade onward, and act as reminders for your use.

8th Grade Checklist

☐ **Get good grades.** The extra work now will help freshman year go better. It sets the habits for better grades in high school.

☐ **Review university web sites.** Knowing some college basics helps you put up with school. "Why do I have to do this?" is best explained if you're thinking ahead. See what's interesting to you.

☐ **See a counselor.** Or see an assistant principal to go over class choices, with a plan for 9th grade. Move up to advanced classes and activities as is reasonable.

☐ **Take the PSAT™ 8/9, and/or the PreACT™.** A middle school should offer the PSAT 8/9, but might not. You should ask your school to add it, even if just for you. The PreACT is given at high schools. If your school or district won't offer these, contact the ACT at (319) 337-1000 or the College Board at 866-433-7728 for locations. It's only $12 to $15. Go for it.

☐ **Take some practice tests at home**. Why would you do something boring like that? Because you are thinking big and looking ahead. The score isn't important, yet. See what's on a test.

☐ **Look up summer programs.** Many universities have summer programs and camps for 8th graders, often at a reasonable cost or for free. It can expand a student's horizons and be included on the college application. Drag some friends along. Try something new.

☐ **Visit a college campus.** At this early age, a visit, mingling with college students, helps a young person feel more comfortable and confident about college (and more motivated about school). Go after school on an early release day or on a Saturday. Visit admissions, eat, and go to the game room. Ever played billiards? Is it earth shattering? No. Is it worth it? Yes.

9th Grade, Freshman Checklist

☐ **Schedule classes with college in mind**, not what your friends want. Let the counselor know college is the goal. Take the harder classes as are appropriate, even if you only see your best friends at lunch from now on.

☐ **Many selective colleges want four years each of English, a foreign language, math and science**. If a selective college is even a remote option, register each year for all of these subjects.

☐ **Get good grades.** Getting good grades establishes a base of knowledge for the future. Colleges look seriously at grade point average (GPA). Get a good start on a good GPA. It's harder to raise it if you tank a 9th grade class. Some scholarships require at least Bs in the core classes from freshman year forward. Don't let an avoidable C in freshman year be a problem later.

☐ **Check for programs for next summer.**

☐ **Visit a college campus.**

☐ **Go to a college forum or fair with admissions representatives.**

☐ **Take the PSAT™ 8/9, the PreACT™ and/or the PSAT/NMSQT®.*** These are practice tests. Create an ACT account and a College Board (SAT) account, which you will use later for the regular ACT tests and College Board tests. Use the accounts for online study guides. The PreACT test and the PSAT/NMSQT* test can also be taken later, but 9th graders are allowed to take these practice tests, to provide exposure to the tests at this early grade. The scores *are not* reported to colleges and *do not* go on your transcript.

☐ **Volunteer or intern.** Follow your interests and passions. Having an area of interest and following it throughout high school looks good. Do something, somewhere.

☐ **Participate in an activity,** if you can keep grades high at the same time.

*PSAT/NMSQT® is a registered trademark of the College Board and the National Merit Scholarship Corporation, which were not involved in the production of, and do not endorse, this product.

53

10th Grade, Sophomore Checklist

☐ **Get good grades,** for knowledge and for success on standardized tests.

☐ **Consider internships, volunteer programs or university programs for high school students.** During the school year, you can volunteer or intern after school or on Saturdays. During summer, many opportunities are available. Try to have something extra. If you are working at a job, that counts for a lot too, so, good job.

☐ **Take the PreACT™, PSAT™ 10 and PSAT/NMSQT®* tests for practice.**

☐ **Visit some college campuses.** If on a family vacation out of town, visit a campus. Visit a local campus.

☐ **Find out more information.** Go to a college fair or forum. Visit a college admissions office. Read the websites. Or call. Tell them your particulars, such as GPA and course work, and see what they tell you.

☐ **Understand how subject tests work. Some colleges require them.** Get a plan ready for these tests, and others, that you want or need to take so you are best prepared for each of them and don't miss the test dates.

☐ **Sign up to get college information.** Do so on an ACT account or College Board account, and on college websites. Maybe set up an extra email address just for college admissions. You'll get a lot of mail and email from colleges, but so what? It's encouraging to look over. Check out all those colleges that you never knew about. This also shows colleges that you are interested, which may help with admissions in senior year.

---

*PSAT/NMSQT® is a registered trademark of the College Board and the National Merit Scholarship Corporation, which were not involved in the production of, and do not endorse, this product.

11th Grade, Junior Checklist

This year is a big year. Take it seriously.

☐ **For those colleges you are thinking about,** sign up on each college's website to receive more information. You'll get notices for events in your area. Signing up may help to show the admissions staff that you are interested.

☐ **Do *all* your schoolwork and homework.** Lay off the chit-chat, games and shows. Spend more time reading and studying. Really, this is a big year.

☐ **Get an ACT account and a College Board account.** Use the account for on-line practice, some of which is free. Double check things. Get information.

☐ **Practice on the standardized tests. Practice on subject tests, if you'll need to take them. Do this regularly every month.**

☐ **Take the needed, recommended subject tests at the best possible times.** Have a detailed schedule.

☐ **Figure out when to take the ACT test or the SAT test. That can include junior year.**

☐ **Starting in November and December, work on a summer plan.** Summer seminars are not needed for a college application, but some activities can enhance an application. Interning, volunteering, jobs and studying for the SAT test or ACT test are recommended for summer. Look up summer programs on winter break, as early deadlines are in January or Feb. 1, especially for financial aid. If you can't afford a program, some are free or offer aid.

☐ **Work on figuring out where to apply:**

    ☐ **Consider a community college to start.** You can attend a community college locally or in another state and later use the credits as a transfer student to a four-year college. Everyone should explore this option.

    ☐ **Read through guides to U.S. colleges. Go to college forums and fairs. Visit colleges.** Look at rankings. Read college blogs. All of this is informational and motivational to know about colleges you could attend and find some you didn't know about.

☐ **Start to save money for the application fees** that are due in first semester senior year, at about $40 to $50 per college. Or have a plan to use waivers if you are eligible.

11th Grade, Junior Year — Summer

☐ **Study for the standardized tests. Be aware of the June, July and August test dates.** It could make sense to take some of these tests in summer. Know the options. Have a plan.

☐ **Start your application essays.** You will need one essay that tells your story, so you should start.

☐ **Do something extra.** This can include a job, volunteering, interning or research, or lots of test practice if you haven't taken your final ACT test or SAT test, or all your subject tests yet.

☐ **Research early admissions options and commitments.**

11th Grade, Junior Year - August is Important!

☐ **August is important** to be ready for September of 12th grade, senior year!

☐ **Create timelines and checklists to check for September tests that you should take.** Register for September tests.

☐ **Set up an account on the Common App, Universal App, Coalition App or Common Black College App; or set up individual college accounts on the college websites.** Select some colleges and start a new application see what you need to do and what information you need to complete the applications later. Nothing is viewed by a college until you finalize it and submit the whole application later, so this is practice. You will just start to fill in the information and save the account information for later.

☐ **Look at the FAFSA** (Free Application for Federal Student Aid) financial aid information to be ready for later. The FAFSA on the Web Worksheet gives you a preview. Earlier applicants might get more money. Some scholarship deadlines are in Oct. and Nov. Be ready. (You can start to fill in the FAFSA online on Oct. 1.)

12th Grade, Senior Year Checklist

12th Grade, Senior Year, September

☐ **Don't goof off on your homework and schoolwork.** Don't switch to easiest courses. The grades for senior year, first semester, will also be sent to the colleges you apply to. If you tank them, it could hurt admissions chances. Also, the schoolwork and homework that you do now still helps you on any tests you will take.

☐ **Use your checklists and timelines to register for and take the required and recommended tests.**

☐ **If using an early application, have a full, detailed plan ready.**

☐ **Watch out for earlier deadlines for scholarships, general merit aid and other financial aid.** Get ready for those due on Sept. 30 or Oct. 1. The FAFSA and CSS can be filled out and sent starting on Oct. 1.

☐ **Begin or continue to practice for the standardized tests.** You can do a practice test one section at a time, not take it all at once, if that helps.

☐ **It's crunch time, but get ample sleep, by cutting some fun out. Really.** If you are always sleepy you will not learn as well, or do as well on tests. Get homework done on the bus, in study hall, and right after classes end. Get to sleep early enough by doing schoolwork early enough. Do the work first, then relax, not the other way around.

☐ **Continue to fill in college applications online and save them to your online accounts.**

☐ **Meet submission deadlines for art, research papers and other such portfolio work.** These deadlines can be a month before the regular application deadline. If this involves having a teacher submit it, start early and follow up, so you will be less of a pest.

12th Grade, Senior Year, October

☐ **You can start to fill in your FAFSA for free and CSS (for a fee) on Oct. 1. Review the requirements for financial documentation,** as information may be due or recommended with early applications. Though the deadlines for financial forms may be later in February and March, general wisdom is to finish these forms as early as possible to increase chances for aid. If you need to estimate, you can, and still submit the form. You can also get data from the IRS starting on Oct. 1. The CSS/Financial Aid PROFILE® is also very important. Pay the fee, it's worth it, or check for a waiver. The CSS fee is $25 for the first school and $16 each for additional college. Yes, it's time consuming. Fill it out anyway.

12th Grade, Senior Year, November

☐ **Be aware of Nov. 30 application deadlines. Check every college that you are even remotely interested in for the application deadline. Some are early.** The State of California University System, for example, has a regular application deadline of Nov. 30.

12th Grade, Senior Year, December

☐ **If you have any tests left to take, continue to practice.** Even at this late stage, extra practice *will* help.

☐ **December 31 or Jan. 1 is the deadline for many college applications, so start or continue to work on the applications.** Even if you only have one application, *do not wait until the last week of December.* While any one application is not overwhelming, if you are applying to multiple colleges, it can add up to many, many hours of work, especially for good essays.

12th Grade, Senior Year, Jan. Feb. & March

☐ **Complete financial forms and other extra forms.** Find the numbers, or estimate from last year, and fill in the blanks. So what, if it is a lot to do? Figure it out. Money is money. Sometimes students go to college without filling out the FAFSA or the CSS and miss out on the money. Do *not* do that. Fill out the FAFSA and CSS, no matter how long it takes, so you can get any extra aid money you should get.

Chapter 6

For Those Who Aren't Getting a Lot of Help:

The next few pages go over some advice that may apply to a student, parent or guardian having more difficulties, frankly, than most readers are experiencing. The U.S. has many students in less than ideal situations. Some students are in foster care. Some 1,300,000 U.S. grade-school and high-school students reside in shared or doubled-up housing, motels or shelters.[16] If that includes you, then you are obviously not the only one. Many families don't know much about college. My hope is to provide someone extra encouragement to overcome such problems. So, that's what the next few pages are about.

Are you, as a student, feeling unsure about the future?

If further training or college is on your mind, but no one else is helping you right now, that is even more reason to make up your mind to get training, or to go to college, and to get the help you need to do so.

Are you, as guardian or parent, not sure how to proceed?

It takes a lot of time to figure everything out, then more time to do all the follow-up. This is even more reason to make up your mind to find additional help if needed.

Often, the adults are not around much to help students, due to work or other factors. That can be just as true for middle-class parents who work long hours as it is for working-class parents who barely make ends meet.

For a student facing such factors, these are important reasons to improve the situation by finishing high school or a GED and getting into a training program, a community college or a four-year college. Your future can be more stable. There are people who want to help. Often you must go to someone, not wait for someone to come to you.

For a parent or a guardian, if you truly want to help but need more guidance, then take small steps, asking for help along the way.

Go to a library and start with a few books. Visit a high school counselor. Look for college apps for your phone. Look online, perhaps with a library's computer, to search websites, such as YouCanGo!™ and BigFuture™E. Other informational websites are listed on pages 80-82. Stop by any local college to get information and talk to someone. Get through the basics first, then continue. It will take effort on a regular basis. It will be worth it.

Students, What If You Need More Help?

If you are a student who is not getting much encouragement or guidance, well, don't give up. Sure, it's hard to ask for help sometimes. It can be embarrassing at first, and later. This is, however, your future. If some people around you are bad examples, then you must decide to do things differently than those people. Your future does not have to be the same as the indifferent kids who sit next to you in class, even if those kids are your friends. If there are some bad examples in your family, as are in many families, your future can be different.

Friends and Family are Important,
But Don't Listen to the Goof-Offs or Follow Bad Examples

Your friends and family are important to you. They should be. But your friends or family may not be spending time with you in the best way for you, if you're more serious about the future than they are. Make the smart choice and prepare for your future.

Goof-off friends and down-in-the-mouth family members will eat up your time. "You don't need to do *all* that," they'll tell you. "Let's chill." Sure, hang out a little, but not *all* the time.

You have to make up your mind to separate yourself on a regular

---

E YouCanGo!™ and BigFuture™ are trademarks owned by the College Board, which is not involved in the production of, and does not endorse, this product.

basis from people who aren't serious. They may not care about grades. If you, however, can get higher grades, you had better do so, and not let them hold you back.

If you must save face, when you have homework to do, you might blame it on someone else, such as mom or dad, your guardian, your aunt, your uncle, your big brother, your little sister, the teacher, the counselor, or even the admissions person at the college, who said you had to do it.

You might boldly go where you haven't gone before, to say:

"I have work to do. I have to go."

Then get up. And go. And do the work.

Who Really Does Care About You and Your Future?

Is a person really a true friend, if they aren't looking out for what is best for you? You may be starting the process of passing them up, and they're uncomfortable about that, preferring that you just hang out, as in the past. It's time, however, for you to start to move forward. While remaining friends, if you have to bypass people so you can study, so you can go to college, so be it.

Turn it around for a minute. What kind of friend would you be if your good friend really could go to a good college, but you made them miss out? Just because you wanted them to hang out with you. You would mess up his or her future? Just so you can hang out. That's not a true friend. That's a misguided, selfish young person.

Should you take life-altering advice from those types of people? Maybe let them pick a movie, but don't let them pick your future. Grow up. Toughen up. Tell them no.

If It Is Up to You, Then It Is Up to You

If it is up to you, then it is up to you. You can do it. With effort, doors will open. For your own sake, take the first steps and find out more. At whatever level works for you, go forward.

If a student needs remedial classwork, so be it. Wherever you are at, if you haven't taken school seriously so far, then change your ways.

If you are about to graduate or have graduated from high school, and you need remedial classes, then get going. Some students graduate, thinking they've done OK, but testing at college shows they need to retake some classes, or a lot of classes. Well, get going.

Take such classes. Find a tutor. Some free help is usually available, if you ask around. Use Khan Academy online for free. If you got a bad start, be mature enough to admit it. If you do the work to correct it, then you have a bright future.

Lacking Computer Access? Don't Let That Stop You!

Students, parents and guardians, if computer access or internet access is a problem, do not let this stop you. A whole lot of people don't have faster internet, or any internet, at home, certainly when money is tight.

Use the municipal library and school library, school internet, or wireless at a restaurant or coffee shop on a school laptop, personal laptop, tablet or phone to work on things. Use McDonald's Wi-Fi. With an account, the college application websites save your account information as you go along filling in applications.

A public library should work, but to cover all contingencies, if you have no workable internet options, request a paper application. If need be, you can insist. That would stand out in a positive light, proving that you were a determined applicant.

Another option for a local college is to ask if you may use a computer terminal at the college to complete the application.

Being Broke is Hard: Make Adjustments

In this book, you will read many suggestions whereby I mention costs as being reasonable. But if you have no spare money, the smallest costs can hold you up.

Some of us are broke at times, depending on varying conditions, and are not guaranteed any money in our pockets, including $10 for an extra score report, $2 for some file folders, or $3 to get coffee and leave a tip.

For those who are in a tough situation with money, I've tried to give low-cost or free options. Getting a student from temporary housing into college is so important that I must stress that students, parents and guardians not give up. When you read about this cost or that cost, don't automatically think that you still can't go forward. See what can be done.

Ask and Improvise

When the road is blocked because of money, don't give up. Try to improvise. If a deadline is nearing and you don't have the money for something, what should you do? I recommend that you let someone at the high school or college know. At times, it's easier to ask for help and at times it is the last thing we want to do. At times, it is very hard for any of us to get past the reluctance to admit that we don't have money for something.

On fees for tests and applications, see if something can be worked out. Sure, the high school won't put up a sign offering every kid a free SAT Subject Test, for example. But if you need one, it would show you are very serious if you were to go to the principal, the assistant superintendent or the superintendent and ask if the district, or a local agency or charity, would pay for it, explaining which colleges you need it for. Ask.

Many school districts now pay for a school-wide SAT exam or ACT exam. Ask. If that is coming up for your district, plan to use one or more of those tests for your college applications at no cost.

Hundreds of colleges have free applications. Fee waivers are available, as explained in this book.

Whatever it is, try to improvise.

Transit fare, gas money or parking fees can be a problem to travel to an internship, for example. Rather than not go, let them know, "My funds are low for travel some weeks." If they won't pay for transit, then explain that's why you won't be there sometimes so they won't think you missed out of negligence or lack of interest. They'll appreciate knowing, so it is worth getting over the reluctance to bring it up.

Money for Social Events

Not having money is awkward, that's for sure. If you should go somewhere and you'll need to eat to get through the afternoon or evening, then eat before or after you go somewhere. I've eaten my food right out of my backpack on a bench or in a hallway with a spoon or fork and paper napkin. When everyone else is chipping in for pizza, I've skipped it, saying I ate before I got there, then eaten later.

If it's good socially to hang out in a restaurant with other students, do so, but you can just order a decaf, or say you have an upset stomach and have water, leaving a dollar tip, if you have it.

You can still get in on the conversation and make a good impression, without having to spend money. When you have some good things to say, that's what people will remember, not what you ordered, or didn't order.

Ask for Help, No Matter What

Students, no matter what the reasons, if you are having problems getting ready for job training programs or colleges, in completing applications or in understanding the options, ask for help:

- ☐ Talk to a fellow student who is also applying.
- ☐ Talk to a friendly teacher. Talk to the principal. Sure, the counselor is busy. Keep going back.
- ☐ At your job, talk to an adult, a supervisor or a college student.
- ☐ Talk to a librarian.
- ☐ The nearest college admissions office will help you, if you will just walk in and talk to them: "I need some advice."
- ☐ Ask at your place of worship if someone can provide assistance. Stop at a nearby church when it's open to see if the staff or pastor knows someone who could help.
- ☐ Track down a college readiness or college assistance program, if available in your area.

Bad Stuff on Your Record

Colleges certainly do accept people who have unfavorable items in their record, so send in the application, despite something less than ideal in your record. Discuss this with your counselor or an assistant principal. Some disciplinary items may not be reported by the school. Juvenile records may not have to be disclosed.

You definitely should still complete your applications and send them, even if you have to disclose something.

If you see a question about such things, do not think the worst and let it keep you from completing the application. Colleges ask such questions because they have to, not because they can't wait to find a reason to turn anyone down. Answer the question accurately based on what must be disclosed and submit the application. The odds may be that you will be accepted due to the good things on the application, not the one bad thing.

In the future, when you complete a degree it will help offset any stigma of a bad mark, much to your benefit, so apply.

Ignore the Jerks. Move Around Them

In navigating high school, a college bureaucracy and life, you will deal with rude people who will brush you off and stand in your way. Arrogant, rude people, for whatever reasons, are insecure about themselves, so they overcompensate by acting superior to others. Some are focused on themselves, oblivious to the equal importance of others.

Work around such people, not letting them stop you.

A Lot of People Want to Help, Once You Get Things Going

Mature people will respect you for your effort. Be proud of your effort. Hey, a lot of others are not even trying. Boldly keep asking for assistance. If something might be embarrassing, such as a lack of money, or not knowing about something, or past mistakes, don't let that hold you up, because everyone has had such situations.

Go ahead, ask. If it doesn't work out the first time, the second time, or many more times, keep going, adjusting things, until it does work out. It will be fine.

Educational opportunities have never been better in the U.S. In 1940 only about 11 percent of people had a bachelor's degree or higher. Now it's about 33 percent.[17] The good benefits of a completed relevant degree done at a reasonable cost last a lifetime. That is for you as much as it is for anyone. It will be worth it.

Chapter 7

The Basics for an Associate's Degree & a Bachelor's Degree

This next section is for students, and their parents, for whom community college or a four-year college is a new venture. It is also for parents and guardians who went to college long ago and need updating.

Let's review some college and university basics.

And by this, I mean exactly that, the basics. I stress this because for many households, let's be honest, knowledge of the details of the college and university system is lacking.

Millions of students are willing to work to better their lives. Many guardians and parents want to help. But what can hold them back?

Often, other kids do not support academic achievement, making it hard for a student to buck up against his friends and social groups to say, "I have to study now," or "I care about going to college." Sometimes brothers, sisters, cousins and friends discourage the serious one from extra schoolwork. "It doesn't take all that."

Often middle-class and working-class parents and guardians are working at irregular hours, not being at home evenings and weekends. When they are home, everyone's exhausted, ready to catch up on sleep or veg out on TV, not double check homework, or college emails.

But, students, parents, and guardians, to get ready for college, you must have longer conversations about school than: "How was school?" asks the parent. "Fine," says the student. "Did you do your homework?" "Yes." That's polite and all, but when it's time to get serious, it's going to take much more than that.

Basic College Terms

First, some definitions: A *college* issues one-year or two-year certificates and diplomas, or two-year associate's degrees or four-year bachelor's degrees. A *university* issues master's degrees and other advanced degrees. A university may have a college within it. The term *liberal arts college* or *liberal arts degree* refers to studies in math, science, or humanities with a major and with some classes in other topics, rather than studies that are primarily technical or vocational, such studying to be an aviation mechanic. In this use, the term liberal does not mean liberal as a political label. A college with a conservative political reputation, for example, still offers liberal arts degrees, such as in math, science or English. With college studies, the term *liberal arts* refers to a type of study, not a political or social ideology.

Parents and Students, What is Your Commitment Level?

Making good decisions about college requires attention to details, guidance from others, encouraging yourselves and each other and follow-up. High school students must understand job markets and the effects of education.

College Readiness, Admissions and Scholarships

College readiness means a student must know the material; not guess on the material, to progress through the first two years of college to an associate's degree, for example.

Further, to get merit scholarships to state colleges and private colleges, a student must prove he or she knows the material very well. Further still, to be accepted to more selective colleges, a student must prove she or he knows the material very, very well.

What's the proof? Good grades and good test scores. If a student has Cs and a below average test score, how can he or she claim mastery of the material and readiness for more rigorous college programs? He or she can't. The offers will not occur. Nor should they.

Let's not, however, discourage the C student with average scores from completing a degree and proceeding to great business and career success, but let's acknowledge that getting a merit scholarship isn't probably in the works. (Remember that lower-cost options are available to all. Also, some aid for low-income students is based on that low-income, even for C to B students.)

You Can't Guess Your Way Through the Tests

The ACT exam and SAT exam measure college readiness.

- For English and reading, the student must read and reread several paragraphs of writing at a steady speed to understand the vocabulary, sentences and the logic of the ideas.
- For math, problems and equations must be mastered. The problems must be completed at a steady pace.

Sure, that's common sense, but many students don't take these basics seriously, especially in freshman and sophomore years. They get lazy, rather than thoroughly learning the English and math their school is presenting to them. Avoid that mistake.

Hey, freshmen and sophomores, you'd better take it seriously, study enough, and request tutoring if needed, so you can know this material in senior year. That's what it takes if you want better choices in college. The people who design the standardized tests make sure a student can't guess his way through.

In math, the student has to know how to do the problem, not commit a calculation error, and not take forever to do it. In English, the student must know grammar and punctuation to avoid guessing.

For College-Bound Kids: Those Standardized Tests?
They Come from the Classwork and the Homework

Because the tests are used for admissions and financial aid, I recommend that students as early as in 8th and 9th grade take a practice standardized test. Some readers will take issue with this advice, but hear me out. Students should have fun and happiness in life. I'm pointing out that taking practice tests with the right information and right attitude can make this process less stressful and tiring, not more so.

cognition (kag nish en)

the brain's process to obtain knowledge
with experience, senses, thought,
and study

Cognition is Obtaining Knowledge.
Anyone Can Improve Cognition.
No One is Stuck.

Research has confirmed that our brain pathways improve with more effort, such as increased studying. Research proves that students who accept that they can do better and then act accordingly, do get higher grades and test scores, no matter where they start from.[18] Anyone can build good stores of knowledge. Certainly, success starts with a willing mind. But to reach mastery, any and all, must complete extended, diligent work.

Any student of any background can improve, if he or she decides to. A person is a combination of his or her level of cognitive ability and his or her level of determination, both of which can improve. On the other hand, there are many very smart, but lazy people who will accomplish little of importance.

We can improve our skill in reading, writing and studying. No one has to say, *I'm stuck*. Determination can be improved substantially, which improves cognition and results. Anyone can become a faster reader by reading more. Any student can increase math speed by repeating the equations, mastering the little details. There is no shortcut. Einstein and Mozart didn't reach the end result just from intelligence. They worked and worked and did not quit, or we would never know their names. They had to learn each detail over years. Just like you. Go over it again. Then some more. Increased effort will mean higher grades and test scores for any student.

And that means you.

But I'm not good in Math

But, I'm not good in English.

That is Incorrect.

Evidence Proves That Students Who Decide To Do Better, Will Do Better in _Any_ Subject.

That Includes You.

Yes, you, as a student, may like one subject over another. That's natural. But don't base grades only on that. That is wrong.

Intelligence (Your Brain) Grows with Effort

Here's the proof: Research shows that students who were shown information that intelligence can be improved, such as the brain is a muscle that grows stronger with effort, had grades rise significantly while the grades of classmates who learned only about good study habits did not. The students doing better are likely to make greater effort, getting As and Bs instead of Cs. [19]

Students had a college GPA increase over four years from a B+ to an A-, for example, when shown that they weren't stuck and they could improve academic performance, compared to students that weren't shown this concept.[20]

Adjust your attitude and you can do better in any subject. These are facts.

I'm not good at it, is not a fact carved in stone forever, if you do more to get good at it. _I'm stuck_, is not fact, after you get unstuck by adding one bit of knowledge upon another. Move mental barriers.

If you're behind, get off the phone and redo the basics. If you do so, in any subject, your grades and test scores will improve.

College Degree Levels in the U.S.

Type of Degree	Years to Complete That Degree Level	Notation	Cumulative Total Years to Complete	Official Name
Certificate or Diploma	1 year or 2 years		1 year or 2 years	Certificate or Diploma
Associate's	2 years	Can include transferred credits	2 years	Associate of Arts or Science
Bachelor's	4 years	Can include transferred credits	4 years	Bachelor of Arts or Science
Master's	2 years	Requires bachelor's first	6 years	Master of Arts or Science
Law or J.D.	3 years	Requires bachelor's first	7 years	Juris Doctor
Medical or M.D.	7 years (includes 3 years as a resident)	Requires bachelor's first	11 years	Doctor of Medicine
PhD	3 to 5 years (varies)	Requires master's first	9 to 11 years (varies)	Doctor of Philosophy* (includes most science and humanities subjects)

*Doctor of Philosophy does not mean that the study of philosophy is included. It's just the title, unless it is for a PhD in philosophy. The PhD can be for English, economics or chemistry, for example.

The student should be exposed to what college readiness means, and not by just skimming a few practice questions, but by actually taking a practice test, so it sinks in.

It will force him or her to face the facts of how detailed the information is. Then a student will be able to relate what he or she learns in class throughout high school to how it is tested on the standardized test. Part of the age-old question, "Why do I have to know this stuff?" will be answered.

Not only is the knowledge from high school important for personal life, careers, business and academics, but *it is on the test*.

Test-Optional Colleges: You Can Get Accepted to a Great College Without Even Taking the SAT Test or the ACT Test

Many well-regarded colleges do not require or do not emphasize the SAT test or the ACT test for admission. One list is on www.FairTest.org. How about Bowdoin, Skidmore, Smith, Trinity or Wake Forest? All are top colleges, with no test requirement. Many of the U.S.'s liberal arts colleges do not require either test, nor do some state colleges. So, if you are suffering from test anxiety, you can breathe a little easier. Maybe that will improve your test scores.

If you have good grades and accomplishments but get bad scores, consider some of the colleges that don't require a test. The colleges may allow you avoid reporting the worst scores.

Or just skip the tests completely and use the colleges that don't require the test. Hey, that's up to you. One student I knew was going to use Pima Community College in Tucson to apply to transfer to University of Arizona Nursing. So, she didn't take an ACT test or SAT test, but got As at the community college. She got into U. of A. Nursing, a highly-rated program.

Students who apply with transfer applications can take an ACT test or SAT test well after high school graduation to enhance a transfer application. After a year or more at the community college, for example, take a test. If the score is good, it can be included in the transfer application.

Remember that some colleges that require the tests do offer a lot of financial aid to lower-income families, so if you're shooting for those colleges specifically, then yes, you better work on the test prep.

At selective colleges that are test-optional, however, many accepted freshmen, about 80 percent to 90 percent, did still submit test scores, as shown in Common Data Set statistics.

Even that leaves a lot of students who got in with no test scores submitted.

Take the Practice Tests, but Don't Sweat the First Scores and Don't Get Discouraged

Here's a risk with my advice to take early practice tests: The student gets a lousy score, gets discouraged and gives up. I've seen it happen, where students may not say much, but they become convinced that a lousy score is their fate forever. They incorrectly conclude that improvement is not possible.

I know very strong arguments can occur over this, which is why I know this is so serious. "I'll never do better," says the student. "Yes, you can," says the parent. "No I can't. Leave me alone!"

Practice tests are vital, but with the wrong understanding of what can be a long and winding process, a bad practice-test experience can sabotage a student's mindset.

Let's avoid that, not by skipping the practice test, but understanding the long process and by expecting, in advance, a lousy practice score. Students, you're going to get lousy scores on a lot of practice tests. So what. That's fine. It's part of the process.

Before you take a practice test, you must realize some, or a lot, of the material may not have been covered yet in your classes. Thus, a lot of answers will be wrong. That's OK. These point you in the right direction, that's how to think about it.

This situation is helped a bit in that the PSAT™ 8/9 test is geared for grades 8 and 9 and the PSAT™10 test,[F] is for 10th grade. The

F PSAT™ 8/9 and PSAT™ 10 are trademarks owned by the College Board, which is not involved in the production of, and does not endorse, this product.

74

PreACT™ test[G] is for 10th graders. Even then, good students may get lousy scores, due to unfamiliarity with testing logic and timing. Such tests offer review on wrong answers.

A student shouldn't be discouraged by the wrong answers, so that he or she lowers expectations of future success or lowers his or her determination to strive.

The wrong answers show that there is a lot to pay attention to in school.

It also shows that these tests take a lot of practice to get the hang of, for some more than for others.

Even for students with good grades who have good understanding of the material, these questions are designed to be a tricky pain in the neck. It takes practice to get the logic down of the reading questions and not take forever. In math, it takes practice to combine different types of math together, remember how to do each equation, and do it quickly enough.

Seeing questions that one cannot answer can be discouraging. Thoughts such as "I didn't know how to answer a lot of those questions. This is hopeless. I'll never make it. Why bother?" will crop up. Such conclusions are incorrect.

Rather, the wrong answers help you focus on future schoolwork and future extra study on your own. Think of this as great news, that you can go over the wrong answers, while it is only practice. A student should not be discouraged one bit by the unanswered questions and wrong answers. They are your roadmap, your tools, to a good score, sitting there right in front of your face.

The type of questions you don't know how to do now will be the ones you will get right later, if you study and practice. By the end of junior year and in first semester of senior year, a lot of the material will have been covered in class, if you are paying attention.

Practice tests are crucial to learn how to keep your place and keep up your speed. I hear it over and over from students after a test that they

---

[G] *PreACT™ is a trademark owned by the ACT, which was not involved in the production of, and does not endorse, this product.*

wish they had been able to go faster and with more confidence. Upon questioning, they admit that they didn't practice nearly enough on taking the test under timed conditions.

This is Boring. Yes, It Is. It Was Boring Way Back When Too and It Will Be Boring in the Far Distant Future. Do It Anyway

With schoolwork, hopefully at many times, the love of learning comes out in all of us and we enjoy the process of learning, of getting things right, of understanding, of liking the knowledge. Let's all try to keep that in life.

Let's admit, however, that for most teenagers at most times, taking tests and studying for them is boring, and especially irksome after being nagged to do it for the millionth time. Boring. Boring. Boring.

Taking practice tests, unless one is in the mindset and mood, isn't a fun thing to do, but it is important.

☞ Chapter 8 ✍

Resources

College Guides, Admissions Books, Study Guides, Websites, Tutors & Counselors.

Use the many books, articles, blogs and online sources of information out there. The advice, discussions and debates about colleges include changes recently in some respects, while much of the discussion has been the same for twenty years.

Visit A Bookstore, Search Your Library, Look Online

At one bookstore, you may find up to 30 different titles about college admissions, college selection, college applications, college costs, scholarships, financial aid and essay writing. Sit down and peruse them. You will see study guides for every test. To save money, write down book titles to check if a library has them, and to check if you can buy them used online or at a used bookstore.

Many books are well worth getting from a library or buying, considering how important college decisions are. A pizza or a book? Two movie tickets or a book? Get the books. If you need to buy one now and others later, do so, but get the information.

For any book, look at the new copy offered to find the year of the most current edition. Sometimes a current-edition book is available used, or even new, at a lower price in the "other sellers" section. A used older edition may have most of same information, at a discount.

College Guides

Use college guides, available at libraries or for purchase.

One great college guide is: *The Other College Guide: A Road Map to the Right School for You,* by Jane Sweetland, Paul Glastris and the staff of the Washington Monthly, 2015, The New Press, New York. It ranks best-buy colleges, (including some overlooked ones). See instructions on how to find a good match for you, such as colleges that go out of their way to help students graduate.

Colleges That Change Lives: 40 Schools That Will Change the Way You Think About Colleges by Loren Pope, updated by Hilary Masell Oswald, 2012, Penguin Group, New York, profiles 40 colleges that nurture scholarship and discovery. Many are not excessively hard to get into, although some still cost a lot.

The book *Cool Colleges for the Hyper-Intelligent, Self-Directed, Late Blooming and Just Plain Different,* 2007, Ten Speed Press, Berkeley, CA, by Donald Asher highlights interesting colleges for all fields and types of students, along with thoughtful, detailed discussions about selecting a college. The last edition was 2007, but this remains a valuable book.

Study Guides:

New test study guides at bookstores or online cost around $12 to $25. You can buy used current-edition study guides online or at used bookstores and sometimes save several dollars.

Most tests remain the same in the type of content and logic from year to year, with the notable exception being the new SAT test in 2016, so use new SAT test guides for 2016 and afterward.

Often libraries order new test guides each year. You may ask a librarian to order a book, and many will do so. Seriously, if you need a guide, the librarian may just order it. If you're in a pinch, ask.

With a library book, you can photocopy the answer pages to mark them, or prepare an answer sheet by hand or mark the pages lightly with a pencil and then erase the marks.

If you need to save money by using a test study guide that is a year or two old, the practice is still relevant. The practice score will still be relevant. It's good to double check, but most tests haven't been revamped recently, so English, history, math, and science test prep books that are a year or two old are fine.

Internet Resources:

Search for sites by college topics. Many college applications, admissions, testing and tutoring blogs, articles and sites are available with valuable information. On page 309 is a list of state university system websites for all 50 states, D.C. and 5 U.S. territories.

Navigate every nook and cranny of websites. Plan on taking some time. Click on every available tab that might remotely relate to you to find information. Some tabs just hint at the information there. Make a notation. Don't rely on memory. Bookmark it, or cut and paste the URL address into a file, or write it down and file it with the college file.

Searching Websites Can Be Problematic

When a website's own search box results are spotty, get out of the college or agency website and use a regular search engine with, for example: "Coolidge College Test Percentiles."

Then you might find a link with the sought-after information, sometimes on the very website you were just endlessly searching.

If Needed, Make Contact

Don't be reluctant to call, visit or email a college office. Before you call, prepare a message to leave. State your name, phone number and email address at the beginning of the message, not the end, so it's easy for the person to replay the message to get your number. Provide a few details, so the right person can respond. Interaction with people, talking to people, brings new, vital information. A knowledgeable person can elaborate with information not listed elsewhere. Always ask the adviser an open-ended question such as, "What further advice can you give me?"

INFORMATIONAL WEBSITES

https://blog.ed.gov/2016/09/affordable-four-year-schools-with-good-outcomes/

From all the statistics, 26 public colleges are highly notable as: **Affordable Four-Year Schools with Good Outcomes.**

www.act.org*

For ACT®, Inc., the PreACT™ Test and the ACT® Test

Includes college planning, financial aid, careers and test preparation. For a free practice test click on Prepare for the ACT / Download a Free Study Guide. A paid online tutorial service starts at about $40 with another for about $180. Students, parents, guardians and mentors can use a free service, the ACT Profile, to plan for college majors, degrees and careers, and to get free information from colleges. Helpline: 319-337-1000.

www.CollegeBoard.org*

For the College Board®, the SAT® Test, SAT Subject Tests™, PSAT Tests, Big Future™ and Advanced Placement® Tests

Includes eight free practice test to print and take at home. (Use the question box to find "SAT practice test.") Has the Official SAT Question of the Day™. Tutoring is free from Khan Academy. You can order study guides. Includes college planning, financing and preparation. With a College Board account, households can receive information from colleges. BigFuture™ sorts colleges for you. General helpline: 212-713-8000. SAT test helpline: 866-756-7346.

www.CollegeResults.org

Create your own group of colleges for comparison with a lot of data available. It's from the Education Trust.

* ACT® is a trademark registered by ACT, Inc. PreACT™ is a trademark owned by ACT, Inc. which is not affiliated with, and does not endorse, this book. The College Board®, SAT®, Advanced Placement®, and AP® are trademarks registered with the College Board. SAT Subject Tests™, PSAT™, BigFuture™ and The Official SAT Question of the Day™ are trademarks owned by the College Board which is not involved in the production of, and does not endorse, this product.

https://CollegeScorecard.ed.gov- U.S. Dept. of Education:

All U.S. colleges are indexed, sorted and ranked by many categories. Searches are by: public, private nonprofit, private for profit, degree, state, region, zip code, college size, name, specialized mission and religious affiliation. It has full college profiles with sorts by categories such as earnings, graduation rate, average cost, name and size.

www.nces.ed.gov/CollegeNavigator

College Navigator – U.S. Department of Education Index:
Data on all U.S. colleges. Has net prices based on family income.

www.nasfaa.org

See extensive financial aid information in the Students, Parents and Counselors section. Read every tab. From the National Association of Financial Aid Administrators.

www.collegecost.ed.gov

The College Affordability section has colleges with high and low tuition and fees and colleges with high and low net prices.

www.CommunityCollegeReview.com

See articles on community colleges, including costs and benefits.

www.nacacfairs.org - Free college fairs with hundreds of colleges.

www. FairTest.org

Some colleges are test optional, meaning students may apply without supplying an ACT test score or an SAT test score. This site lists colleges that do not emphasize standardized tests.

www.CollegeFish.org - Helps transfer students.

https://nces.ed.gov/ipeds - Detailed, sortable data on colleges.

www.ImFirst.org

Helps those who are the first in the family to go to college.

www.FeedThePig.org

Financial information / student loans
American Institute of Certified Public Accountants, Feed the Pig®, Select: Master Credit & Debt;   Select: Student Loans.

www.MySmartBorrowing.org

National career selection and college cost information; from the Pennsylvania Higher Education Assistance Agency.

www.GetMeToCollege.org - Covers a range of college topics.

www.StudentAid.ed.gov - Federal government student aid - U.S. Federal Government site for grants and loans.

http://CollegeAffordability.urban.org

This site has articles to explain college costs. The Breaking Even section examines at what point you make your money back on college, which by one estimate is at age 30.

www.MappingYourFuture.org

College planning, from Mapping Your Future®, from the non-profit Mapping Your Future, Inc.

www.EducationPlanner.org

For parents and students, with sections on careers, college selection, student aid, FAFSA, scholarships and campus visits, among others, from the Pennsylvania Higher Education Assistance Agency.

www.KhanAcademy.org/college-admissions

Has articles and video interviews with advisers on Getting Started; Making high school count; Exploring college options; Applying to college; Paying for college & Wrapping up.

http://new.time.com/money/best-colleges/

Make your own college ranking list **based on your** test scores and **your** finances from MONEY Magazine's Best Colleges with 706 colleges by location, majors, school size.

www. StriveForCollege.org

A non-profit site for students whose parents did not go to college, which provides information and a mentor for specific questions.

www.PublicUniversityHonors.com

Honors college information for public colleges and universities.

All 50 States: Public University System Websites

50 states, plus D.C. and 5 U.S. territories are in a list on page 309.

Lists of Summer Programs and Extra Curricular Programs for High School Students

A) Imagine Magazine from Johns Hopkins Center for Talented Youth has a national listing of programs and resources at: www.cty.jhu.edu - select: Resources, Imagine Magazine, Opportunities and Resources for Gifted Students.

B) MIT: www.mitadmissions.org - search for "summer programs."

THE COMMON DATA SET IS GREAT

For One College, You Can See:
→ **GPAs, low test scores, middle test scores, high test scores of admitted freshmen in Sect. C9.**
→ **Admissions waitlist information in Sect. C2.**
→ **How many transfer students applied and were accepted in Sect. D2.**

The format is easy to compare between colleges. The Common Data Set is a very valuable tool. There is a lot of information to sort through. But that's a good thing. You can find out a lot about different colleges. Try it.

A) Use a web search for:

College Name Common Data Set, such as

University of Maryland Common Data Set

or

B) Search for Common Data Set on a college's website search.

The Common Data Set (CDS) initiative is a collaborative effort among data providers in the higher education community and publishers as represented by the College Board, Peterson's, and U.S. News & World Report, per www.commondataset.org, as of Nov. 22, 2016.

Paid Tutoring and Paid Admissions Advisers

Regarding paid test tutoring, paid academic tutoring or paid admissions advisers, these are optional services.

If you have the money to spend, such services may be worth it to you, to avoid extra research on your part, although this book provides a solid tutorial, with low-cost referrals, on these matters. Services cost from $59 to $99 for test practice. It goes up: $200, $300, $1,000, $3,000, $10,000 to $20,000.

With individual paid tutors, or a paid-for class, let's recognize that some companies do, in fact, have tutors who have gotten perfect scores on the standardized tests.

Regarding paid admissions counseling, let's recognize that some college advisers have in fact worked in the selective admissions field and can provide insights tailored to the specifics of one student.

Learn About Selective College Admissions: For Free, $50 or $105

Any parent or student can get a solid explanation of the process of selective college admissions by starting with chapters on selective admissions in this book and reading one or more of the four books listed on page 200. Four other books about choosing colleges are listed on page 197. Many of the eight books are in libraries, so you can get started for free.

For about $50, you could purchase four books. A recent total of all eight books at regular prices on one bookseller it came to about $105, including shipping and tax. That's a lot of information and expertise for $105. E-books are less. If you find some of them used, the price is lower.

Get Personalized Help for Free, or at Low Cost

Students, for a tutor, find a classmate who will help you out, as a favor. A short call or text can make the difference when you are stumped on homework or test prep on some nights.

Lower-priced tutoring can be found. Visit a college employment office for listings of tutors. Post some flyers: "Tutor Needed." On campus billboards, student tutors post flyers. Is a student at your high school available? Parents could pay $10 to $15 an hour to a student tutor, depending on prevailing wages.

The College Board has continued to offer Khan Academy for free SAT test tutoring for a few years now. Khan Academy also offers free classes on specific subjects from algebra to history.

Chapter 9

College Visits, Fairs & Forums

College visits, fairs and forums during high school are important for motivation. Students, get out there to see what's ahead of you. Parents, help your student by visiting a college.

As far as finding a fit, that is part of the goal as well. If a student sees a great fit out there, then he or she becomes more motivated.

Go See a College to Get Motivated

OK, parents and guardians, your stubborn kid may need some, or a lot, of encouragement to take college seriously, and thus take high school seriously. Without fail, take them to see a college, the sooner the better. No matter how stupid they think it is, find some time, call in sick from work if need be, and go.

OK, students, listen up, you need to take going to college seriously and see what's out there. Forget about what everyone else is doing, or *not* doing. Go see for yourself. The whole family could use the extra stimulus that college is a real, pending step in life.

Visits to colleges can show the student that there is a big world out there, other than the high-school world of friends, fools, gossip, fashion, boredom and drama.

A visit to a college reminds a student:

❖ That there will soon be a life for him or her at a college;

❖ That he or she needs to get ready for it;

❖ Why he or she is supposed to learn in class and study every night;

❖ To bypass hindering, lackadaisical classmates; and

❖ Why a scholarship to a state college or admission and a scholarship to a selective college would be beneficial, and could be possible.

What about a Selective College?

If a selective school is a possibility, then college visits, even to local state colleges, are important to reinforce that goal. At the local college, in addition to discussing its own college, the admissions staff can confirm to a student and parents that high scores and great grades can open admission doors to other more selective colleges as well.

Selective colleges send staff around the U.S. for recruitment sessions. Attend such events to meet admissions staff from selective colleges. Visits are recommended. See the chapters about selective colleges.

Not Sure About Different Colleges? Go and See

College fairs and forums can be very encouraging for a student who might not yet conclude that a selective college is possible. Skeptics say such events are designed mostly to boost the application totals of the colleges. Even if you are skeptical about their motives, or doubt your chances at any of these colleges, what if learning about selective admissions from these people helps you out? Go and see.

At these events, dress business casual (p. 283), and you'll be ahead of those students and parents who don't.

College Fairs and Forums

College fairs and forums allow students and parents to speak with admissions staff. Sign up for more information on an admissions website for notices. You will find these events by looking in the admissions portion of college websites. Sometimes the admissions events section is hard to find. Search for *Coolidge College in your area* or *Coolidge College in your town*. Once you find these pages, bookmark them into a separate college events folder, so you can check the sites regularly. You can also call.

Combined College Forums and College Fairs

www.nacacFairs.org

National fairs in all regions: The National Association for College Admission Counseling (NACAC) has college fairs in all regions of the U.S. with no charge to attend. These fairs each have from 75 to 275 colleges from around the nation.

NACAC also has college fairs specializing in science, technology, engineering and math (STEM) colleges and performing and visual arts colleges.

www.CoastToCoastTour.org

Dartmouth, Northwestern, Princeton, University of California-Berkeley and Vanderbilt

www.ctcl.org - Colleges That Change Lives

Agnes Scott College	Allegheny College	Antioch College
Austin College	Beloit College	Birmingham-Southern
Centre College	Cornell College	Denison University
Earlham College	Eckerd College	Emory & Henry College
Evergreen State	Goucher College	Guilford College
Hampshire College	Hendrix College	Hillsdale College
Hiram College	Hope College	Juniata College
Kalamazoo College	Knox College	Lawrence University
Lynchburg College	Marlboro College	McDaniel College
Millsaps College	Ohio Wesleyan Univ.	Reed College
Rhodes College	Saint Mary's (CA)	Southwestern University
St. John's College	St. Olaf College	University of Puget Sound
Ursinus College	Wabash College	Whitman College
Willamette University	Wooster, College of	

www.8ofTheBestColleges.org

Claremont McKenna, Colorado College, Connecticut College, Grinnell College, Haverford College, Kenyon College, Macalester College and Sarah Lawrence College

www.ExploringCollegeOptions.org

Duke, Georgetown, Harvard, University of Pennsylvania and Stanford

www.ExploringEducationalExcellence.org

Brown, UChicago, Columbia, Cornell and Rice

www.NavigatingEducationalOpportunities.org

Colby, University of Florida, UChicago and University of Vermont www.ChristianCollegeFairs.com

Fairs with 30 to 50 colleges, many from the region of the fair's location.

☞ Chapter 10 ✍

College Rankings

Rankings generally aren't very important, but can help guide students among different colleges. Perhaps a high ranking in a certain major can alert you to a college you did not know about. Reputable educators have made the argument that these ratings are imprecise, and thus not important at all, which is often a valid conclusion.

Therefore, use the rankings for information, but certainly not as the most important reason to make a college choice decision.

This book seeks to help students who may not expect at first to have any options at top-ranked colleges, such as students from low-income families at working-class high schools. Students who can meet the requirements should apply to well-ranked colleges, from the Ivies on down.

But let's avoid having any more students join into a fixation on seeking status by attending a college with a high rank that creates excessive self-imposed pressure. "If I don't get in, I'm doomed." Disappointed? Yes. Doomed? Hardly.

Research confirms it is more the person, than the college[21] that is the more important factor for success, which follows a person's good attitude, a work ethic, and an ability to get along with others. Such people use colleges of all types to find satisfying careers, make good livings and have vibrant lives.

U.S. Accreditation Counts for a Lot

U.S. colleges and universities, including tax-payer supported, government-run (public) ones, are among the world's best.

Students worldwide seek to attend U.S. colleges. Both private and public colleges are accredited by the same agencies, including community colleges, so standards for accreditation are quite uniform, meaning high, from one corner of the U.S. to the other.

The quality of many government colleges can and does match, or exceed, that of private colleges.

Certainly, at a top-ranked college, public or private, the tough coursework, the well-qualified faculty, and the ambitious students will provide a great environment. Does a selective college cover more material in greater depth, moving along faster? That could be. The teachers may expect more of students at a selective college.

When educational authors such as Frank Bruni, Paul Glastris, Jay Mathews and Jane Sweetland stick up for public colleges and universities, they're not denigrating the Ivies as if Princeton is handing out diplomas from a bubble-gum machine. Further, we expect that a student at Princeton, for example, meets people who know people who know people, if you get my drift. Hiring managers know that the high-ranked colleges have good people.

How Important is a Ranking? Not at All, Really

But hiring managers also know that all the other colleges have good people too. I've read comments that each level of course work covers similar material around the country, regardless of college reputations. Is the ranking of a college the most important factor as far as a student obtaining competency in any given field and excelling in any given field? No, not at all.

If you want to obtain competency and even further exceed expectations in any given field, opportunity to shine exists in U.S. accredited colleges in all states, starting with community colleges and regional colleges. Corporate managers report that graduates from regular colleges routinely bypass graduates from higher-ranked colleges.

Differences in College Salary Averages

Community colleges and regional colleges show lower salary averages for attendees, for example, than large four-year colleges, but that doesn't mean quality is lacking at the smaller colleges.

A lot of students at community colleges are correctly choosing jobs that fit their abilities, such as being x-ray technicians or dental assistants. They don't try be doctors or dentists, because their abilities don't match those jobs. That's smart. Then they choose the community college to save money. That's smart. A community college that serves more students who become x-ray technicians than students who become doctors will have a lower salary average. That does not indicate a lower quality of instruction.

At such colleges, siting in the same classes are a smaller number of students who will go on to be doctors. The instruction from the community college, though less heralded, will start such students on the path to achieve competency and excel as doctors.

Some colleges have lower salary averages because so many of their students go into social work, government, teaching, research, the arts and other careers that pay less. This can include expensive, private colleges and good public ones with top academics. Again, lower salary averages do not indicate lower quality. Some colleges serve regions that have a lower cost of living, thus lower salary averages. Again, it does not indicate a lower quality of instruction at such colleges.

Who Cares Where You Go?

Is your life going to be a social and financial failure if you don't get into one of the perceived top colleges? Of course, not. If that happens, just get going on life somewhere else, ASAP, in order to reach your same goals. The goal of only getting A Degree From That Place misses the point. You still have to do something after the degree, right?

Students, don't worry too much about perceived prestige to impress or outdo others. The people you may impress if you get into some fancy college will be thinking about themselves, not you, when you're sitting in class. Some will be happy for you, for about the five minutes you have their attention. Your parents will be proud. None of which will help your grades, employment or business later.

And if you don't get into the fancy college, the same people won't care much about that either. And your parents will get over it.

Who deals with the real consequences of where you go? You and your immediate family. That's about it. If you're a good and capable person, take a deep breath, be happy with yourself, and go forth to do some good, no matter where you start out or end up.

People can look at rankings among many factors in making college decisions. If you have the option, and the money costs are pretty close, you very well ought to consider a higher-ranked college. But not if you can't afford it, such as if the loans will be like a battleship anchor around your neck for 20 years. Should rank, or prestige, or what other people think, be the main factor then? Not at all.

Get Excited, Curious, and Optimistic

Parents and students, it's exciting to see all these options, with all kinds of great fits for all kinds of different reasons. Don't get overwhelmed, get curious. Don't get worried, get optimistic. It takes time to sort through the information, so get going.

Start with the state system websites (p. 309) for your state and nearby states. They list public and many private colleges, with links. For students who want to get away from home, remember that some colleges in the same region offer reduced rates (p. 103).

College Guides

To spark your interest, here are some colleges from the guides recommended in Chapter 8, Resources, (p. 78): Do you know about Agnes Scott College for women, Beloit College, Berry College, Cook Honors College, or Earlham College? You ought to.

Public colleges include Eastern Carolina University (NC), Eastern Oregon University, New College of Florida and Truman State (MO), so they offer lower in-state rates. Truman State and Eastern Oregon offer discount rates for students from other states in their regions, thus offering even more students access to a high-quality, small liberal-arts college, but one that isn't $40,000 a year net.

While downplaying rankings overall, I advise that looking at rankings can point a student in the right direction, including for specific majors.

World rankings also show what may be a surprise to many; just how good U.S. public colleges are, including their State U.

Forget About Oxford or Cambridge; Head to UCSD or UW

To modernize one world ranking, the Academic Ranking of World Universities purposely did not count Nobel Prizes and Fields Prizes, categories that overly favor the oldest universities.

Which colleges then moved into the World's Top Ten? Right after England's bastions of prestige, Cambridge and Oxford?

- the University of California at San Diego and
- the University of Washington

So, UCSD and UW are just as good as Cambridge and Oxford?

A respected rating agency came to that very conclusion based on academic and research indicators, except for those awards won back from 1902 to 1950.[22] High school students and parents in those states may not know this, or be inclined to believe it, but times are changing.

A mistake in perception is to underestimate the level of opportunity at U.S. state colleges for ambitious students. Who is making this mistake? Too many ambitious students and their prodding, ambitious parents, that's who.

U.S. public colleges and universities are very, very good, but because we grow up around them, we're used to them, or we often hear more about the sports teams than the academic programs.

More people in the state of Washington can probably give you an idea of about how long it's been since the UW Huskies or the Washington State Cougars were in the Rose Bowl, than know about the honors colleges at UW, WSU or Western Washington University.

In U.S. minds, the comparison between UW and Cambridge or Oxford would be that the Huskies would trounce Cambridge or Oxford in sports.[H]

But does it come to mind that UW's research, professors, scholars and students can equal Cambridge's or Oxford's?

It should.

U.S. Honors Colleges are Producing Great Results

In addition to the usual high-ranking public colleges, your state's top colleges have great programs in place for ambitious students. Sure, the overall acceptance rates at a state university may not be as exclusive.

This is by design to give more students a chance at college.

This is praiseworthy, not detrimental.

While not slamming the door in the face of average students, your state's colleges have honors colleges in place for ambitious, top students to move up.

The website www.PublicUniversityHonors.com has information, including recent press reports. Wikipedia has a list.

Benefits include:

◆ Advanced, demanding classes are available.

◆ Top, award-winning professors have been hired.

◆ Research projects are ongoing, waiting for you to join in.

◆ Business startup programs are available, with links to venture capital.

◆ Students in your state's colleges are compiling the accomplishments to be accepted to the most elite graduate programs, law schools and medical schools.

◆ Graduates will be hired at the top corporations.

And all at lower in-state prices, plus, perhaps, some scholarship money.

[H] Before any Brits complain, I'll note that Cambridge and Oxford athletes might match up with the UW athletes. Attendance is 250,000 for the Cambridge-Oxford rowing match on the Thames River, a lot more than Rose Bowl attendance, so those British squads are probably pretty good.

Local Schmocal U.? Or Top Worldwide University?

I'm from Tucson, Arizona, home of the University of Arizona. To Tucson kids, the University of Arizona can seem average and blasé. It's us local schmocals, right?

Students in Phoenix might think Arizona State University is no big deal. A check of rankings and accomplishments shows otherwise.

Worldwide and national rankings publish results for about 500 colleges and universities, after analyzing perhaps 1,000 colleges and universities.

The University of Arizona and Arizona State University in recent years have ranked *worldwide* in the top 100 or top 200 by various rating agencies. In some majors, ASU and UA are ranked ahead of Ivy League universities and other top world universities.

Arizona State in 2017 joined Harvard, Stanford and the University of Chicago as the only U.S. colleges to produce a Rhodes Scholar, a Churchill Scholar and a Marshall Scholar in the same year.

That's an elite accomplishment.

ASU announced it was ranked #1 in the U.S. in Innovation, ahead of Stanford and MIT and that it has 40 programs ranked in the top 25.[23] ASU's Barrett Honors College is highly regarded.

Phoenix and Tucson kids don't know that their public universities beat out the majority of 500 universities that are ranked nationally and worldwide and a few thousand other colleges around the U.S. and worldwide.

In many objective measurements, they are truly among the best universities in the world.

Not too bad, for good ol' State U., just down the road.

<u>Various College Rankings</u>

Academic Ranking of World Universities (Shanghai)
>   www.ShanghaiRanking.com

Acceptance Rate
>   www.AcceptanceRate.com (see Browse by State)

Affordable Colleges with Good Outcomes - U.S. Dept. of Education
>   https://blog.ed.gov/2016/09/affordable-four-year-schools-with-good-outcomes/ (26 colleges)

Forbes Magazine
>   www.forbes.com/top-colleges

Kiplinger's Best College Values
>   www.kiplinger.com (select Menu, Tools, College)

Money Magazine's Best Values Ranking
>   www.time.com/money/best-colleges/rankings/

Niche rating service
>   www.niche.com

QS World University Rankings
>   www.TopUniversities.com

Times Higher Education
>   www.TimesHigherEducation.com

U.S. Government Department of Education College Scorecard
>   www.CollegeScorecard.ed.gov (Use sorts for listings.)

U.S. News and World Report
>   www.USNews.com/Rankings

Washington Monthly
>   http://WashingtonMonthly.com/college_guide

Websites may change or discontinue.

☞ **Chapter 11** ✍

Benefits of Community College

You can start out at the community college for a certificate or associate's degree for a job, for example, as a dental assistant, nurse's assistant or welder, among many others, if that's a good level for you. With steady employment, and steady investing, you can build a good retirement.

For jobs requiring higher credentials, from a community college, you can, as well, continue to a bachelor's degree, and even end up with a law degree, a medical degree or a PhD.

I know a student who enrolled at the University of Illinois, but to save money he took most of his early credits at Parkland Community College in Champaign, IL. He was careful to take classes that would transfer for credit. At Illinois, he completed a bachelor's degree in English with honors. He went on to Notre Dame Law School. He's busy at a good firm, making very decent money, and it all started with community college credits.

If, after applying at a four-year college, you don't get a scholarship or much financial aid, you should consider skipping the four-year college for now, and starting at a community college.

If You Start at a Community College, Will You Finish?

Before we go over the benefits of a community college, please understand that statistics show that many students who start at a community college do not end up with a degree.

As far as that goes, a lot of students who start at a four-year college don't end up with a degree either, so this warning goes to all students.

You must plan and persevere to get a degree. Being in a four-year college during freshman and sophomore years can help some students maintain the made-up mindset to finish a bachelor's degree. Determine whether that is a factor for you.

If you need the extra motivation and support you get at a four-year college, consider paying the higher cost.

If you will be just as motivated to finish your associate's degree, then check on how much you will save in money, while triple-checking how to transfer the credits.

Be Sure the Credits Will Transfer!

It takes planning to have your credits at the community college transfer properly to count towards a bachelor's degree. Most of the time, this will be a standard procedure, but I'm raising an alarm for when it isn't. I had one family member who took verbal assurances from a private college, and then most of her transfer credits weren't allowed. She lost a lot of time and money.

"We can't evaluate the credits until you apply two years from now," is a runaround from lazy staff people and you do not have to accept that. College staff knows that transferring is a standard, common practice. Now, so do you. Thus, insist that the college provide guidelines or an evaluation of your planned courses in writing. If this is not available, the staff is being irresponsible. Don't take verbal assurances or maybes.

Community colleges have standard transfer agreements with four-year colleges. Use those agreements and guidelines to plan your associate's degree to transfer into your bachelor's degree. Then a transfer can be properly done at a significant savings without losing credits, time and money.

Benefits from a community college can include:
- Some community colleges offer four-year degrees in some majors;
- Qualified professors in smaller classroom settings than you may find in the first two years at a four-year college;
- Significant cost savings on tuition and fees compared to regular four-year colleges and for-profit schools;

- One-year certificates that can match or exceed certificates at much more expensive for-profit schools;

- Two-year associates degrees that can match or exceed degrees at much more expensive for-profit schools;

- Staying local allows you to keep your current job and housing arrangements or more readily find other job or housing arrangements using your local contacts.

- If you move to another area, tuition costs may still be reasonable;

- Extra activities that you can initiate, such as:

  - Opportunities for extra projects with close interaction with professors; and

  - An honor society, clubs, activities and study groups with other students seeking high academics. You can find students who share your goals, and professors to help you at whatever level, regular or higher, for a great academic experience.

Community College Review

See www.CommunityCollegeReview.com for articles and information.

Save Money on the Way to a Bachelor's Degree

Students can obtain an associate's degree and then apply as a transfer student to a four-year college, including selective colleges.

One service, www.collegefish.org, assists with transferring. It is run by the honor society for community colleges, but it is open to all students.

A student can finish the last two years at the four-year college and it counts as a full bachelor's degree from that four-year college.

If you, for example, transfer to the University of Wisconsin, the bachelor's degree will be that of the University of Wisconsin only.

Transfers to other colleges are also often allowed after freshman year or when semesters or quarters change.

An Honor Society to Meet Other Academic Achievers

Phi Theta Kappa is the official honor society for community colleges. The website is www.ptk.org. The society has information on scholarships, advisers and mentors for community college students. Scholarships may include money towards completing bachelor's degrees as a transfer student.

Community Colleges Can Give You a Good Start in a New Town

To start in a new location, look at a community college in another part of your state or in another state. Even in another area or another state, costs can be lower than at a four-year college. See information in the next chapter on moving to a new location.

☞ Chapter 12 ✍

Transfers, Moving to Another State & Study Abroad

Want to get away and spread your wings? In a new setting, away from parents, relatives, and the old crowd?

Want to head for the big city? Or do you want the ocean coast, or the countryside or the mountains?

Or study abroad? How about sipping espresso while reading textbooks in Paris or Rome? What about Mexico City or Shanghai? In some cases, it costs about the same, or less. Tuition in France and Germany is free, even for U.S. citizens, who can enroll there and get degrees. For whatever your level of adventure, here are some details.

Hadn't thought about it? Go ahead and do so. Around the U.S. or around the world, it is possible with some effort. It could be great, and even working-class and low-income students have options.

Within your state, or in another state, you might transfer in the future, maybe even to a college you didn't get into the first time.

Read on about transfers, moving to other states and study abroad.

Transfers

In any given year, semester, or quarter, all colleges, even highly selective ones, have students who have left, thus creating openings for transfers. The Common Data Set (p. 83) shows transfer data in Section D2.

Here are general possibilities for transfer applicants:

- Transfers are allowed from most four-year colleges to other four-year colleges.

- Transfers might be allowed after any semester or quarter, not just at the beginning of the traditional academic year in the fall. So, halfway through freshman year, or halfway through sophomore year, or for summer semester, you might be able to apply as a transfer student to somewhere else.

- If a student was denied admission to a college as a freshman, the student can apply to the same college later as a transfer student. If the student has improved his or her record with great grades and accomplishments, there is a chance of admission.

- Transfer openings are fewer, often in very small numbers, although far fewer people apply.

Moving to Another State

You could move to a new region or state for education by starting at a community college. Moving to another state to attend community college can make sense, but a student might have to pay higher rates for tuition at the community college for the first year, than do established residents. If you move, these rates can be:

(a) more than back at your home-state or home-district community college, (b) but less or about the same than regular rates back at your home-state four-year college. Later, after one year, lower, in-district rates often apply.

Here's one scenario:

- A student could move to another state and attend community college at about the same price as he or she would have paid with in-state rates at his or her old state four-year college.

- After one year, being careful to document residency, reduced rates would apply in the new state for the second year of college.

- After two years, a student would have an associate's degree and be ready to apply as a transfer student to a four-year college in the new state with in-state rates. Have a plan, confirming all the details.

Low Rates Within Your Region

You can still get out of your home state at good prices with regional exchange rates whereby you may attend college in the region at lower rates. Atlanta and Dallas kids can head for the Gulf Coast, and vice versa. Arizona kids can go to California. Oregon kids can get some sun, finally, in Arizona. Many larger universities, however, don't offer the discounts.

The National Association of Student Financial Aid Administrators
www.nasfaa.org/State_Regional_Tuition_Exchanges
This site links to the sites below and to financial aid programs for all 50 states and five territories. Select Students, then Financial Aid in Your State.

Southern Regional Education Board Academic Common Market
www.sreb.org/academic-common-market
www.sreb.org/regional-contract-program (medical, dentistry and veterinary)

The Midwest Student Exchange Program
msep.mhec.org

New England Regional Student Program
www.nebhe.org/programs-overview/rsp-tuition-break

Western Interstate Comm. for Higher Educ. Student Exchange Programs
www.wiche.edu/studentExchange

Establishing Residency in a New State for In-State Tuition: It's No Sure Thing

Be warned that in-state tuition is not automatic after moving and working in another state. Such a move may be worth the time, considering the huge savings for in-state college rates, if you conclude that a public college in another state is the best fit for you. The time does not have to be wasted. You can earn money from work, earn credits from a community college, or do both.

On the other hand, you can stay in your home state to enroll at lower rates without delay.

To be eligible for in-state tuition in the new state, just moving, getting a job, a state ID, or starting classes may not suffice. You may have a new state ID and pay taxes, but still not get in-state tuition.

Want Someplace New?
Get Your Start at a Community College

☐ <u>LA or Orange County?</u> There's L.A. City College, Valley College, Santa Monica College, Pasadena College, Orange Coast College and more. Hit the books, sitting on the beach.

☐ <u>New Orleans?</u> For this city with balmy winter weather, try Delgado Community College.

☐ <u>In the heart of Texas?</u> Austin has Austin Community College; Dallas has the Dallas County Colleges; Fort Worth has Tarrant County Colleges and Houston has Houston Community College.

☐ <u>Seattle?</u> Seattle Central College on Capitol Hill.

☐ <u>Manhattan in New York City?</u> Take the A Train? Yes, or the C, 1 or 2 to the Borough of Manhattan Community College in the city that never sleeps.

☐ <u>The California redwoods?</u> Mendocino College.

☐ <u>The North Atlantic coast?</u> York County or Southern Maine Community Colleges.

☐ <u>A small town out west with mountains nearby?</u> Northwest College in Powell, Wyoming is an hour from Yellowstone National Park. Snow ski in the Bighorn Mountains. No traffic jams here.

A student who has moved can get in-state prices only if he or she meets very specific requirements set by the college. These requirements vary, but generally could include:

- ☐ working at a job, or
- ☐ attending community college, or
- ☐ a combination of both
- ☐ for a full year or more in the new location,
- ☐ perhaps also while being independent of parental income,
- ☐ while moving <u>not</u> primarily for educational purposes.

Being Independent of a Parent's Income: What Counts?

If the new state requires the student to be independent of parental income, that means the student must show his or her own income from a business or job, or money from a loan in his or her name that pays expenses such as housing, food, transit and utilities. Yes, you can live cheap, staying with a relative or friend for cheap or free, riding a bike, taking the bus or driving a beater, but you have to show that expenses are paid from the student's income or loan proceeds with bank statements and expense receipts in the student's name. Sure, the parents can give the student a little spending money, but bills must be paid from the student's earnings or loans.

What is "Not for Educational Purposes Only?" Find Out

I have looked at different college requirements around the country and some mention only showing clear presence for one year, such as a lease and driver's license.

Others stipulate that the move to a new state cannot be "for educational purposes only." Thus, if you are moving only for college, and that's how they see it, it could mean the higher out-of-state prices for you.

I'm warning everyone very clearly and strongly that you had better figure out what everything means. Ask the people in the new state what they will accept as "other-than-educational factors," such as if family members are in the state or in the area, or if an employment offer will count. Be sure to know the exact requirements to get in-state prices. Triple check everything. Try to find cases of people who have done it. Ask a lot of questions.

Some colleges are more welcoming, if the demand to attend there is not as great, and other colleges are very stringent, if a lot people want to attend there.

If the college and state you want to move to will make it clear that you can do so and obtain lower rates later, then it can be a good thing to do. Many people flourish in a new setting.

Study Abroad: Want to Really Get Away?
College in Another Country

U.S. citizens are wanted as foreign students in other countries, just as foreign students are reserved some spots at U.S. colleges. You will be welcomed if you wish to go, and it's possible to do with lower net costs than here in the U.S. This can be true for a future master's degree, so keep that in mind. I know a student who is off to the University College London for a master's because it's a very highly-ranked university that costs less than a lot of U.S. universities.

Study in English

There are a lot of ways to do it, some very affordable. For instruction in English, one option is to go to English-speaking countries such as Canada, the United Kingdom and Australia. Additional programs in English include:

o Some U.S. colleges have locations in other countries with instruction in English. New York University, for example, has such programs in Abu Dhabi in the United Arab Emirates and Shanghai, China. Saint Louis University (MO) offers degrees in Madrid, Spain with instruction in English. Wikipedia has a list of American colleges and universities abroad with instruction in English.

o For study in English, there are several American Universities in foreign nations that are fully accredited in the U.S. These are private colleges, such as the American University of Paris or of Rome.

Study in the Foreign (Local) Language

Otherwise, instruction is in the local language.

To learn a foreign language while in high school, you had better start freshman year, or sooner.

Here's one example.: Italy has extra financial aid for low-income families, even for U.S. students (and Italy will consider good SAT test scores).

So, from a U.S. working-class neighborhood, you could head to Rome or Florence for a respected, and inexpensive, bachelor's degree, and who knows where that might lead? If you learn Italian first. Spanish speakers might like Spain for college.

A gap year is a year off from college classes after high school graduation. U.S. students can be accepted to a U.S. college and use the gap year to travel, work or conduct research, for example. This delays graduation by one year in the U.S.

With a study-abroad plan, students can use a gap year in a foreign country to work and get the language down, before starting classes abroad.

In Europe bachelor's degrees are completed in three years, so even with a gap year to practice the language, you can graduate four years later with a bachelor's degree, just as you would in the U.S.

International Study Can Help Your Career

Many U.S. students study abroad. For many jobs and careers, experience and knowledge of a foreign country or language helps. Graduates can work for global corporations, international agencies and in academia all over the world or in the U.S.

Study abroad can be linked to a U.S. college. Students may obtain a degree in another country that is valid for U.S. jobs and further university study in the U.S. Below is a short list. With research, you will find more programs.

A U.S. college may recognize a significant amount of credit from study abroad, for one or more years, all while enrolled in a U.S. college.

107

Countries with Costs About the Same as in the U.S.

I noticed many listings for scholarships and aid for U.S. students to attend college in Europe, including from the foreign colleges.

In some countries costs are like U.S. costs. These countries include Australia, Canada, China and England.

- London? Tuition costs are like U.S. costs, or lower, but a bachelor's degree takes only three years. The University of London's colleges include City University of London, University College London, St. George's and the London School of Economics.
- Beijing, Hong Kong or Shanghai? Perking University, Hong Kong University and Fudan University welcome foreign students.
- Australian instruction is in English. Costs are like U.S. costs.
- Many U.S. students get degrees in Canada, which offers instruction in English (and in French) and costs may be like, or lower than, U.S. costs.

Countries with Lower Costs than the U.S.

In France, Germany, Italy, Mexico and Russia, net costs at well-regarded public colleges and universities can be lower, often by a lot, than in the U.S.

You must still pay for registration fees, books, renting a room and food. Again, in Europe, bachelor's degrees are awarded in three (3) years, not four. You might be able to work for wages in the other country while in college. Here are some examples (taught in the foreign languages):

- Paris? Espresso on the Left Bank. The Sorbonne is a major college. Tuition in France is free. Let's see, that comes to $0.00. Registration fees are low. Savings on tuition will help you get a room with some Parisian students.
- Berlin or Munich? Follow in footsteps of Du Bois, Einstein, Heisenberg, Planck and Weber. Tuition is free and fees are reasonable at public colleges. There's Humboldt, The Freie University or the University of Munich. Heidelberg and Leipzig have 65 Nobel winners between them.
- Rome or Florence, Italy? Great scenery to enjoy as you read textbooks. Public universities have reasonable tuition, perhaps

around $2,000 a year. In Italy, tuition is based on family income. So, lower-income students, including U.S. students, may qualify for more aid. High academics are also figured in. And get this, they take the SAT test scores into account, so if those are higher, merit aid may increase.

- Mexico City? U.S. students may attend the National Autonomous University of Mexico (UNAM). Instruction is in Spanish. The tuition for U.S. students is about $500 a year, due to taxpayer support. The UNAM has an online program for U.S. students in Spanish with an office in Los Angeles.

- Moscow or St. Petersburg? Historic cities. The Higher School of Economics in Moscow is recognized by the London School of Economics and has some classes in English, as well as in Russian. The Moscow Institute of Physics has had 10 Nobel winners. Tuition is only $4,700 a year and living expenses are a lot lower than the U.S. or the rest of Europe. St. Petersburg Polytechnic has 4,500 foreign students.

Other programs are available in Africa, Asia, Central America, the Middle East and South America. Search for international study programs or study abroad.

For Very Serious Students and Very Serious Savings
The University of London International Programme

Do you love to read thick books on your own? The University of London's International Programme is a well-regarded degree at a very, very low price. Eight Nobel winners have attended the University of London International Programme. *This is not an online program.* You read and study on your own, anywhere in the world, with no classes, but with the same syllabus, books and final exam as the regular students use, but you don't pay the tuition of the regular students. The definition of *tuition* is "paid personal instruction". (Remember that, regular students, when you are paying your tuition bills.) Because you don't use a professor's time in class or online with U of L International, there's no tuition.

The International Programme began under Queen Victoria for the British Empire's officials around the world and their college-age children. It includes the renowned London School of Economics and Political Science, Kings College, University College London and more. A theology bachelor's degree is available for ministers. About 50,000 students are enrolled for bachelor's, master's and PhDs, compared, for example, to 31,000 enrolled for such degrees at Columbia University in New York.

This is for serious students who, on their own, can plow through books for eight months from September to May and then take the annual final exam, which is sent to a location closest to the student. U.K. bachelor's degrees take three years. Extensions are allowed.

It requires discipline, yes, but with books included it costs only $2,500 per year for three years, not counting costs for wherever you're living. That's $7,500 for the bachelor's, with room and board extra.

This might appeal to independent types, as it is rigorous, prestigious, very affordable and it does not tie you to one location, to commuting to class or to sitting in class. You may visit or live in the London area to use the University libraries and find study groups.

Live the Bohemian lifestyle. Coffee, a stack of books to read, no classes to attend, and you're getting a degree. That's the life. Where is Bohemia, anyway? Or maybe surfing in Australia or Costa Rica for an hour every morning before hitting the books? The world's your oyster with this deal.

☞ Chapter 13 ✍

Regular College Costs & Finances

This chapter will discuss college costs for regular colleges, those that are not selective for admissions. For selective colleges, Selective College Costs & Finances on page 239.

College costs fall into these categories:

1) private non-profit, four-year colleges

   1A) wealthy and generous

   1B) of more average means

2) public four-year colleges

   2A) in-state rates

   2B) regional colleges at in-state rates

   2C) in-state rates in a nearby state

   2D) out-of-state rates (much more expensive)

3) public community colleges

   3A) in-district rates (much cheaper)

   3B) out-of-district rates, which are higher, but similar to 2A, 2B and 2C

4) for-profit private colleges

A Lot of Students Pay Full Price, or Close to That

While some states are starting to offer more tuition assistance to students, most U.S. students will pay full price at state colleges, or similar or higher costs at private colleges.

For the lowest-income families in the U.S., making $30,000 a year or less, some reductions may be offered. But for many middle-income and higher-income families, $10,000 to $15,000 a year, not including room and board, is a starting point, even at in-state rates at a public four-year college.

1) Private Colleges Do Offer Discounts

(1A) Private non-profit colleges that are wealthier may be more generous. These are often selective. See Selective College Costs & Finances (p. 239).

(1B) Private non-profit colleges of more average means do offer aid to lower the price for middle-class and working-class families, so a $45,000 annual cost may be reduced to a $20,000 annual cost, for example, not including room and board.

Higher-income families will not usually receive such steep discounts. Thus, a middle-income family might face a choice between a $15,000 bill at one of their state colleges, plus room and board, or a $20,000 to $30,000 bill at a private college, plus room and board.

2) Public Four-Year Colleges: In-State Rates Are Cheapest, while Public Out-of-State Rates are High

(2A) Public four-year colleges at in-state rates are the least expensive and can be a good deal, at least compared to most private colleges.

(2B) Smaller public regional four-year colleges can be $3,000 to $5,000 lower in price per year than the flagship public colleges, as shown in the chart on page 114.

(2C) Some states offer discount rates to students from nearby states, under a regional tuition-exchange arrangement (p. 103). Public regional tuition-exchange rates can be reasonable.

These discounts are offered within regions, but not at some flagship and larger universities.

Here's an example from the Midwest.

For a Midwest resident, a lower rate is offered at:

Indiana State	University of Kansas
Kansas State	University of Nebraska
Missouri State University	University of North Dakota
North Dakota State	University of Wisconsin - Milwaukee
University of Akron (Ohio)	and many more regional colleges and universities

For a Midwest resident, a lower rate *is not* offered at:

Illinois State University	University of Illinois at Champaign
Indiana University (Bloomington)	University of Michigan
Michigan State University	University of Minnesota - Twin Cities
Ohio State University	University of Missouri at Columbia
Ohio University	University of Wisconsin at Madison

(2D) Public four-year out-of-state rates are much more expensive, yet still may compare with net costs at private colleges, especially for higher-income families.

3) Community College Rates are More Down to Earth

(3A) Public community college in-district rates cost the least and still offer the quality of U.S. accreditation for college credits that are transferable to all other U.S. colleges, private and public, if the credits match up within the same major.

(3B) Public community college out-of-district rates cost more, but may be comparable to 2A, 2B and 2C, i.e., in-state public rates. This means that paying higher rates for one year at a community college in another region of your state, or in another state, may cost about the same in-state four-year college rates.

Thus, a community college in another region or state can be a starting point. See Benefits of Community College (p. 97) and Transfers, Moving to Another State & Study Abroad (p. 101).

There is just no getting around how low the in-state rates are at public colleges and community colleges, compared to other college options. That doesn't mean going to an in-state college is dirt cheap. A few states offer better discounts, but those are not common.

4) For-Profit Colleges

For-profit colleges are easy to get into, but charge a lot more.

Flagship State College Costs vs. Regional State College Costs

(Some Regional Colleges Save You $5,000 a year, $20,000 on a bachelor's degree)

(from College Navigator, 2017)

Type of College	Four-Year College	2016-17 Tuition & Fees
Flagship	Ohio State University - Columbus	$ 10,037
Regional	(Ohio) Kent State University at Salem	$ 5,664
Flagship	University of Illinois – Champaign	$ 15,058
Regional	Northeastern Illinois University	$ 10,138
Flagship	University of Texas – Austin	$ 10,092
Regional	University of Texas – Permian Basin	$ 5,774

College Navigator Lists Full Prices, In-State Rates, Out-of-State Rates and Financial Aid Information

The College Navigator lists the full costs charged, without any aid, under "Tuition, Fees and Estimated Student Expenses" For public colleges, this includes the in-state rates and out-of-state rates. For all colleges, it shows cost differences between on campus housing, off campus housing and living with family.

In College Navigator's Financial Aid section, you can see on the 7th line, Institutional grants or scholarships, how many students the college itself gave money to, with an average. Along with the net price section, you can use this information to compare colleges, as to their overall generosity and their generosity to your income bracket.

Easy to Find Net Cost Estimates for Any College Based on Your Family Income

You can get net cost estimates for any college in the U.S. on the College Navigator at https://nces.ed.gov/collegenavigator. Estimates include room and board.

Here are the steps: type in the name of the school, select the college from the list; go to Net Price, (the fourth category listed). College Navigator (from the U.S. government National Center for Education Statistics) uses this format, for example:

University of Missouri, a public college in Columbia, MO:

AVERAGE NET PRICE FOR FULL-TIME BEGINNING STUDENTS

Full-time beginning undergraduate students who paid the in-state or in-district tuition rate and were awarded grant or scholarship aid from federal, state or local governments, or the institution.

	2015-2016
Average net price	$16,317

Full-time beginning undergraduate students who were awarded Title IV aid by income.

AVERAGE NET PRICE BY INCOME	2015-2016
$0 - $30,000	$12,060
$30,001 - $48,000	$12,746
$48,001 - $75,000	$15,203
$75,001 - $110,000	$19,545
$110,001 and more	$21,444

Saint Louis University, a private college in St Louis, MO.

AVERAGE NET PRICE FOR FULL-TIME BEGINNING STUDENTS

Full-time beginning undergraduate students who were awarded grant or scholarship aid from federal, state or local governments, or the institution.

	2015-2016
Average net price	33,222

Full-time beginning undergraduate students who were awarded Title IV aid by income.

AVERAGE NET PRICE BY INCOME	2015-2016
$0 - $30,000	$21,970
$30,001 - $48,000	$23,085
$48,001 - $75,000	$25,110
$75,001 - $110,000	$28,875
$110,001 and more	$33,849

Use a Net Price Calculator: It's Easy to Do

For four-year colleges, the net price calculator in the financial aid sections of their websites gives an estimate. The College Navigator links to these calculators in the bottom of the net price section of each college. Another site is www.collegecost.ed.gov. You can also do a general web search, such as: University of Georgia Net Price Calculator.

You can enter in rounded figures, and not have to dig out the W2s, as you must with the FAFSA form. Once you get the hang of it, you can get an estimate in about five to ten minutes.

You can do so anonymously by choosing guest, just entering in a generic name and approximate figures. Don't choose to save the information if asked (such as with a student account) and then you can see your estimated costs anonymously.

Not All Online Net Price Calculators Work the Same
Some Ask About Grades and Test Scores, Some Do Not

Some online net price calculators include questions about grades and scores, which implies that academic merit aid will be figured.

I checked several of the colleges that had questions about grades and scores. I methodically entered in different grades and scores to see the results. I found some calculators that provided the same price when I entered high grades and scores as when I entered low grades and scores. Thus, for some net price calculators, the GPA and test score questions had no effect.

Those colleges probably have some merit aid, but you won't get an estimate even after entering in grades and scores. So why do they ask? I don't know.

This glitch may mislead you, not estimating aid, when your high grades and scores could indeed increase your aid when your full financial-aid application is evaluated.

For one state, the net-price calculator indicated that very high grades and scores result in a $9,500 annual scholarship for in-state students, which is a big difference, and certainly nice to know.

The FAFSA4caster doesn't show any college aid or state aid, just the federal aid. It will show you a Pell grant estimate. If you don't see any Pell money, your family income may be too high for Pell grants.

Remember, these estimates could vary greatly from a final offer. A detailed conversation about your specifics with a financial aid staffer could give you a better idea of what to expect. Will higher grades result in higher college aid? Staff may confirm what the net price calculator has, but what if there are other factors?

Bona fide aid offers only occur after acceptance to the college and completion of the financial aid forms.

You Have to Look to Find Things You Don't Know About How's About Getting $36,000 Out of the Blue?

Here's an example of why proactive paying attention and poking around is important. I know a senior student and her parents who used one college's calculator, took five minutes to put in her general grades and expected scores to get an estimate for about $9,000 for an annual scholarship, for $36,000 total for the bachelor's, most of the in-state tuition.

They had had no idea it was available, and poof, there it was.

Then, looking at the details of the program, the girl found out that one C she got in freshman year in a core class meant she wasn't eligible.

Oh well, that went down the drain. Right? Rather than give up, the girl called the financial aid office. She could take one make-up class. She could take tests even after she was accepted for more chances to reach the needed scores. The program wasn't limited to a certain number of students. As long as she had those grades and scores, she was guaranteed to get the aid.

None of this was clear from the first look at the website.

By looking, the family was alerted to a $36,000 scholarship, and by making contact, the student avoided missing out. Had they not been looking around and dug deeper, they might have bypassed that college, paying much, much more elsewhere.

Vital information was not on the website, but took a call to find.

Full Scholarships Are Not That Common

Large merit scholarships are not very common for average students. Certainly, scholarships are listed on college websites, but look further and you often find that only a few students get a full-ride scholarship.

At private colleges, average amounts of aid can be around $20,000+, which sounds like a whole lot at first. Wow, $20,000 would cover the full tuition and fees at a lot of state colleges. The problem, however, is that $20,000 doesn't come close to covering the full tuition and fees of a private college, which can hit $45,000, not counting room and board.

Public or private, aid and grants are generally compiled into a financial aid package based on family income, with more money sometimes going to lower-income students.

In the U.S., the vast amount of aid awarded every year, about 94 percent of it,[24] goes through the standard college financial aid system, not from individual scholarships from outside private sources.

Often when you provide your financial information for a college, including the FAFSA and the CSS, you will be automatically considered for all scholarships offered by that college. But some colleges have other procedures, so check.

Here's one scenario. With the regular financial aid forms and deadline, you are considered for the President's Scholarship. The Chancellor's Scholarship uses the same forms, but with an earlier deadline. Then, the Founder's Scholarship require a separate application.

Private, Individual Scholarships from Various Sources, Social Organizations, Faith-Based Groups, Foundations, Companies and Corporations, etc.

These outside scholarships are in total only about 6 percent of what is offered compared to the 94 percent that comes from regular state, federal and college aid packages given out through the FAFSA and CSS form and regular financial aid offices of colleges.

Individual private scholarships are still significant in number and nationally total into the billions of dollars, even if a lot of them individually are only $1,000 for one time. This is why articles, websites and books can have headlines such as "Billions in Scholarships Are Available To YOU!" a statement that is by itself an accurate one, but the premise is very misleading. Here's why. It takes time; one must have matching qualifications and hundreds of others may also apply, and that's for a one-time $1,000 scholarship.

I heard yet again recently from a parent who said that "Millions in scholarships go unused," which is also very misleading, as if large amounts of money are just sitting unused, to be picked up with a quick search that will easily match to you. That's not true. Yes, millions in FAFSA aid isn't used when people don't submit the forms. With private scholarships, of all the $500 and $1,000 awards out there, perhaps enough of them aren't used that it adds up to a million bucks. But really, most companies and foundations see to it that the $1,000 ones are given out, certainly the $10,000 ones. And for most $10,000 scholarships, a lot of people apply, so those scholarships aren't easy to pick up.

Again, for comparison's sake, remember that for $10,000 in aid given out on average, roughly $9,400 comes through the financial aid offices of the colleges and only $600 comes from elsewhere.

Yes, you might apply to individual private scholarships that relate to you but it takes a lot of time to apply to a lot of them.

Is a Private Scholarship Search Worth the Time?

Should you spend 20 hours, 30 hours, or more, on miscellaneous scholarships? If you meet the requirements, perhaps. Many who work at it do see results. Don't lose out, just to watch more junk on your phone or TV, or chit chat with friends. Certainly, you should spend a few hours on an exploratory search. (This is after you've checked for special scholarships from the colleges you will apply to.)

After you find some leads, should you spend 20 or 30 more hours filling out the applications? Or spend 20 or 30 extra hours studying for the SAT exam or ACT exam so your score is higher? A higher exam score could increase your aid packages from multiple college financial aid offices. Moving your test score up even by a few points can increase your chances of admission and increase your aid by thousands. That's not an exaggeration, as many college advisers state this in articles and books. The ACT shows examples on its website.[1] You should not neglect test prep to chase random scholarships.

Certainly, well-produced applications to local, statewide and national scholarships will produce results for some students. Someone will be awarded the money and it could be you.

Private Scholarship Searches

If you decide to try for private scholarships, use internet search categories for yourself, but not with your name or any personal information. Thus, for a student from Texas going to a Texas college with a biology major, search: scholarships in Texas; scholarships in Texas for science; scholarships in Texas for biology; and scholarships in Texas first to go to college; and other various combinations.

The College Board has a scholarship search function. Some scholarship search sites have been around for many years, with good reviews. Some are free, if you agree to join marketing lists. Set up a separate email for scholarship searches, since you may get a lot of college marketing emails. Searches charging higher amounts could be a scam, or just not worth it. There are no fees to apply to individual scholarships. Zero. If an individual scholarship application asks for a credit card number, debit card number, bank account number, or other personal financial information it is a scam.

Report scammers to:
https://www.consumerfinance.gov/complaint/

---

[1] From the ACT home page, select any item to advance past the home page, then at the top, select Scores, then on the left select Should I Retest? and see Why Every Point Matters on the ACT test.

The Free Application for Federal Student Aid (FAFSA)

The FAFSA is free and should be filled out by every family. Do so to find out about the federal government Pell grants which are offered for full-time and part-time students to community colleges and four-year colleges up to about $5,900 a year, i.e., $23,600 for four years. Pell grants may extend two more years, but the total might not increase.

Pell grants are highest for low-income students, but the award is on a sliding scale, so middle-income students may still get a partial Pell grant.

Then the FAFSA is used to help calculate aid from the state and the college.

Is the FAFSA convenient? No. Yet, there are worse things in life. Fill it out anyway. A few hours of work can be worth a decent amount of money. How about a few thousand dollars to start, on up to $5,000?

If I offered you $1,000 an hour to mow my lawn for two hours, would you do it, even if my lawn is quite inconvenient to mow? For two hours on FAFSA you could get $2,000. That's getting paid $1,000 an hour. And it may not take that long and you could get more. If needed, do it in several sessions, saving it to go back to finish.

You will need exact figures from the household tax returns, (including the separate income total for each parent from the W-2s, etc.) plus rounded figures on the parent's savings, home value, mortgage balance, retirement accounts, and other investments.

Fill Out the FAFSA! It Really is Free Money

To belabor this point, I just read yet another article stating *that large numbers of working-class families do not fill out the FAFSA even though they **will get money***, so fill out the FAFSA!

Perhaps some people are nervous about giving data to the government or haven't filed taxes. Folks, the government already sees the income on the 1099s and W-2s you got last year, and that's all you are being asked about here, so get the free financial aid by filling out the FAFSA. If you haven't filed a tax return, see the footnote below.[J]

I repeat! Adults and students, do what's needed to fill out the FAFSA and get up to $5,900 of money for a person's college cash every year for four years, perhaps $23,600 in total.

The CSS/Financial Aid PROFILE®

The College Scholarship Service (CSS) Financial Aid PROFILE®[K] is a $25 service for one college from the College Board. For each additional college that a student uses, the CSS is reduced to $16. This cost is well worth it to find out if the college will provide more aid.

If applying to a private college that uses CSS, the fee is $25 for the first college and $16 for each additional college. Pay the extra $16, as these private colleges will give aid, but the CSS is needed. A fee waiver is available which covers eight colleges. Eligibility includes families with $45,000 or less in income, those with an SAT fee waiver, orphans and wards of the court.

A Student Work Contribution up to $5,000 is Standard

Most colleges require a student work contribution of about $2,500 to $5,000 a year, from a summer job or a part-time job during school. Some of this may be covered by a work-study program. (A loan in place of this might be able to be mixed in at the student's choice.) This is the starting point.

[J] Parents, there are several free online services for a federal return. For free, you can input your information to see if you owe, without having to officially file or contact the IRS. With the IRS, you can get on payment plan, $50 to $95 a month, for example. Once you're on a payment plan, you should be in good standing with the federal government, thus the kid can get money from FAFSA aid, so the family might come out ahead, even with the IRS payments.

[K] The CSS/Financial Aid PROFILE® is trademark registered by the College Board which is not involved with, and does not endorse, this product.

Typical Assets are OK

Assets are not treated the same as income. Family assets are not expected to be sold off to pay for college. Families can still get financial aid with typical assets of $500,000, or more.

Aid is based much more on annual earnings, than on assets, unless assets are very high. A family can have savings, own a home, have retirement money, and still get a decent deal if the annual household income is average.

Financial Aid Tips

There are books and articles that explain the financial aid process. There are details to know about federal loan programs, varying rates, terms, college savings plans, etc., so read up, but honestly, I didn't find any methods to a sudden, unexpected windfall of lots of money. Here are some tips:

Fill It Out! Fill *everything* out. Just follow the directions. Usually, you can save the information and return later. Next, do so as early as possible to get in line sooner, so to speak.

Need a Free Dorm Room and Meals? This tip is for sophomore year or later, so keep it in mind for later. Some colleges give a free dorm room, a free meal plan and a small stipend to students who are supervisors of a dorm room section. You'll need to show good grades. It's not the easiest job. But it can be worth about $10,000 or more per academic year.

Negotiate: After receiving offers, if you still need additional money, very politely but seriously contact the financial aid staff with specific information about your situation, including details about other offers. The packages can be adjusted. Being a demanding jerk about it won't help, as the people know what they have to work with. I have seen offers increased, after some give and take between the family and the college. A visit to the college may help.

Use tax-exempt 529 accounts: If you know you will have to pay out of your own pocket for part of the package, place the money in 529 college savings plans. These are tax-exempt accounts for putting money aside for educational expenses, so that's adding another 15% to 35%, for example, to the deal. For more savings, most states allow savings up to a certain level to be deducted from state income tax.

Pay Credit Cards Off from Savings: For people with large savings accounts who also are carrying some credit card balances, here's a tip. Take some of the savings, which is counted by financial aid formulas, and pay off credit card balances, which are not counted by financial aid formulas. You would have more emergency availability on your credit cards, but not as much in the saving account. Don't run up the cards. Keep them for an emergency

For All Loans and Special Programs; Know All the Details; Read Everything Yourself; Don't Take Verbal Assurances Only: There are many, many accounts of students and parents who were told one thing, but another thing happened, so they ended up:
- missing out on the best deal,
- later, after many years of payments, not getting the benefits that they thought they signed for, or
- paying higher costs,

due to them not knowing the real details.

Know for certain that you know, by having it in writing, and *reading it for yourself*, highlighting it, so you know where to find it in writing. If you need someone to help you understand the terms, have the person processing your paperwork show you the specific benefits and guarantees in writing for you to highlight. Or find someone else who can show you in your paperwork where to read it and highlight it for yourself. Typically, people sign things without reading them or understanding what something means. Don't be typical. Know what it means, *before you sign anything*.

☞ Chapter 14 ✍

The Standardized Tests

The ACT® test score and the SAT® test score count permanently in college admissions, if used. Most colleges use them. A student can take one or the other, or both. These test scores usually affect which colleges will admit you and how much financial aid you will get. Like it or not, that's the deal. Students, start freshman year to build a solid base of knowledge to score higher on the tests.

Here is what you must understand for higher scores: The tests measure math and English up to a certain level, as explained by the test practice guides. You can master this material. Whether that takes you a lot of time or not as much time, the level of the material remains the same. The *only variable* involved is how much time you will devote to learning that material between 9th grade and 12th grade.

Stress will go down when you are well prepared. This chapter explains many details about the tests. The Practice Tests chapter (p. 151) covers test preparation. Both tests cover reading comprehension, reasoning, vocabulary, grammar, punctuation, data analysis, and math up to and including trigonometry.

Many colleges do not require either test, including some major colleges and some selective colleges. Community colleges usually don't require them. Some regional colleges and smaller state colleges do not require them. With multiple scores for the same test, many colleges now count only a student's highest scores for admission, known as super scoring. Unless a college insists on seeing all scores, which some do, a student can choose which test dates to report.

Super Scoring

Super scoring is the practice of taking the highest scores of the different test sections to be counted for admissions purposes. This is most often done with the SAT test, but is also done for the ACT test.

SAT® Test Super Score Example

First Test	Reading	640
	Math	620
	Total Score	1260
Second Test	Reading	600
	Math	**740**
	Total Score	1340
Third Test	Reading	**710**
	Math	720
	Total Score	1430
Super Score	**Reading**	**710**
	Math	**740**
	Total Super Score	**1450**

Essay scores are super scored the same way.

The highest reading score, 710 on the third test, and the highest math score, 740 on the second test, are used. In this example, the student's first test scores would not be used in a super score, so if a college didn't require all scores, the student could exclude the first test.

ACT® Test Super Score Example

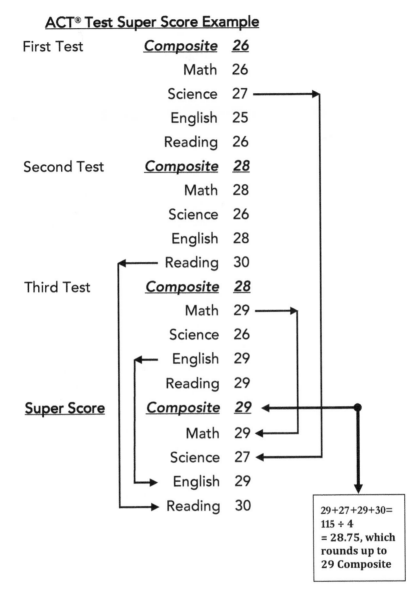

First Test   *Composite*   **26**

Math   26

Science   27

English   25

Reading   26

Second Test   *Composite*   **28**

Math   28

Science   26

English   28

Reading   30

Third Test   *Composite*   **28**

Math   29

Science   26

English   29

Reading   29

Super Score   *Composite*   **29**

Math   29

Science   27

English   29

Reading   30

> 29+27+29+30=
> 115 ÷ 4
> = 28.75, which
> rounds up to
> 29 Composite

Essay scores are super scored the same way.

For any ACT composite score, the four section scores are averaged and rounded to the nearest whole number (i.e. 28.25 rounds down to 28 and 28.50 rounds up to 29). In the example above, the student benefits from super scoring, which rounds up the composite to 29, instead of the 28, which was the highest regular composite score.

Super Scoring Details

◆ Colleges that require all scores negate the student's ability to select which scores to send. Other colleges allow students to select scores.

◆ If a college allows you to select which test dates to report, then confirm if the college super scores. If so, then analyze how the scores on each test date will affect the super score. You could not report a test date, if it didn't help your super score.

◆ When the college super scores, the lower scores are still available for admissions officers to see, if they wish, but often those lower scores are disregarded, placed on a back page of the file, so to speak.

◆ A student may not super score for herself or himself, however, by selecting that a math score be reported for one date, and on another date that a math score not be reported, for example. For each date selected, all scores are reported.

◆ Different options apply to subject tests. If more than one subject test is taken, and the college requires all subject tests to be reported, then the college will likely consider the highest score in each subject test the most relevant, which is like super scoring. The student may be able to report only his or her best subject test scores.

Test agencies state that most students do better the second time. Thus, taking a test more than once to try for higher scores makes sense, even without extra practice.

Significant improvement is possible with practice and test prep. If the scores are higher, you can report them. If not, then don't. For colleges requiring all tests, with test prep, your scores shouldn't drop much, at the worst, but should go up. A lower score does not negate other good scores. See page 326 for the actual transcript of a student who had lower scores that improved significantly in a short time by the student's determination to do better.

Data-Analysis and Science-Style Questions

With both tests, the science and statistics questions are about how to read and interpret information in tables, charts and from statistics.

The questions don't quiz students on knowing scientific facts, such as how many electrons are in hydrogen, or on knowing statistical facts, such as what the population of the U.S. is. The tests give you the facts to answer the question.

The ACT test has a specific science reasoning section labeled as such. This section includes data analysis.

The SAT test has the same type of science reasoning and data analysis questions placed throughout the exam instead of a section labeled for science questions.

Students should practice reading and interpreting charts and tables to know how to solve such questions. Again, you don't need to memorize scientific facts or statistics, but know how analyze facts in the charts, tables and text.

Vocabulary

The SAT vocabulary-related questions changed in 2016, whereby students don't need to know as many less commonly used words. Your knowledge of harder vocabulary words, however, is still tested. My niece, for example, got a question wrong when she did not understand the meaning of the word pertinent. Turns out it was pertinent.

The exams also test your understanding of words that have more than one meaning, depending on context.

Students will see more difficult words that are used in serious writing. Use the up-to-date study guides to see how word knowledge applies. Know college-level words that may not be in everyday use at school, or with friends and family (p. 137).

Check Out Both Tests, Then Decide

Most colleges have no preference and accept either or both. About half of U.S. students take one and about half take the other. Get advice from your high school counselor and teachers. Perhaps a student may choose to take both. A student could take one ACT practice test and one SAT practice test to compare them.

An internet search will provide websites, blogs and articles to provide information about differences between the tests.

ACT Test		SAT Test
45 minutes	English	65 minutes Reading
60 minutes	Math	35 minutes Language
35 minutes	Reading	25 minutes Math
35 minutes	Science Reasoning	55 minutes Math
[Optional 40 minutes Essay]		[Optional 50 minutes Essay]

Both tests are about three hours long, broken into four sections. Both have an optional essay as a fifth section, which is offered after the regular three-hour session.

The ACT test is 2 hours and 55 minutes, plus breaks.

The SAT test is 3 hours, plus breaks.

Students get break times between sections, so students are at the testing center for about three and a half hours, not counting the optional essay.

Some colleges require the essay, some recommend it, and for some it is optional.

Students, You Can Learn This Stuff

High scorers use discipline to master the material, finishing the schoolwork, learning one step, then the next, with regularity, for years.

For example, the fundamentals and finer points of geometry can be repeated and practiced so that they are well understood. That can be true for a student that started with a natural affinity for math. It can also be true for a student who dislikes math.

For either student, $A^2 + B^2$ equals C^2.

Don't Like Math? So What?

For a student, who does not like math, so what?

Each equation can be learned. By going over it again and again, an algebra equation can be mastered, then done faster, then answered quickly and correctly on the test, whether a kid loves math, hates math, is a brainiac or isn't. It is the same with geometry, etc.

Don't Like English? So What?

It's the same idea in English. Look harder words up. Use them. Learn the right punctuation. It may take some students less time, and some students more time, but diligence leads to mastery, not brilliance.

Diligence Is Important

Many brilliant people have too little discipline to accomplish something substantial. Yes, they're clever, and they know a lot about a fair number of things, but being clever and able to spout off with some facts is not a durable accomplishment.

Use the many hours of your life spent in class to absorb the material, to get more information out of your teachers and the curriculum.

Students, do you want an offer to a better school or perhaps additional financial aid, or are chit chat, gossip, and Teen Drama more important to you? Which are you committing your time to?

Sure, you are not guaranteed to get any offers of scholarships at all. Perhaps your only offers of admission might be the local colleges, or the local community college. But I'll guarantee you only average results, or worse, if you zone out too much in class; if after class you spend too much time on entertainment.

By this, I don't mean that you shouldn't take breaks, explore things, or ever have any fun. Read books you like? Spend hours talking with friends about who knows what? Binge on a great show? Sure. Creativity and inspiration take many forms. Relaxation recharges us. That's fine.

What to avoid, however, is non-stop inconsequential blah, blah, and blah. If that's what you choose to spend your time on, then expect the results of that choice, such as limits to your academic, professional and business opportunities after high school.

The U.S. offers any citizen a chance to better themselves, to even create themselves anew. U.S. students should treasure this opportunity.

Do not fritter away your high school years.

Sure, have some fun, but also get something done for your future, for the United States of America's future, and for the world's future. We are counting on you.

Improve on Tests by Knowing Why You Got a Wrong Answer

After a test, figure out why your wrong answers are wrong. One's tendency is to not do this, thinking ahead to the next test, but going over wrong answers is the best thing to do. Here's why.

With math questions, the close-to-correct answers might match up with common calculation errors that are made. See what those are.

With reading questions, the logic to find the correct answers will be similar. Each time you find out why you got the logic wrong, it helps you get the logic right later. The correct answer is not clearly apparent by the careful design of the test writers. A wrong answer will appear to be technically correct or a "close" answer, but it will have a flaw of some kind, keeping it from being the best, correct answer.

Sometimes, You Will Swear They are Wrong, But They Aren't

I remember going over wrong answers with John (from the story) on an official practice reading test. On one question, we went over it for twenty minutes, debating the nuances of different sentences and words. We just knew that our answer was correct. We couldn't see the test writers' logic. I was ready inform them that we had discovered this obvious error in their book. After a break, we reread everything again. Finally, we saw it; how our answer was indeed not the best answer. They were right. Learn to find what they're looking for.

Rachel's Lament, "I'll Never Get A 700. This is Stupid."

Here's an important example. Rachel was a girl whose parents took her to Harvard and Yale using their vacation time. Her father told me what happened. A Yale student they talked with said he got a 710 on his SAT test for reading. As they walked away from the Yale student, Dad

132

said to her "You read a ton of books and you speak as well as he does. You can get a good score."

"I'll never get a 700. This is stupid. Let's leave," she said.

Later, Rachel took a practice SAT reading test. It was 600. She could see on each wrong answer, how she got it wrong. She knew that she could get more right. She took another test and got 650.

"See," dad said, "you can get to 700."

"Yeah, right," said Rachel, feeling dejected with the 650 score.

"Let's look at the scoring chart again," the father said. They found out that if in one section, out of 52 questions, she could get 4 or 5 more right; and if in the other section, out of 44 questions, she could get 4 or 5 more right; she could be at 700.

"Rachel, if you keep working on it, can you get four more of these right in each section?" the father asked. She literally paused for a while, thinking about those questions.

"That's possible," she said. Her dejection disappeared.

It was possible, and it was not just some parental positive-thinking hype. No longer was it the untouchable Ivies with the kids from the better high schools that she could never match up with, since she came from a working-class family and went to working-class high school.

Now it was four more right answers in each of two sections.

She never would have believed it, had she not personally tabulated her own answers, seen how the test was scored, found her mistakes on her wrong answers and seen for herself that she could get them right.

She could see exactly where she was, which was, she now realized, getting close to a top college level.

Practice? Or Relax? How About Both?

I recommend a lot of extra practice for the standardized tests and point out many ways to practice. Some advisers do not recommend as much practice. Let kids be kids and don't stress them out, is their advice. Well, a student can still be prepared for the tests, and not be stressed out.

Students and parents will hear and read admissions officers, college guides and advisers generally state something along these lines:

(A) That after two or three official tests, taken near in time to each other, many student's scores do not change dramatically.

(B) Colleges take a student's high scores and view them as if the student is in a range around that score and could likely score a little higher or a little lower on any given test day.

Those are generally fair and accurate statements. But, they are far from true all the time, such as when a student is *not* serious about the test at one time, but *is* serious later.

Then, very significant increases in the scores can occur. Look at the case of the student, John, in the earlier story.

In only three (3) months, from October to January, his SAT math score went from 620 to 740 (of 800 possible).

An equivalent ACT math score would have gone from 26 to 32 (of 36 possible). His SAT reading score went from 640 to 720 (p. 326).

A Huge Increase on a Score: What Was the Difference?

The big difference was attitude, which led to proper test prep. He didn't care *at all* about his first test, but he cared *a lot* about his last test.

On the first test, he didn't think anyone would ever see the scores, because, in his mind, he was just heading off to the state college with no scholarship.

But three months later, he took the test *very, very seriously*. He realized that he did, in fact, have a decent chance for a scholarship, maybe at a top college.

From blasé, he became attentive. He did extra test prep, which for him meant that he didn't need endless hours of catch up. His base of knowledge was good, but he needed to track down those math equations he was getting tripped up on. He learned from his wrong answers in the reading sections, where his mistakes in logic were.

Sure, young people should have some carefree fun, *along with* making a reasonable effort for their own self-interest, for their own futures.

I have seen too many good students caught off guard by these tests. Lower scores result from a lack of familiarity with how the material is presented, and with how the test flows. Solve that with lots of practice over time, rather than just last-minute cramming.

How Comfortable Are You When You Take the Tests? How Familiar Are You with the Tests?

Master the flow, using proper techniques, not getting bogged down. Is your level of speed solid, without being in a panic? Panic or anxiety during test taking is a disaster. We freeze up or our thoughts get so frantic that it is hard to work logically.

Math: How long will Algebra questions take you? Does that leave enough time for geometry and trigonometry? For juniors and seniors, practicing Algebra I and II could increase their speed. First get fast at algebra. Then get faster at geometry. Then increase your speed on trig. Keep going over this until you don't get wrong answers and you do it fast enough. Can you do that? Sure. Will you? Go ahead. Do it.

Reading and Writing: Can you jump back and forth in the reading section and the possible answers and not lose your place, while also keeping track of the logic involved?

Are you able to reread one paragraph again to eliminate one wrong answer, and then a different paragraph again to eliminate another wrong answer, working carefully, yet quickly enough, to track down the tricky correct answers, repeatedly, before your time runs out?

Pacing and Timing Are Tangible Skills to Master

Correct pacing is crucial for success. Each section is its own, stand-alone challenge. Bomb just one of them and your score drops a lot. For each section this is what is needed:

☞ When half the time is gone, are you on track to finish all questions?

☞ With ten minutes to go, see if you on track to finish all questions.

☞ You might have plenty of time left, but if you aren't familiar enough with each section, you may not know it and panic.

☞ Or you might need to speed up, but not realize it in time.

☞ How long do you stick with the tough questions, before making a choice?

☞ Can you go back to the questions you weren't sure about?

If you can't finish a section, and cannot even read five questions to narrow them down, you should still guess. There are no penalty points for guessing (except on the SAT Subject Tests). But if you have to completely guess, it could be a lot of points missed. It takes several tests to get the hang of where you need to be when time is half up, with 20 minutes left, and with 10 minutes left, to keep on pace to get to all the questions.

Do you see why it would take many practice sessions to get to the point of strong familiarity? Do you see why strong familiarity will be such an advantage?

Classroom Tests Don't Come Close to the ACT and SAT Tests

Students, just because you took tests well in your classes, doesn't mean you can waltz through these tricky exams. They are designed in minute detail to trip you up, by world-class experts at doing so, in ways far cleverer than your high-school teacher has time to think up for a class final.

There are 154 questions on the SAT exam. There are 215 questions on the ACT exam. Take your pick. You get three hours. You need to be ready.

The College Board states that its SAT test has harder answers at the end.[25] Blogs state that ACT math questions are harder at the end, but I don't know about the other sections.

Get to Know Your New Best Buddies

Get to know your new friends. On the SAT test, those will be Section 1 with 52 questions, Section 2 with 44 questions, Section 3 with 20 questions and Section 4 with 38 questions.

For the ACT test, your new best buddies will be Section 1 with 75 questions, Section 2 with 60 questions, Section 3 with 40 questions and Section 4 with 40 questions. Get to know them very well.

Next, Do You Need Some Cramming on the Material?

With practice, you may find that you can keep up the speed, but that you need to better understand the material. With some concerted effort, you can shore up your base of knowledge, nail down loose ends and get more questions right.

Vocabulary

Khan Academy's SAT site, states that an authoritative vocabulary list doesn't exist for the SAT, suggesting that students learn harder words from the Atlantic Monthly, Economist, New York Times Book Review and Wall Street Journal, among others.[26] At a library, take an hour or two to skim for words to create a list. Get a subscription on your phone for a month just to find such words. Show off your Economist app to your friends. On an internet search, I found vocabulary lists that looked reasonable. For more correct answers, learn new words.

Grammar and Punctuation

When you must find the correct punctuation or grammar, are you on autopilot, or stumbling? Look up common grammatical and punctuation mistakes and nail this stuff down. Do you know the use a semi-colon (;) compared to a colon (:) and a dash (-)? How about an apostrophe (') with a word ending in an 's'? Free grammar websites and articles abound. The Associated Press Stylebook and the Chicago Manual of Style are used by professional editors. These are in some libraries or are available for purchase.

Math

Specific types of problems may be holding you up. Find out which ones you need to learn, refresh or relearn. If it's trig questions, don't only redo them once or twice. Do them ten times. Or more. Get fast.

When Should a Student Schedule the Official Exams?

Three test date windows are most often used for regular decision applications in varying combinations:

(A) second semester of junior year

(B) summer between junior and senior year

(C) first semester of senior year

Early decision applicants (pp. 236-237) must use earlier test dates. In addition to the regular test dates, some high schools add in their own test dates, so check for those if you wish to use them.

If you're not ready for a school-sponsored test, you may opt out.

Junior Year (2nd Semester) & Summer:

Many students take their first test in March, April or May of junior year, or in June or August after junior year. This can include taking the test two or three times within these months. Later, a student may take more tests to try to score higher.

If a student concludes that his or her scores are strong enough to submit, he or she can concentrate during senior year on the applications.

Summer & Senior Year:

Many students take their first test in June or August after junior year or in September at the start of senior year for the ACT test or October for the SAT test.

This still lets them to take the test a second and third time. For the 2017-2018 example, some colleges will *not* use the February ACT test for fall 2018 admissions, while others may, if the score arrives in time.

National Testing Dates Calendar
ACT® Test and SAT® Test

Sample Calendar for Junior-Year Second Semester and Senior Year. (2017-2018 dates are shown, to be adjusted for any year.) These are test dates for individual students to register and pay for. In addition, some schools give tests at no cost on different dates. (SAT Subject Tests are generally available on these SAT test dates. A student must select either to take SAT Subject Tests or to take the SAT regular test on one test date.)

Junior Year: 2nd Semester

Jan. (2017)	Feb.	March	April	May
	ACT Test (10th) (Not New York)		ACT Test (14th)	
		SAT Test (10th) or Subject Tests		SAT Test (6th) or Subject Tests

Summer after Junior Year

June	July	August
ACT Test (9th)	ACT Test (14th) (Not New York)	
SAT Test (3rd) or Subject Tests		SAT Test (26th) or Subject Tests

Senior Year: 1st Semester and 2nd Semester

Sept.	Oct.	Nov.	Dec.	Jan. (2018)	Feb.
ACT Test (9th)	ACT Test (28th)		ACT Test (9th)		ACT Test (10th) (not New York)
	SAT Test (7th) or Subject Tests	SAT Test (4th) or Subject Tests	SAT Test (2nd) or Subject Tests		

SCHEDULING SAT SUBJECT TESTS
Do Not Forget SAT Subject Tests, If You Need Them

For selective colleges' admissions, students might need two (or three) SAT Subject Tests in total. This is very important.

The SAT Subject Tests are given _on the same day_ as the regular SAT test each month, so it is an either/or decision that month on which type of test to take. You may take up to three (3) SAT Subject Tests on one day.

Test Dates for Early Decision Applications

For early applications to selective colleges, students must factor in earlier test dates, including for the SAT Subject Tests.

Early Deadlines for Scholarships Might Mean
Earlier Test Dates Are Necessary

Some special scholarship deadlines are early, which means the college might want to see test scores then. Here's one example: Georgia Tech has an Oct. 15 deadline for a few scholarships. That's a lot earlier than the regular decision deadline of January 1.

How Many Times Should a Student Take a Test?

Advice on when and how many times to take a test is all over the map in books, blogs and articles.

- Many admissions advisers recommend taking a test two times at least.
- Some say taking tests three, four or five times is even better.
- Other advisers say to stop at three, as after that it may look as if the student is trying to luck into a better score.
- I lean towards two at least, and if you think you can improve, take three or four as long as you are taking concrete steps to increase your score.

If you have taken practice tests, then an official test will not be, in effect, a practice run. Avoid using an actual ACT test or SAT test as a practice run because that score record is permanent, unless you cancel it. Regarding how many times to take a test, students may:

◆ seek advice from a counselor

◆ seek advice from admissions staff of colleges

◆ read the discussions in books, articles and blogs

Most students do better the second time. That is statistically proven, as stated by the College Board and ACT, Inc. on their websites.

From a March or April junior year test date to a November or December senior year test date, are six to eight months to improve scores through study, practice, tutoring and additional classroom instruction. Even just a month between a first test and a last test provides time for improvement.

Tests Paid for by the School or District: These Are Usually Good, But with A Serious Warning

An ACT test or a SAT test may be scheduled school-wide or district-wide and paid for by the school, the district or the state. Let's refer to these as school tests. These are free and are most often a benefit for students. Some students may not take a test otherwise and might find out they can get into better colleges than they expected.

Students aiming for a selective college, beware. Do not take it unless you are ready. If you are already planning for more test prep and taking the test later anyway, then stick to that plan and opt out of the school's test. If the free test helps financially, then be sure you're ready.

For a school ACT test and a selective-college applicant, the most important thing may be that a school test score cannot be removed from your record if you tank it, while a regular ACT test can be removed from your record if you tank it.

So, if you have plans to apply to a selective college that requires all test scores, be sure to be ready for that school-sponsored ACT test because you cannot cancel it, unless you do so before you leave the testing room.

Read This Story About the Serious Problem a School-Given Test Can Cause

One girl was all set with a summer/fall study plan to get a good ACT score in senior year with two tests in Sept. and Oct., and a backup in December. She had a 4.4 GPA out of 5.0, so her knowledge base was good to build on with the planned test prep. It was a good plan.

Then in April of junior year, the school ACT test came along, which she hadn't planned on. She didn't understand that she could opt out of it. The school staff herded her into the test, along with every other junior, although she should *not* have taken it, as I'll explain.

She took it unprepared and tanked the math especially, getting a 19 composite.

The mom called the ACT helpline. The gentleman told her, "Sorry. We hear this occasionally, but the score can't be deleted, as with regular tests."

She still expects around a 28 composite, maybe higher, based on practice tests since, but now she has a 19 ACT composite on those applications to colleges which require all scores, along with the explanatory sentences.

For those of you also at around the 19 level, don't take this wrong. That's about at the 43rd percentile, so you're near the halfway point of U.S. students, so with some more work you could be up at 22, which is the 63rd percentile, which is respectable for colleges to see. You can be shooting for 24, which is about the 74th percentile, which is a very strong accomplishment, or trying for even higher.

The same applies for an SAT test when the school gives it. If you are not ready, and the selective colleges will ask for that score, then opt out and take the test later when you are ready.

You may skip a school test if you are not ready. Though it's free and everyone else is taking it, that doesn't mean you must take it. Go to the library. The staff asks all students to take it because many students wouldn't take it otherwise, but for you the circumstances are different, so explain this and insist on opting out.

If You Skip or Cancel a Test, Can You Take It Again?

Let's go over skipping or cancelling a test, so a student who is serious about these tests knows all the options.

Skip the Test

If a student is too sick, or has an emergency or has any other circumstance that will ruin the student's performance on that day's test, then the student may just not show up. The student usually loses his paid fee, although a partial refund may be offered.

The student may take the test in another month, paying another fee, but perhaps not at full price.

Cancel During the Test or After the Test, Before You Leave the Room

A student can cancel before finishing. (Maybe a student was too sick to concentrate, or even finish. Maybe a death or an emergency occurred and the student could not concentrate.) The student may take the test in another month, paying another fee.

Cancel in the Next Days After the Test

After a test is completed and the student has left the testing room, a student can still cancel an SAT test or ACT test within a few days of taking the test.

Cancelling tests is not to be done on a whim, especially for the SAT test as the cancellation is immediately permanent.

Be aware in advance that you may feel uncertain just after the test, but do not assume the worst and cancel right away. Who's to know? Consider the student John in our story at the start of the book. His father asked about his last test,

"How do you think you did?"

John replied, "I really don't know. Those questions are tricky."

"Can't you estimate? Did you feel you knew most of it?

"I really don't know."

He wasn't at all certain, even after taking it twice before. His first score was in the 87th percentile. This last test turned out to be his best score, hitting the 98th percentile, but he really didn't know in advance.

Colleges look mostly at your best scores, not your worst, so if the score turns out lower it isn't the end of the world. Take the test again, if possible.

Further Details on Cancelling Tests

Further details of cancelling are in the Appendix (pp. 327-328).

Stalling on the ACT Test Score

With an ACT test that a student pays for, he or she can place a stall, in effect, on the score, which allows the student to see the score before anyone else sees it. This costs extra money if you end up using the score, as you must pay $13 per each report to each college, instead of the four free reports provided. So, this costs $52 to stall on sending the scores to four colleges in total.

To use this procedure, a student could first *not* put any college codes on the form at the beginning of the test. If you put college codes in, they can be removed after the test, by phone or online by removing the report codes to the colleges by the Thursday noon deadline after the test was taken. This stops the score reports to the colleges. The student will get the score report. Later, if the score is OK, the student can pay the $13 fee to report the score to one college.

If the score is terrible, the student can cancel it in writing. Later, the student should request that a cancelled test be removed from his or her transcript. Test scores paid for by the student are considered the property of the student, not the of a school. Once it's cancelled, a test doesn't exist on ACT records.

This procedure is not available if a school or the state pays for ACT test, which cannot be cancelled.

The SAT Test Score Can't be Stalled, Only Cancelled.

An SAT test cancellation is final, but must be done within a few days of taking the test (pp. 327-328).

SAT Score Choice™

The SAT test offers Score Choice™ at no extra charge, which allows a student to select which SAT test dates to include in reports to colleges. Some colleges, however, require all scores to be included, so Score Choice™ should not be used to exclude a score for them.

Order Your Right and Wrong Answers

If you will take the test again 60 days or later after a test, then ordering the report of your right and wrong answers can help you. It takes about six weeks to get this report after a test date.

For the ACT test, this is only available for some of the national tests, and not for school tests. ACT calls it a TIR, a Test Information Release. It costs $20, with no fee waiver available. In the past it was available for December, April and June.

For the SAT test, this is available only for certain test dates, recently for October, March and May. It is called the Question and Answer Service. It costs $18, with a fee waiver available. A less specific SAT Student Answer Service, with just the type of question listed, costs $13.50, with a fee waiver available. This covers the other dates.

Score Verification

If your score was much lower than it should have been, look into score verification for a fee.

ACT Essays Rescored

If your ACT essay score is a lot lower than you expected based on your writing ability, it could be well worth the $50 to ask for an essay rescore. If the score goes up, you get the $50 refunded. The essay score cannot be lowered, so there is no risk, other than being out $50.

SAT Essays Cannot be Rescored

An SAT test essay cannot be rescored.

Put Test Scores in Your Transcript, if you Cannot Pay for More Score Reports

If you are out of money for score reports but have applications due, be sure that the scores are on the high school transcript. Then inform the college of your situation. Include an explanation in your application. Don't be shy about this. Colleges want your application and staff from top colleges have told me that they will often accept this procedure.

Between Tests, How Can You Improve Your Score?

A student may use free tutoring and practice; or services that cost money. Check for free or low-cost apps. Use tutoring online with a laptop, tablet, home computer, school computer or library computer. Use practice books. Some of the tutoring services have affordable rates starting from $39 to $99, then $200 to $300, and on up. They have free trials. If you can afford them, they may be valuable.

At some point, a student should sit down with a paper practice test, and a No. 2 pencil to take a timed test in a silent room, as those are the actual test conditions.

Free and Low-Cost Tutoring and Practice

ACT®, Inc.

- From ACT.org look under TEST PREPARATION for a range of free items and some products for a fee, at reasonable prices. The ACT, Inc. publishes its own study guide with practice tests for about $33. This book is available from the ACT website store, from booksellers nationwide and at libraries.
- The ACT offers an online tutoring program for about $40.
- The ACT website offers a free practice ACT test to download and print. From the ACT.org homepage, (as of 2017) select TEST PREPARATION then find DOWNLOAD A FREE STUDY GUIDE and select PREPARING FOR THE ACT. You may need to save to a pdf or export to a pdf to get a clean printout.
- Scroll down in the TEST PREPARATION section to see free online practice, including free detailed information on the essay option. You can get 100 free questions with Question of the Day if you sign up for ACT Profile.

The College Board®

The College Board website is a source of good information about the various tests that it administers.

- It offers its own study guide for the SAT test with practice tests for about $25. This book is available from the College Board website store, from booksellers and at libraries. This is a good value, coming from the company that creates the actual tests.

- The College Board offers a free, well-regarded online tutoring service (Khan Academy) specifically for the SAT test.

- The College Board's website has eight free practice tests.

Other Publishers and Libraries

There are study guidebooks on the standardized tests and subject tests from various publishers for about $20 to $30 available from booksellers and at libraries. These companies also have phone apps and online practice, some free and some for a fee.

Most school and local libraries have these study guidebooks. Often the books may be out, but with a hold request, you'll have it in a week or two. If not, you can ask your school librarian or municipal librarian to purchase a book you need. The librarian will often do so.

Students and parents, seriously, if you don't have the money right now for a book you need, go ahead and ask your librarian to buy it. Librarians have told me that they have a budget for such requests.

If using a library book, photocopy the answer pages to mark when you take the practice tests, or mark the pages lightly with pencil and erase the marks when done.

How to Take a Practice Test Without a Lot of Stress

What's highly valuable about practice tests in books and online is to immediately get a math score, or an English score, or a complete score.

You can see where you are at, and start going over the wrong answers right away. How exciting.

Here's a way a student can take a full practice test with less stress and fit the testing time into the demanding schedule of a busy student.

This method also works well for a student whose attention span for practice tests is only from 35 to 50 minutes. Thus, everyone is covered.

Here's How:

- Select English or Math/Science. Take only one practice test segment at a time, in the 35 minutes to an hour allowed for that section. So, that takes a half hour or an hour.

- Busy? Yes. That's true. But you can fit in a half-hour or an hour practice section sometime during the week.

- Then, the next day, or later in the week or the next week, just do the second English or math section. Take a look at that English score or that math score. Your first score!

- After two more sections. You're done! Tally the full score.

- Thus, in a week or two, or within a month or two, a student, can find out his or her score that matches the official scores. How will you do? Get going to find out.

For an accurate score estimate, the student must match official test conditions by putting forth serious effort without *any* distractions.

Do's:

- Do so when rested and ready to focus.

- Do so in a quiet location, sitting down at a table or desk, without distractions. The room or house must be silent. Do not have a TV on or music going. If you usually study with music or shows on, *that will have to change for practice tests*. This test is in a silent room, so practice that way.

- Perhaps use a study hall or the corner of the library, which aren't 100 percent silent, but are close enough.

- In a house, use the kitchen table, the living room table, or a desk, with other people staying in other rooms for the duration.

- Guessing on answers is OK, with no penalty, except for SAT Subject Tests (p. 165).

Do not:

- Do not take a test lying on a couch or on a bed.

- Do not have your friends or family hanging out jabbering away in the background or anywhere where you can hear them at all.

Consider These Points About Practice Tests

✏ With his or her best effort, when not tired or distracted, then the results will indicate the student's ability and score at that time.

REGARDING PRACTICE TESTS

☢ 🚨 WARNING! ATTENTION! WARNING! 💣☢
EXPECT LOUSY, LOW,
EMBARRASSING SCORES AT FIRST

Students, parents and guardians should expect low test scores on the early practice ACT tests and practice SAT tests, and possibly on the first regular tests. If that's the case, do not conclude that you cannot get to the quartiles for your targeted colleges.

Your scores will rise with more classroom instruction, test prep and familiarity with the test. Take another practice test. Check the score. Then again. Then again. You must go over the wrong answers. Then again. If you do that:

Your scores will go up!

✏ Each test score doesn't mean the student will be stuck at that level. With more school instruction, the scores can improve.

✏ Further test prep improves scores. Student can review wrong answers, study on their own, and get help from teachers. The ACT and the College Board give students information based on their practice and regular tests. Using library books, or the free practice tests online, any student can see where they are and take steps to improve.

A Practice Test Can Show You Where You're at Today

Don't be caught off guard as to where the student is on these important tests. If the student needs a lot of improvement, it's best to find out earlier.

When the student gets a halfway decent score it's great to have that good news, and the student and parents are encouraged to take even more steps to get better results.

Then, when a student is doing well, it's time to go all in towards a great score.

Chapter 15

Practice Tests

The PreACT test and PSAT tests are preliminary tests. Let's call them practice tests. They are not required for college applications. The scores for these tests are not reported to colleges. They are for practice and evaluation. For students who might apply for scholarships and selective colleges, practice tests may help to increase scores on the regular ACT tests and SAT tests.

There are four (4) different practice tests. They are designed for use in the following grades and include:
1) PSAT 8/9 Test for 8th and 9th grade
2) PreACT Test for 10th grade
3) PSAT 10 Test for 10th grade
4) PSAT/NMSQT®* Test for 11th Grade: [Only in October]
   (Also the National Merit Scholarship Qualifying Test)

The PreACT test and each of the PSAT tests, however, may be taken by any student in any year, starting with 8th grade. ACT, Inc. rules and the College Board rules allow this. A summary of rules on page 158.

The PreACT
- PreACT scores are not reported to colleges.
- The PreACT test costs $46 for the test given directly by the ACT, with a fee waiver offered. For a school-given test, it costs $12.
- Students can take a PreACT test to compare it to a PSAT test to help decide which test, the ACT test or the SAT test, to take later.
- The PreACT test is geared to 10th graders, but if you are serious about practice, you may take it in any grade.
- Thus, you can take it multiple times, one time each in 8th, 9th, 10th and 11th grades, for example, and each year you get a new test.

---

* The PSAT/NMSQT® is a trademark registered by the College Board and the National Merit Scholarship Corporation, which are not involved with the production of, and do not endorse, this product.

- If you take it twice in one year you would see the same questions, but this might change in the future.

Keep the test booklet, which is allowed and encouraged, to go over the wrong answers when you get your score report. Ninth-graders would benefit from taking the PreACT test, which is allowed, rather than waiting until 10th grade. Eleventh-graders may benefit from taking another PreACT test to get more practice in a test-day setting.

If your school does not offer the PreACT test, you can ask that they do so (p. 329), but it's worth the $46 to get a test day experience at a testing site as well.

The PSAT Tests

♦ PSAT test scores are not reported to colleges.
♦ A PSAT test costs $16, but a school may waive the fee if asked. The student registers and pays at the school, not on the College Board website.
♦ Students can take a PSAT test to compare it to a PreACT test, to help decide which test, the ACT test or the SAT test, to take later.
♦ Only one PSAT test factors into college admissions, but not in the usual way, as the score is not reported. That test is the PSAT/NMSQT®* test (National Merit Scholarship Qualifying Test), taken during junior year (11th grade) in October.

During junior year, the PSAT/NMSQT®* test is used to qualify students for the National Merit Scholarship, which goes to 7,400 students nationwide. The awards vary, starting with a $2,500 one-time award. Different corporate and college scholarships go to some winners, sometimes for more money for more years, but they are not full-ride scholarships.

1. Regarding admissions, juniors who score well are designated as National Merit semi-finalists, (and with additional work can become finalists), which should be put on an application. This is the only way any PSAT test could affect a college application. The score is not seen by colleges, but they know it was high for semi-finalists.

---

* The PSAT/NMSQT® is a trademark registered by the College Board and the National Merit Scholarship Corporation, which are not involved with the production of, and do not endorse, this product.

2. The PSAT 8/9 Test and PSAT 10 Test do not count for college admissions. They do not count towards scholarships. They are only practice tests.
3. The PSAT/NMSQT®ᴸ* test can be taken by any student in 9th and 10th grades but when a 9th-grader or 10th-grader takes the PSAT/NMSQT®* test it does not factor into the National Merit status, unless that student is finishing high school early. Otherwise, it is only for practice during 9th or 10th grades.
4. The PSAT/NMSQT®* test offers a fee waiver in 11th grade only for low-income families. The local school could pay the fee for a student, so a student should ask if need be.
5. The College Board has two free PSAT/NMSQT®*practice tests on its website.

The National Merit Semi-Finalist Designation Can Help with Admissions

Because National Merit recognition enhances an admission application, a junior seeking a selective admission should take this test seriously, with extra study and practice prior to the test in October of junior year.

That being said, if a student does not get a recognized score, so do many others accepted to top colleges as shown below.

Approximate Annual Totals[27]	
Freshmen at 50 Various Top Colleges	100,000
Freshmen at 100 Various Top Colleges	200,000
National Merit Semi-Finalist Scorers	56,000

A good ACT test score or a good SAT test score later will help offset failing to make National Merit high scorer status. The highest ACT test score or SAT test score is the most looked at test result.

Take These Valuable Practice Tests!

⇒ If a student just doesn't have the money when it is time to sign up, he or she should ask the school to cover it, or ask to pay later. and ask.

ᴸ * The PSAT/NMSQT® is a trademark registered by the College Board and the National Merit Scholarship Corporation, which are not involved with the production of, and do not endorse, this product.

⇒ The student gains from a real-time testing experience on practice tests that are like the standardized tests. That's important and valuable.

⇒ After the test, guidance is offered based on correct and incorrect answers to see where to improve.

⇒ All these benefits mean that students should take these tests at the modest cost and with the reasonable amount of time required.

But Wait! There's More!

Parents and students will be glad to know, or not, that in addition to practice tests listed so far, a student can mix in even more tests if he or she wishes. Yes, even more. What a deal. In summary, here's how to maximize all practice opportunities.

- How about a freshman takes a PSAT/NMSQT®* test in October? Seriously, for serious students, why not?
- The counselor's office might have a free practice test booklet.
- Several publishers offer study guidebooks with up to 10 practice tests in one book. Many of these are at libraries.
- On free phone apps, The ACT and College Board have test questions.
- Other phone apps are sold at reasonable prices, such as $5.
- On the websites, the ACT has one free practice test, and the College Board has eight free SAT practice tests.
- Some paid tutoring services offer a free practice test online.
- Some paid services are reasonable in cost, (less than $50 online) offering tutoring from experts who have aced these tests with perfect scores. The ACT, Inc. and the College Board have lower-cost online tutoring (and they wrote the tests). Khan Academy has free online SAT test tutoring.
- Online, phone or take-at-home tests are easier to fit into a schedule, but don't offer the same test-day experience as a preliminary exam test at a school or a practice test at a tutoring company.

8th- and 9th-Graders
Say Hello to the PSAT 8/9 Test and PreACT
Sophomores
Here are the PreACT and PSAT 10 Tests

These Tests Are Your Friends

Yes, I'm repeating this, but for 8th-, 9th-, and 10th-graders, it should be strongly emphasized that they benefit from taking these practice tests, even if school officials and fellow students do not know about it. It is great practice and no one at the colleges will ever see the scores.

Eighth-graders, 9th- and 10th-graders and parents, call the College Board student/parent helpline at (866) 433-7728 to ask about test sites (8 AM to 7 PM, Eastern Time Sept. to early June and 9 AM to 7 PM Eastern Time mid-June to Sept, Mon-Fri. and on test weekends). Call the ACT at (877) 789-2925 (8:30 am to 5 pm Central Time, Mon.-Fri.).

School staff can call the College Board at (888) 477-7728 to verify rules and set up the test and call the ACT at (319) 337-1000 or 1270. See a request memo in the Appendix (p. 329).

In summary, on a well-spread-out schedule a student could take 10 to 15 full practice tests combined at school, home or with tutors, many for free, by the end of junior year. Many motivated students take more than that.

Find Test Taking Methods That Work for You

Regarding test-taking strategies, I am not qualified to offer advice, other than this: Keep your place, as discussed below.

Please look up test-taking advice.

The Official Guides from ACT, Inc. and the College Board have detailed advice on taking-taking skills on their websites and in their guides. They're not hiding anything.

Be willing to sift through these tips and explanations from all sources for a good understanding. It is not nearly enough just to know that you should keep up a good pace.

For your own best results understand these details on test reasoning. This is important. Don't wing it.

Test Taking Flow: Keep Your Place

Losing your place repeatedly over a three-hour test will lower your score. This isn't nit-picky. It is vital. You will take the Official SAT Test or the Official ACT Test only a few times in your life, and the results can have a huge impact on college selection and financial aid, so this isn't nit-picky or stupid to think about.

OK, it sounds dumb to bring up, but this works: Keep one index finger firmly on your place in the selection or mark it with your pencil, and keep the other index finger firmly on A, B, C, D, or E as you move your eyes around. Develop that habit. Keep one finger firmly on your place, while you look elsewhere or must turn a page.

You can also use an eraser as a place keeper.

You May, Can and Should Write on the Test Book

Writing on the test book pages is officially allowed, so write all over the test book whenever it will help you. This is the opposite of what we are used to. But you better do so for these tests. Develop a new habit. Write on the test booklet to help you.

- Cross off the A, B, C, D and E answers as you eliminate them.
- Circle A if it looks correct and put a '?' next to B if it looks possible, for example, as you cross off the other answers.
- Circle, underline or put X, ? or ↦ to help you.
- Write notes anywhere and connecting lines to guide you.
- For math, write on the test book to help yourself. Write down calculations so you don't have to keep figures in your head.

Overall:

- Make the practice conditions as close to the conditions that will be experienced during the test.

- None of these practice tests are required to apply to college. None of the scores are reported to colleges.
- The $12 and $15 tests are very reasonable, and $46 still isn't too bad.

In Summary, Regarding Practice for the Standardized Tests

Students, with all these practice options, if you don't use them and then do not know what types of questions are on these tests, and you don't know the level of difficulty, and you aren't comfortable taking the tests, then you have only yourself to blame.

Conversely, to use positive language, if you practice regularly, you will know what to expect. You will be comfortable and confident and you will do much, much better.

HERE ARE THE REAL TEST RULES

The ACT, Inc. and College Board rules allow:

☞ *Any* student, starting in 8th grade, (or even earlier*)

☞ or in *any* year of high school

☞ may take *any* preliminary, practice test

☞ *any* time it is offered

☞ *anywhere* it is offered

☞ at the student's choice.

☞ Any student may take all four preliminary exams (PSAT 8/9 Test, PSAT 10 Test, PSAT/NMSQT Test** or PreACT Test) in one single school year.

☞ Any student may take any exam at another school or another school district.

☞ Any student may take the regular ACT exam and the regular SAT exam in any year, although it is recommended for junior and senior years.

☞ Any student may opt out if he or she is not ready, (and prefers to take it later) including for school-ordered tests.

☞ Any tutor, parent or guardian may take a test to better understand the test. (One mom took seven SAT tests.[28])

☞ Anyone who doesn't go to college right away, may continue to study for a test, taking it after high school as an adult for future college applications or credit.

Those are some of the test agency rules.

*Usually, 8th grade is the first year for a practice test, but students in earlier grades are allowed to take a preliminary test, for special programs, for example.

** The PSAT/NMSQT® is a trademark registered by the College Board and the National Merit Scholarship Corporation.

DO NOT ACCEPT INCORRECT INFORMATION

A misinformed person may tell you "This is not available to you," when *it is available* to you. School staff people make mistakes sometimes.

You students are smart, able and ready. Get a head start on practice tests, internships, projects and whatever else you can dig up and dream up. Don't let misinformed, timid people who avoid anything new or different hold you back. If you're the only student doing it, so what? That means you're the smart one. Wisdom is justified of her children. Ignore faint-hearted do-nothings. Take a practice test! Go see about something! Try your idea! See what happens! Find out! Go and ask! Call and check! Get it done!

Here's an actual case: School staff incorrectly told a 9th-grader that the PreACT test and the PSAT/NMSQT®* test were not available to 9th-graders. They didn't want to sign her up, *until the 9th-grader insisted.* (Both tests are available to any high school student in any year.) Later, a school staffer incorrectly said it would be bad on her record, which was not true, because a 9th-grader's score on a preliminary test is not sent to colleges, nor is it part of the transcript, nor is it part of any scholarship.

The 9th-grader was aiming for top colleges and was very wise to take the preliminary test, experiencing what was on a standardized test and how to take it. She got an answer report for tutoring and a preview of what she'd need to learn over the next four years. All for $15 and a few hours of time. But what if she had let the misinformed school officials stop her? She would not have gained these valuable benefits. She would have been held back.

Do not let people hold you back.

*The PSAT/NMSQT® is a trademark registered by the College Board and the National Merit Scholarship Corporation which are not involved in the production of, and do not endorse, this product.

POSSIBLE PSAT PRACTICE TEST SCHEDULE

GRADE		1ST SEMESTER		2ND SEMESTER
8TH	#1	PSAT 8/9 Test (Sept. to Jan.)	or	(Feb. to Apr.)
9TH	#2	PSAT 8/9 Test (Sept. to Jan.)	or	(Feb. to Apr.) and/or #3 PSAT 10 Test (Feb. to Apr.)
10TH	#4	PSAT/NMSQT* Test (Oct.)	and/or	#5 PSAT 10 Test (Feb. to Apr.)
11TH	#6	PSAT/NMSQT* Test (Oct.)	and/or	#7 PSAT 10 Test and/or Move on to regular SAT Test and/or
12TH		Move on to regular SAT Test		

POSSIBLE PreACT PRACTICE TEST SCHEDULE

GRADE		DURING SCHOOL YEAR WHEN SCHEDULED	
8TH	#1	PreACT Test	
9TH	#2	PreACT Test	
10TH	#3	PreACT Test	
11TH	#4	PreACT Test	2nd SEMESTER Move on to regular ACT Test and/or
12TH		Move on to regular ACT Test	

Taking one practice test a year, or two, certainly isn't hard to do. If a student takes even one or two of these practice tests, he or she will benefit. A student who takes even more will benefit even more.

*The PSAT/NMSQT™ Test is a trademark owned by the College Board and the National Merit Scholarship Corporation, which are not involved in the production of, and do not endorse, this product.

Things to Do for a Standardized Test

Here is a long, nit-picky list. Students who will benefit from a higher score, please read the tips to help you on this important test day.

Two Weeks Before the Test

Why two weeks? To have it out of the way. Read the list and see.

1) Get a photo ready and download it for your test pass on the ACT or SAT website. Print it early, so in case there's a glitch you have time to fix it. No pass, no test.

2) Purchase #2 regular wood pencils. <u>Mechanical pencils *are not allowed.*</u> <u>Pens are not allowed.</u> It says this on the test instructions at the test. This rule isn't easy to find on websites clearly stated as "no mechanical pencils are allowed," but wooden No. 2 pencils work with the scanners and mechanical pencil marks might not. I hear of test proctors who allow mechanical pencils, but students should follow the rules so the answers scan properly. Do not use a pen on the essay, which will then be disqualified.

3) Purposely make a few pencils dull and rounded on the end because a dull, rounded end fills in the circle faster on the answer sheet.

4) For the essay portion, have several sharp pencils. Have a hand-held sharpener. You will write for nearly an hour and a dull pencil is hard on the hand.

5) To erase wrong answers, consider using a hand eraser so you can also use it as a marker to keep your place in the test booklet.

6) Have an approved calculator. Don't wait until a few days before the test to buy one, as the week before the test I've seen local stores sell out of these calculators, as a bunch of students show up to buy them. Calculators cost from $10 on up to $90 or more. You'll need to buy or borrow one, and leave enough time to learn how to use it

properly. Know how to use that model. Ask a math teacher or a math whiz, if need be. The ACT and College Board websites list approved and prohibited calculators. Have fresh batteries.

7) Have a watch in case the wall clock is hard to see or is broken. (It happens.) If you hate wearing a watch to the point of distraction, put it on the desk or on the floor, but have one in case you need it. (You can't use a phone to check the time.)

A Week Before the Test

1) If you haven't already, print your test pass. If there is a glitch, you have several days to fix it.

The Day Before the Test

1) If the test is at another school, know the drive time and the route.
2) Put gas in the car the day before.
3) Buy or prepare a few snacks and drinks for the five-minute breaks in the hallway.

The Night Before the Test

1) Check the test website for a test site cancellation or change. You're supposed to get an email or text, but check the site too. (Changes happen all the time so you must check.)

2) Set your clothes out. In case the room is hot for you, have a regular shirt on. In case the room is cold for you, take a jacket or sweater.

3) Pack your bag. If you forgot something, get it. Thus, the next morning, you will have it all, and you may sleep a little longer.
   a) The supplies include:
      (1) Test Pass
      (2) ID Card
      (3) Watch
      (4) Calculator with fresh batteries
      (5) Pencils (No. 2, wooden, two of them dull. If writing an essay have 6 to 10 sharp ones, or have a sharpener. No pens or mechanical pencils are allowed.)
      (6) A hand-held eraser for a place keeper
      (7) Extra shirt, sweater or jacket
      (8) For hallway breaks; snack, juice, electrolyte drink or water

4) Unless you still have material to cover (i.e., the post-Cold War period for the History Subject Test) do not study the night before. You might recheck a tricky math equation, but that's about it.

5) Eat a healthy dinner, so you'll be fresh and have energy for the morning, but not be over stuffed.

6) Let's be honest here students; of all the Friday nights of your youth, this is the one night not to party at all and be impaired in any way the next morning.

7) Have a light, relaxed evening. For you ambitious types, do not start a new project with this spare time. Do not get the adrenaline flowing and stay up. Don't get caught up in a book plot, video game or TV-show binge so you stay up late. (I read a history book to help me nod off.) Have everyone be quiet. Wind down. Sleep.

8) Don't get home too late. School activities are important, but the others should also respect a teammate's college goals. Students and parents, this is one time to insist that academics come first. Sure, don't skip a playoff game, but leave right afterwards.
   a) The coach or director can let you leave early, or be excused for that event entirely if it's an away event with a very long drive.
   b) For an away event, the school can make the reasonable exception to allow a parent to drive the student home. If needed, go over someone's head, such as to the superintendent's office. Seriously, insist on this.

9) The average light spectrum with blue light interferes with your body's natural melatonin production. (Blue blocker light bulbs and reading glasses are available for night reading.) Melatonin is required for a full sleep cycle. So, turn out or cover all lights and shut the door tightly. Cover the windows to reduce the morning light, so you'll sleep until your alarm goes off. Turn an alarm clock light away from your bed to reduce light. Get a full sleep cycle in a dark room.

10) Set one household alarm, and one or two phone alarms. Thus, in case there is a power outage at 4 a.m. that messes up the household clock (which happens) and in case a phone operating system glitches (which happens), one of the other alarms will still go off. You will sleep better, if you're not consciously or subconsciously thinking about whether an alarm will ring. Seriously, set at least two alarms, or even better, three.

The Morning of the Test

1) Don't roll out of bed and go straight to the test. To be alert at 8:30 a.m. when the actual test starts, it takes some time to fully wake up a human brain. Exercise a few minutes. Take a shower. If you feel tired, have coffee, tea, cola, juice or fruit to wake up, but not too much so you get jittery. Get your brain working by reading something that requires concentration for ten minutes that morning, such as a news article. Be ready to think fast when the questions start, not still shaking off the morning cobwebs. A slow start will hurt your score. Every point counts.

2) Eat some breakfast if that is your routine or take a snack for a bite in the hallway if you usually eat later.

3) Leave with extra time for no stress. After you get in the car, pause to remember to have everything. Avoid a U-turn. Avoid a disaster, like forgetting the calculator. (A student I know zoomed to a store to buy one, barely getting to the test site in time.)

4) Stay focused on the way over. Leave the phone off. Look out the window. With friends before the test, keep calm and focused. Late-breaking drama can wait.

5) Turn off your phone and leave it in the car or in your bag by the room door. Pulling out a phone could invalidate your test.

6) Use the bathroom at the test site before doors close at 8:00 a.m. You may not get another break until as late as 9:30 a.m.

In the Testing Room

Be bold with the test proctor to correct any problems. There could be, for example, confusion on timing with a problem with the wall clock. (Which is why it's good to have a watch.)

Insist on Using the Five-Minute Test Breaks

Between test sections, the rules allow a full five-minute break. Use the time to use the bathroom, stretch, and walk around a little. Get out of your chair and move around. The break will help you concentrate on the next segment. Have juice or a snack for glucose for your brain.

Should You Guess on the Tests?

For most tests, yes, you can guess with no penalty. As explained on the agency websites, here are the rules on penalties for wrong answers:

ACT Test   OK to guess; no penalty for wrong answers.

SAT Test   OK to guess; no penalty for wrong answers.

AP Subject Tests OK to guess; no penalty for wrong answers.

CLEP Tests   OK to guess; no penalty for wrong answers.

PSAT/NMSQT   OK to guess; no penalty for wrong answers.

It is different for:

SAT Subject Tests: 1/4 point penalty per wrong answer, with 1 full point for each right answer. If you have no idea, don't guess. If you have eliminated 2 as wrong answers out of 5, statistically, a guess could be in your favor (1 of 3). If you are down to two answers on one question, statistically, a guess (1 of 2) could be in your favor.

Some proctors want to skip the break. *Do not let them skip the break.* Say, "I have to go to the bathroom and we're supposed to have a break." Even if you don't need to use the bathroom, use the break to walk around and stretch.

Make Notes and Write on the Test Booklet

Write on the test booklet. In the official test guide, and on the agency websites, you are advised to mark the book as needed. Cross off wrong answers and circle the right one. Make calculations. Mark things to double check if you have time at the end. Not writing on the test book can put you at a distinct disadvantage and you are allowed to write on the booklet. If the proctor says otherwise, hold your ground and insist that he or she call the helpline in their test packet.

Finally

Remember, girls do very well on standardized tests.
Remember, boys do very well on standardized tests.
You'll do fine

☞ Chapter 17 ✍

Other Tests

Other tests include:
> **SAT Subject Tests™**
> **Advanced Placement® (AP®) Tests**
> **International Baccalaureate (IB) Tests**
> **CLEP® Exams – College-Level Examination Program**

Only some colleges, the selective ones, *require* SAT Subject Tests to apply, and they don't require any of the others listed above. Other than at those colleges, these tests are optional, but can be beneficial.

SAT Subject Tests™

For admissions, some colleges require or recommend two SAT Subject Tests, which are wholly different and distinct from the SAT Test, although they are offered on the same day. Many colleges request one math or science test and one humanities test, for a total of two. Some colleges require or recommend both one math and one science SAT Subject Test, but do not require a humanities test. Thus, to cover all cases, some students would need three (3) tests. SAT Subject Tests do not result in college credit. If you want to highlight your major, a good score on the related test helps.

If the colleges you wish to apply to do not require SAT Subject Tests, you can skip these tests.

Strong scores on these tests, however, look good on an application, so if you get high grades in some of these subjects, consider taking the tests, even if they are not required. If a college didn't require an SAT Subject Test in the first place, you do not have to report the score if it's not beneficial to your application.

To Take Required Tests, Plan Ahead

If you may even remotely consider applying to a college that requires SAT Subject Tests, then you should know about them. Do not have to forgo applying to a college only because you didn't plan for SAT Subject Tests. It happens.

If a student has done well in classwork, then adding the SAT Subject Tests into the process is not a big deal. Each test is one hour and three tests can be taken on one testing day.

Schedule the tests if possible after the student has recently covered the material. Consult teachers as to timing and how the material from class matches a test. Don't wing it.

Use SAT Subject Test study guides (which have practice tests) available in libraries, or for purchase. If needed, ask the librarian to purchase one. Students should study with a guide and take practice tests.

The College Board website has free subject test practice questions.

Getting an average score on any one subject test isn't the end of the world in admissions, but try for your highest score with adequate preparation. You can retake this test, as your schedule allows, if a score is really low.

Cancellation: A student may cancel the SAT Subject Test before leaving the test center. The second way to cancel is with a form with a signature that must be received by fax or overnight mail or courier by the next Wednesday, 11:59 pm eastern time (1 minute before midnight) at the SAT office. Cancelling a subject test score isn't generally recommended, unless you can schedule another test without interrupting your schedule for the important SAT exam.

Advanced Placement®M (AP®) Tests

AP Exams are only given once a year from May 1 to 12. Advanced Placement® (AP) exams are not required for applications, but can enhance an application. An important benefit of an AP® Exam is that a

---

M Advanced Placement® and AP® are trademarks registered by the College Board®, which is not involved with the production of, and does not endorse, this product.

passing grade can equal one or more semesters of college credit, saving time and money in college.

AP Tests Do Not Require a Class

Any student may take any AP exam without taking an AP class. This includes home-schooled students and students whose schools did not offer that AP class. Students can take regular English, for example, and study on their own with AP study guides to take the AP English literature exam.

If your school doesn't offer the AP test you want, you can take it at another site. The College Board's helpline might help find sites. Your school, with enough notice, can add an AP exam on your request, even if the AP class isn't taught there.

Regarding College Applications and AP Score Reports:

- Before the AP test in May, decide if it is best to select one college for a free score report, which saves you $15. This score report sends all AP tests to that one college. If you want to see a score first, then it will cost you $15 to report the score to one college later. Be aware that if you do get a 1 or 2 score, which is low, then you should cancel that score for free by July 15, or withhold it for $10 per score by July 15. After July 15, the score goes to the college you selected.
- Additional reports to colleges cost $15 each, showing all scores, unless a score is withheld.
- One or more scores can be withheld by the student to that college for $10 per score. This isn't done online, but in writing via fax, mail or courier. A withheld score can be released for free later.
- Cancellation: A student can cancel an AP test completely for free which removes it from his or her record. But if you put a college down for the score report, you will need to cancel before June 15 or the college will get the score. The cancellation isn't online, but in writing via fax, mail or courier.
- See that your high school transcript includes the results you want.

- Good AP scores enhance college applications. The additional $15 cost per college report is recommended to spend for selective colleges and honors programs. Certainly, your top few college choices should know you got 4s or 5s on AP exams. For the top colleges, the cost is worth it. If you have no money for these fees, see below.

- You can self-report AP scores by listing your good AP scores in your accomplishments, mentioning that you can't report them officially yet. The school can list the good AP scores on your high school transcript at your request.

Good Scores on AP Exams = College Credit
Saving Money and Time

Many colleges give college credit for a passing grade (3, 4 or 5 out of 5 possible) on an AP Exam. The highest score, a 5, can get more credits. For the cost, $92, and a few hours of test time, a student can save a whole semester on a college course and tuition costs, as well as move the student further along on the degree requirements. (For low-income students, a fee reduction of $31 is available.)

Many AP teachers encourage students to take the AP subject tests for these reasons, but, one more time, students do not need AP subject tests to complete a college application, including one to a selective college. The student in our story took no AP tests, as he was behind in SAT prep and wanted to focus on the SAT test and SAT Subject Tests exclusively.

A student may skip AP tests until the end of senior year to concentrate on grades, applications and others tests. Then, after applications are in, if he or she passes the AP exams in May of senior year, college credit can still be obtained.

For AP exams, the study guides from the library or from booksellers are helpful. AP Subject Tests are offered in more than 30 subjects. including art, English, history, math, languages, music, science, and social sciences. Check whether using AP for college credit will affect a freshman financial aid package.

International Baccalaureate (IB) Tests

The International Baccalaureate (IB) tests also provide college credit if passed. These also offer significant savings. The IB tests can be a very good deal. IB exams can only be taken in conjunction with an IB course at a high school. Whether to report IB scores for admissions depends on the college, which should be consulted. Check whether using IB for college credit will affect a freshman financial aid package.

CLEP®[N] Exams – College-Level Examination Program

CLEP exams from the College Board provide college credit if passed. CLEP exams require no class and many subjects are covered by the 33 exams. CLEP exams have study guides. The cost savings are significant. CLEP exams cost $80. CLEP exam scores can enhance a college application, but are optional to report.

[N] *CLEP® Exam is a registered trademark of the College Board®, which is not involved in the production of, and does not endorse, this product.*

AP®, CLEP® and IB Exams Provide College Credit.

Students can get cost savings with AP® Exams, CLEP® Exams (College-Level Examination Program®) and IB Tests (International Baccalaureate). AP Exams do not require a class. CLEP Exams do not require a class.
IB Exams require a class.

AP® Exam Scores and College Credit Awarded

These are examples. Consult a college for specifics.
CLEP Exams and IB Exams offer similar savings.

AP® Exam (A Score of 3, 4 or 5 out of 5 is a passing score.)	AP® Exam Score	College Credit Hours	College Course Equivalent Example
Chemistry	4	4	CHEM 151
	5	8	CHEM 151, 152
Physics 1	4,5	4	PHYS 102
U.S. Govt. and Politics	4,5	3	POL 201
Spanish Language and Culture	3	8	SPAN 201, 202
	4	11	SPAN 201, 202, 251
	5	14	SPAN 201, 201, 251, 325

Which is a better deal?
Approximate College Tuition Costs
(+ $150 books cost)
Compared to AP® Exam Cost

Credit Hours (4 credits = 1 class for 1 semester)	Community College Cost	State 4-Year College, In-state	Private College Cost	Example of Equivalent Number of AP® Exams	AP® Exam Cost
4	$ 500	$ 1,350	$ 4,000	1	$ 92
8	$ 1,000	$ 2,700	$ 8,000	2	$ 184
12	$ 1,500	$ 4,050	$ 12,000	3	$ 276
16	$ 2,000	$ 5,400	$ 16,000	4	$ 368

That's a good deal 👆

AP® CLEP® and College Level Examination Program® are trademarks registered by the College Board.

All the Tests	Required for Admissions?	Any Scores Reported to Admissions?	Is Score Selection Allowed?
PSAT 8/9 (Preliminary)	NO.	NO.	NOT APPLICABLE. Scores are not sent.
PSAT 10 (Preliminary)	NO.	NO.	NOT APPLICABLE. Scores are not sent.
PreAct (Preliminary)	NO.	NO.	NOT APPLICABLE. Scores are not sent.
PSAT/ NMSQT Test* (Preliminary)	NO, for National Merit only.	NO, but National Merit status may be noticed.	NOT APPLICABLE. Scores are not sent.
ACT Test	MAYBE. YES for most. NO for some.	YES.	MAYBE. YES for most. NO for some selective colleges.
SAT Test	MAYBE. YES for most. NO for some.	YES.	MAYBE. YES for most. NO for some selective colleges.
SAT Subject Test	MAYBE. YES for some selective colleges. Optional for others, but may be recommended.	MAYBE. YES, if required by that college. Optional for others.	YES. If required, at least one score must be reported. Other scores are optional.
AP Subject Test	NO.	ONLY ON STUDENT REQUEST.	YES.
IB Test	NO.	ONLY ON STUDENT REQUEST.	YES.
CLEP	NO.	ONLY ON STUDENT REQUEST.	YES.

Score selection above means whether a student can choose which test scores to report to each college. All AP Subject Test scores, IB Test scores and CLEP scores are optional on a college application and can be submitted after admission to a college for college credit, although reporting good scores can enhance an application by showing academic achievement.

*The PSAT/NMSQT™ Test is a trademark owned by the College Board and the National Merit Scholarship Corporation, which are not involved in the production of, and do not endorse, this product.

All the Tests: Year by Year Index

Most tests can be taken multiple times. See each college about required tests and scores. See options for reporting or not reporting scores. See agency rules for cancelling tests and scores (pp. 327-328). Test months listed below are commonly used, but may change. Some New York ACT test dates may differ.

8th Grade	**Regarding College Applications**
PreACT™ test	practice, optional, not reported
PSAT™ 8/9 test	practice; optional, not reported

9th Grade	**Regarding College Applications**
PreACT™ test	practice, optional, not reported
PSAT™ 8/9 test	practice, optional, not reported
PSAT/NMSQT®* test (Oct. only)	practice, optional, not reported

10th Grade	**Regarding College Applications**
PreACT™ test	practice, optional, not reported
PSAT/NMSQT®* test (Oct. only)	practice, optional, not reported
PSAT™ 10 test (Feb. to April)	practice, optional, not reported
SAT Subject Tests™	if required, is reported, otherwise optional
AP® subject test (May 1-12)	optional, reported at student's request

11th Grade	**Regarding College Applications**
PreACT™ test	practice, optional, not reported
SAT Subject Tests™	if required, is reported, otherwise optional
AP® subject tests (May 1-12)	optional, reported at student's request
PSAT/NMSQT®* test (Oct. only)	practice, optional, score not reported, but National Merit status may be noted.

In 11th grade, the score is seen only by the National Merit Scholarship agency. Students with high scorer status can put that status on college applications. Actual scores are not reported to colleges, which may, however, notice the high scorer status.

ACT® test Feb., April, June, & July	as required, is reported (and/or)
SAT® test March, May, June, July, & Aug.	as required, is reported

12th Grade	**Regarding College Applications**
SAT Subject Tests™	if required, is reported, otherwise optional
AP® subject tests (May 1-12)	optional, reported at student's request
ACT® test Sept., Oct., Dec. & Feb.	as required, is reported

(Feb. ACT® test is allowed for some regular decisions, is reported) (and/or)

SAT® test Oct., Nov. Dec. & March	as required, is reported

CLEP exams can be taken any year. CLEP scores are not required for applications.

IB exams are in conjunction with classes as coordinated with the teachers. IB exams are not required for applications, but good scores enhance an application.

*PSAT/NMSQT® is a registered trademark of the College Board and the National Merit Scholarship Corporation.

☞ Chapter 18 ✍

The Applications

With Checklists

How Long Will This Take?

For one college, with all the information at hand and with essays ready, the whole process may take one hour or two, more or less. Beforehand, however, compiling information and completing tasks will take several more hours, including writing essays. This includes:

- have an account with a college, or with a joint application (such as the Common App), or a paper application;
- test scores must be ordered to be sent to the college, or included in the transcript;
- complete an essay;
- have an activities and accomplishments list, with contacts;
- recommendation letters (one from a counselor, one or two from teachers) need to be submitted by those people to the college, usually via a download to the application or via email;
- portfolios of writing, art, research, etc., must be downloaded or sent to the college;
- the high school registrar must send an official transcript; and
- have family financial information for financial aid forms, although you may be able to complete those later.

Look Over Applications Early, Then Fill One Out

You must set up an online account with an email address, etc. For a paper application, request one.

Before completing and sending an application, look at an actual application early to see how to do it and see what the colleges want.

See how the actual online application website works by

entering in a full application early, but without sending it. You do not want to wonder on deadline day if you are doing it correctly.

I know from helping a student with applications for 2017/18 that these online applications are, at times, not the most logical websites ever devised by humanity. You may finish typing the essay questions, thinking you are done, but you are not, as further action on the Writing Supplement may be needed.

Yes, I Think It's All Set to Go. Oops. Now What?

Things may happen. A vital supplement or portfolio may unexpectedly not upload. Or maybe the teacher was supposed to upload it, two weeks ago. The student I was helping recently had a crucial video from a year of extra-curricular work, which was to launch him above the crowd. The upload was 250 MB too large. Oops. He had to re-record parts and re-edit it on deadline evening.

Two extra essay questions at 250 words on each app add up. For five applications, that's 2,500 words to write. One senior told me she missed several colleges on Jan. 1 at midnight, because she didn't realize how many essay questions would come up. Each college has different types of questions so you can't copy and paste them.

Many of us will send them on Jan. 1, if they are due on Jan. 1. OK, but send one early in the day, so you can see the result to adjust the next application if needed.

Consider sending at least one application a few weeks early, before the December break. Thus, if something unexpected occurs, you can adjust for the other apps. Find out by doing one application early. If you don't, you might need something from the school, but what if it's closed for the break? Go through each college application well before the break. Know how to navigate each step. Look for deadlines for supplements, research papers and portfolios.

Seniors Can Start Some Applications on August 1

Each college has a date on which applications are open to start entering in the data online. Take a look. The opening date information of the joint application services, and the joint applications of some state college systems are shown on the next pages.

Types of Applications:

individual college applications
> or
joint applications
> the Common App (700 colleges)
> the Coalition App (120 colleges)
> the Common Black College App (53 colleges)
> the Universal App (34 colleges)
> state university systems (p. 309).

With most college applications:

1) It is possible to send the application to meet the deadline requirement and pay the application fee later by selecting the option to send in a check. You may also usually send the application to meet the deadline and finalize the test reports later, so those report fees can also be paid later. Thus, on deadline day, you can file an application with no money to spend that day. Later, yes, but not that day. So, the lack of money on deadline day does not have to make you miss the deadline. For more information on fees and waivers see pages 182-185.

2) You may set up a college account and start your application to see what is required, but you do not have to finalize it until you are ready. You can enter data, exit, and come back later to enter more information. Until you finalize it and send it, the admissions office is not looking at the information, so you can make changes.

3) With joint systems, you may apply to multiple colleges without repeating a lot of the data entry each time.

4) Joint applications sometimes require extra work for each individual college, perhaps extra essays or meeting extra requirements. A student, for example, may not just fill out the joint application once, select four

colleges and be done. Each of those four colleges may require extra tasks on each application.

5) While working on a joint application site, the individual colleges cannot see your information until it is sent as a finalized application to that specific college. On joint application sites, an applicant may finalize each individual college application at different times, except for the Common Black College App, which sends the information to all 53 colleges at one time.

6) Once an application is sent to one individual college and accepted, changes cannot be made, other than to send additional test scores, grades and financial forms. Application opening dates for our purposes are for fall enrollment for freshmen applicants.

Students may enter college at the beginning of other semesters or quarters.

Common App   www.CommonApp.org

August 1 is the opening date. All colleges may not accept applications as of that date, but you can get started.

Coalition App   www.CoalitionForCollegeAccess.org

Opening dates are designated by each college. If you see a green "Start Application" button, the application is open. You must find each college's opening date on your own, or wait for the green Start Application button to turn up.

The student profile account is available to start at any time, all year.

Profiles can be started in any year of high school.

You can agree to share your profile information with the colleges, so they might send you marketing material.

Common Black College App   www.CommonBlackCollegeApp.com

You can preview the application by not entering in any data. This App works a little differently. You can't save it, exit and come back later.

When You Click "Continue" At the Bottom
It is Final for All 53 Black Colleges

With the Common Black College App, don't start entering anything until you are ready to finalize it for all 53 colleges.

Preview it first and make notes. Finalize it when you are ready. The activities, honors and achievements all go into one screen, so have those organized with all the dates, locations and contacts.

This form does not have an essay or recommendation letters, but some colleges may require those later, or you can add them later.

A Unique Deal: Let's See What Happens at 53 Colleges

This application is unique in that for a one-time $35 fee, a student's application goes to 53 historically black colleges and universities (HBCU). An applicant can select four colleges as his or her top choices, but all 53 colleges may consider the applicant.

Students who are not sure of their chances of admission or what financial aid they might receive can use this unique system to see if offers might be available. Students may initiate further contact with the colleges to express interest and ask for consideration.

From Fast Food to a Degree and a Professional Career

I read a story of one girl who hadn't taken school seriously and regretted it. She thought no college would want her, that she was consigned to fast food jobs for the rest of her life.

Someone convinced her to fill out the Common Black College App.

A college she had not known existed took her in, provided mentoring, made it affordable, and she was on her way to a bachelor's degree and professional career.

The Universal App   www.UniversalCollegeApp.com

July 1 is the opening date. All colleges may not accept applications as of that date, but you can get started.

State College Joint Applications

Nine state university systems have their own joint applications online. A list with websites and notations starts on page 309. These states are Alaska, California, Texas, Maine, Minnesota, New York, Pennsylvania, South Carolina and Wisconsin.

To be helpful, for the larger states, here are opening dates.

California: The University of California System opens on Aug. 1 (www.universityofcalifornia.edu) and the California State University System opens on Oct. 1 (www.calstate.edu).

Texas: Look for a full preview of the application, without entering any information, at www.applytexas.org which also has 41 private colleges and 74 community colleges. Some applications open on July 1 and others open later.

New York: The State University of New York (www.suny.edu) and 27 community colleges open on Aug. 1. City University of New York (www2.cuny.edu) and 7 community colleges open on Sept. 15.

All Public Colleges, All 50 states, D.C. and Five Territories

A listing to find all U.S. public colleges is on page 309 for 50 states, D.C. and five territories. Each site has state colleges, with links to application websites, some with links to private colleges. Remember that many public colleges in nearby states offer discounted rates (see page 103).

Deadlines

Admissions deadlines include
    regular decision admission
    early decision admission
        binding
        non-binding
    rolling admissions (no set deadline)
    Financial aid deadlines include
        regular financial aid package
        earlier deadlines for special scholarships

The admissions application is one thing and the financial aid application is another thing.

Common deadlines for the financial aid application are a month or two after an admissions application is due. Some special scholarships have an early deadline, requiring the admissions application at the same time. Such special early scholarships are usually awarded to only a few students.

Most money is given through the regular financial aid packages with the regular deadlines. Financial aid applications may be due on Feb. 1 at a college, for example, but many college advisers recommend completing financial aid applications before the deadlines in case colleges start to allocate money early before the deadline. The FAFSA (Free Application for Federal Student Aid) is available on Oct. 1.

Among U.S. colleges there is a variety of deadlines and admissions decision dates.

It's possible to apply in September, for example, to one college, and apply eight months later in May to another college.

Regular Decision Deadlines

The regular decision application deadlines occur during senior school year. Commonly used regular decision deadlines include

November 1	November 30
December 1	December 30
January 1	February 1 or later
rolling applications with no set deadline	

The commonly used financial aid deadlines for regular decision applications include:

February 1   March 1 or 2   March 15

There are variations:

A. The California state colleges, the University of California (UC) system and California State University (Cal State) system use Nov. 30 for regular decision.

B. Some colleges have a deadline a few days before or after a standard deadline.

C. Many smaller colleges have later deadlines, such as May 1 or June 1.

D. Some colleges have rolling applications which means they accept

181

applications starting in August or September until the slots are filled by qualified applicants, or classes start.

E. A few colleges offer a quick decision option, which is like regular decision, but with a decision in three weeks. This is not the same as the exclusive early-decision options.

Early Decision Deadlines:

Early decision applications have several factors to think about. Early decision options are binding or non-binding.

With an early application that is binding or exclusionary, the student agrees to accept the admissions offer and not apply early to other colleges (pp. 236-237).

This is part of an admissions factor of demonstrated interest on the part of the student.

Fees: Get Ready for the Fees

There is usually a college application fee, although hundreds of colleges have a free application.

Sending test scores can involve fees. Each test will send scores to four colleges at no extra charge.

The fee to send an application to each school is from around $30 or $50 to $75. The fee for extra test scores per college is $12 for SAT test scores and $12 or more for ACT test scores.

Be ready for these fees. If you should apply to a lot of schools, save up the money. If you want to apply to four or five schools, be ready for the $200 to $300 cost. For ten or more, it is about $400 to $500 or more. Compared to all other spending during four years of high school, this amount is vitally important to budget for.

To reduce costs, options include:
- regular fee waivers,
- the hardship waiver form,
- free applications, and
- placing test results on a transcript and in the application.

Is the Application Deadline Looming?
In a Pinch for the Money?
Do Not Miss the Deadline. Select Pay by Check.
That Option is the Last Thing on the Application.
Use That Option if You Have To.

Without money, for one, two, or more colleges, you can apply so you don't miss the deadline and select the

☑ Pay by Check

option to pay later, or to obtain a fee waiver later.

Colleges with No Application Fee

Here are various lists of colleges with free applications.

409 colleges – state by state list

Prep Scholar

blog.prepscholar.com/colleges-with-no-application-fee

462 colleges –

DIY College Rankings lists 462 colleges at

http://diycollegerankings.com/290-colleges-with-free-application-fees/952/

92 colleges –

www.Niche.com lists 92 colleges. Go to College Rankings at the bottom of the screen, go to Admissions, Best Colleges with No Application Fee

217 colleges –

CollegeXpress

http://www.collegexpress.com/lists/list/colleges-with-no-undergraduate-application-fee/1681/

Application Fee Waivers

Generally, colleges want applications, unless you are being frivolous. Generally, colleges do not want qualified applicants to be hindered from applying only because a fee is a financial strain for the applicant, thus they provide fee waivers.

A fee waiver section is on most applications, as well as the joint applications, except for the Black College common application which offers no waiver. If you do not have money for this fee, the school, a charity or a church may have available funds.

For regular waivers, families qualify with income up to about $45,500 for a family of four, i.e., the cutoff for the reduced school-lunch program. Students <u>automatically</u> qualify who are homeless, foster children, TRIO program participants, from families receiving housing assistance or public assistance, orphans, or wards of the state.

The last type of waiver is the hardship waiver as explained next.

If You Just Don't Have the Money: A Hardship Waiver

Perhaps you don't meet regular waiver requirements. Perhaps you've paid to apply to several colleges, and used some free applications. But there are still several more that you should apply to, and you are out of money.

I am not recommending sending frivolous applications, but if you have a realistic chance at several more colleges, then a hardship waiver is appropriate.

What if a college would have accepted you, but you didn't send in the application? Should working-class kids settle for only two or three applications, if sending in several more applications will in fact boost their chances? Definitely, not. I've made this argument elsewhere in the book, and I'll make it again now. Families should pay for as many applications as they can, then use the hardship waiver if students should reasonably apply to several more, but no more money is available.

A hardship waiver must be signed by a counselor, college access counselor, school official, financial aid officer or community leader, who will attest to a hardship on a form from the National Association for College Admission Counseling (NACAC), the "Request for Admission Application Fee Waiver."

To print the form, go to www.nacacnet.org and use the search field; enter "Fee Waiver", then select Application Fee Waiver, then Select

NACAC Request for Application Fee Waiver Form. The last box on the form includes the space for a counselor or another person to state that the waiver is needed. The form is then sent to the college admissions office or the Common App, the Coalition App or the Universal App, which accept the NACAC form.

Usually, after you ask for a waiver, the college or service will not notify you that it was approved. Thus, assume it is approved. Go ahead and apply, checking a fee waiver box as approved. A student may also contact ask college to waive or reduce the fee, explaining the situation.

Test Report Fees

Students get to send reports to four colleges for free as part of the regular test fee. After that, it costs $12 per college. The test fee waiver has eight score reports with SAT test scores and four score reports with the ACT. (In Sept., 2018, the ACT waiver will provide 20 reports.)

If you still need to report test scores but are out of fee money, add the test scores to your transcript and list them somewhere in your application, with an explanation. An Ivy League admissions official told me this year that the college would accept that. For certain, send the application, then work with the college to convey your test scores.

Before Filling in the Application: Test Scores, Grades, Recommendation Letters, Portfolios and Attachments

Applications include test scores, grades and recommendation letters. Community college applications may not require tests or recommendations. Portfolios of art, writing, music, research work and other accomplishments might be attached, or sent separately by teachers. Grades and scores are sent by counselors or registrars. You must arrange this within the deadlines. Some things must be attached with the application and others can be sent later. Know which is which.

Set up your online application accounts. Use a staid email name, like thomas.smith101@email.com or t.d.smith@email.com, instead of tommyboy@email.com. Seriously, start a new account if needed with your first name, or first initial and middle initial, and your last name. That's it. Do not use a cute or clever email for college admissions.

Start early. Save it and exit without sending it. You can go back in, make changes, and exit again without sending it.

For selective colleges, extra attention to everything is highly recommended. Students who will apply to selective colleges will find several chapters in this book on selective college admissions.

Essays

The essays should be started well before the application deadline, so others can read them to offer you advice. Rewrite them, and then repeat the process.

Proofread Everything

After completing an application, wait several days at least before sending it, so you can have fresh eyes when you proofread it. Unless it is the deadline day. In that case, wait an hour, at least, to have fresher eyes. Proofread it several times before sending it.

A Bad Mark on Your Record

With a disciplinary mark, check with your counselor about disclosure requirements. Some disciplinary actions do not need to be disclosed. Juvenile records may be confidential. If something will be reported by the school, then you should without exception, explain the circumstances on the college application.

Still, if you must disclose something, do not assume that you will be turned down because of it. Colleges may have to ask about people's records, but they certainly do accept people who have made mistakes, so complete all applications, with no hesitation on your part. You may very well be accepted, so send it in, no matter what.

Colleges Overall Checklist

Use pencil. Rate each college as yes or maybe. Change to no if needed and cross off those colleges.

Status

	YES MAYBE NO	Application Due Date	College Name	App. Done?	Finance Forms Done?
1					
2					
3					
4					
5					
6					
7					
8					
9					
10					
11					
12					

Application Checklist Page 1

Mark with "Yes", "No", or "N/A" for not applicable.

College Name:_____

Application Deadline Date _____

Admissions Office Phone_____

   Address_____

_____

   Contacts [email/phone] _____

_____

_____

College Account Website:_____

College Username:_____Password:_____

___ Uses Common App   (OR)   ___ Uses Universal App (OR)

___ Uses Own Application (OR) ___ Other _____

Uses ACT® Test? ___ Scores Sent?_____ Dates_____

Uses SAT® Test? ___ Scores Sent?_____ Dates_____

Super scores?_____   Requires All tests?_____ Sent?_____

   Accepts February ACT® Test?___Yes____No / If yes, sent?_____

____ Essay #1 Topic_____ / ____ Essay #2 _____

____ Essay #3 _____ / ____ Essay #4_____

Notes:

Teacher Recommendation 1 Sent? ____ Teacher Recommendation 2 Sent? _____

Counselor Recommendation Sent? _____ Extra Recommendation Sent?_____

Transcript Sent?_____ Date_____

Notes:

SAT Subject Test™ 1 (____)Sent?__SAT Subject Test™ 2 (_____) Sent?___

SAT Subject Test™ 3 (_____)Sent?____

Other tests:_____Sent?_____

Attachments / Portfolio ____ Yes ____ No

   Type_____ Date Sent_____

   Type_____ Date Sent_____

   Type_____ Date Sent_____

Application Checklist Page 2

Financial Aid Deadline Dates and checklist:

FAFSA Due Date_____ Done? ____

W2s   Due Date_____ Year(s) needed_____Done?_____

CSS/Financial Aid PROFILE®* Due Date_____ Done?_____

IDOC? ___Yes___ No   Date_____Format?_____

Done?_____

Authorized to release financial information?____ Date_____

Done?_____

Notes:

Interview?_____Yes_____ No

Date_____Time_____Contact_____

   Phone_____ email_____

   Location_____

   Phone_____

Notes:

College Visits / Orientations / Meetings:

Date_____Type_____Notes_____

Date_____Type_____Notes_____

Date_____Type_____Notes_____

Date_____Type_____Notes_____

   Contacts_____

   _____

   _____

Notes [Also Use Visit Report Form]:

College Visit / Orientation / Contact Report

[Make notes on interaction with college staff and on campus visits.]

College Name: _____

   City/State: _____

State/Regional Contact:

Name:_____

Phone:_____

Address:_____

_____

email:_____Title_____

Notes:

Contact Name:_____Phone_____

Date of contact:_____Location _____

Address:_____

email:_____ Title_____

Notes:

Contact Name:_____Phone_____

Date of contact:_____Location _____

Address:_____

email:_____ Title_____

Notes:

Visit Notes:

Things to check:

Chapter 19

Selective Admissions: Let's Be Realistic

Pros & Cons of Going to a Selective College

A discussion about selective colleges cuts a lot of ways.

Being realistic could mean that if you work at it, you could make it in, maybe to one of the top 50, or 100, or 200 large or small selective colleges. Rather than it being farfetched, as the student in our story thought before he got in, you could definitely be in the running. That's being realistic, for some students.

Being realistic could mean that your B+ grade average in regular courses will get you into some very good colleges but not the most elite.

Being realistic could mean that your C or B average in regular classes is a solid start for your in-state colleges, but that a merit scholarship is not possible.

Selective College or Regular College? Pros and Cons

Not everyone from the Ivies ends up anchoring the nightly news, winning a seat in Congress or making a million bucks a year.

Regular college graduates excel professionally and personally. Some students gain a lot of confidence at a regular college, going on to become experts in a field. In such cases, maybe the state college or a regular private college is a better choice, still offering harder classes when one wants them, but not shell shocking a student into poor performance. At an elite college, some students, especially at first, feel overshadowed by all the seemingly brilliant students around them and can hold back or lose confidence. These same students might feel more empowered at a good regular college, where they stand out more, getting more attention from professors.

Will you feel better right off the bat as a top student at a regular college, with easier interaction with professors and other students? Possibly. But even at the state college, it takes work to stand out, build skills, build confidence and build a good record. And did you know that outgoing people tend to get lower grades than quiet people? It's not necessary for success to be seen as the outgoing, super-confident person on campus. Rather, it's important to be inwardly comfortable, to build inner confidence and thus, success.

It's a serious matter as to where a student should go to best build his or her confidence and skills, so give it some serious thought.

These Colleges Are Rigorous, But Not Impossible

Most colleges, even the most elite, are manageable for a good student. Here are some stories from people I've met.

I spoke with the friend of the family of a recent Harvard enrollee, the first in her family or circle of friends to attend such an elite college. The young lady was nervous about how she would do. Upon arrival in her dorm room, on the back of the door, the student found a list for that room of the previous occupants, to which her name would be added. Let's see, ... oh, she recognized one student. He became U.S. President. Is that reassuring or intimidating? Remember too, that dozens of others on that list became Harvard grads, but are not well known.

At a new student orientation, the staff told all the new students, that, yes, many of them were nervous, but they did deserve to be there, and that they would be just fine, which has been the case for her.

Saturday Night Fun: The Library

I know a student at another top five university, the University of Chicago, known as a place where on Saturday nights students go to the library to study and see all their friends, who are studying.

I asked if he went to see Nobel-Prize-winning professors during office hours, to get to know the people who know people.

He told me that he is busy enough getting decent grades, without trying to impress anyone. He'll get to that, when he knows something. Besides, he had quickly seen that if he wanted to impress a tenured professor at this place, he had better have a question thoroughly researched. He'd seen students try to stand out with an attempt at a clever question, but who had not done enough research, which would have answered the question anyway, which is what the professors explained, in short order.

Was it easy? No way. He studied *a lot*. But, he also got enough sleep. He wasn't up too late, not every night. He exercises, but doesn't goof off too much. Were the other kids all brainiacs? "Well not completely, but you can tell who doesn't quite belong." What do you mean? "Well, there's one guy who just does OK." When he said, "doesn't quite belong,", that wasn't in the sense as if the place was only for snooty, well-to-do high society. He meant belonging intellectually.

Sure, many students are wealthy there. That's not flaunted, just a fact of life there. Either rich, or broke, can you think? Wealth won't buy anyone extra knowledge at this place, only studying will, and belonging there is all about the knowledge, thus the studying.

So, do people at the top colleges know the subjects very, very well? Yes, they do. But can a good student hold his own, get good grades and not make a fool of himself or herself, and even excel? Yes.

Going to a Class at Harvard and a Class at Yale

I accompanied a prospective student, an extended family member, from a working-class family, to Harvard and Yale. She attended one class at Harvard with 30 students and one class at Yale with 20, while the parents and I went for coffee. Were the lectures way over her head? No. Did it sound that tough? No. A lot of students were looking at other things on their phones, she said.

We wanted to speak with students, but not the student tour guides.

So, after each of those classes, we asked a student if we could talk to them for a few minutes. "Sure," said each student. Both were friendly and spoke with us at length.

They told us their stories. Neither had been confident of getting in to one of the most-revered freshman classes in the world.

The Harvard student was from a rural area. She was accepted to Georgetown too, so she was academically qualified, and not helped by a legacy or sports hook.

At first, she was not going to apply to Harvard. Her mom insisted. She said she didn't even know where Harvard was. Upon acceptance, she was very unsure of herself. Now a junior, she was glowing with accounts of support from professors, other students and campus resources. She'd made good friends. She'd studied abroad twice. Not only was it doable, she was loving it.

The Yale student had college-educated parents and had gone to a good public magnet high school in Chicago from which a fair number of students do get into top colleges, so he wasn't nervous about the Ivies. He had worked towards Yale and other Ivies, but he hadn't counted on it. (He said other kids who were sure they'd get Yale offers, didn't.) The student was very upbeat. He liked Yale a lot.

Is the work manageable? Yes, they both said, if you weren't lazy. Neither seemed stressed out, but nor did they seem worried about impressing anyone with perfect grades.

Now is that a good representative poll? Not at all. But I think those two students were telling us the truth.

Ivy League Complaints and Stories

Regarding complaints, I've read about how a lot of classes are taught by grad students, not full professors. But then, have you heard the observation that English 210 and Chemistry 210 cover a similar level of material in every college across America? Thus, if a grad student teacher covers it well, what's so great if a full professor covers sophomore-level stuff? Either teacher should expect more of students at a selective college, as the idea is for higher rigor. But neither the grad student teacher nor the full professor can throw the most advanced material into a Chem 210 class anyway.

Another complaint is that at elite colleges, some students are there just to get to a corporate position, doing just enough work to get by, methodically calculating not a trace of effort too much or too little.

Intellectual debate into somewhat-related tangents? Discovery? Risk taking? Forget that. Some students are there for the big-bucks job, period. They cover what's on the syllabus, nothing more, nothing less.

Some students self-impose a lot of pressure for As and other accomplishments to where they feel stressed all the time, neglecting their health. That's not necessary, but it happens.

One story goes that a student from an elite college studied every night and most weekends, got the good grades and then got a good job offer at a top corporation. For four years, he didn't have much fun. He didn't even date anyone. He studied.

Another new hire at the same pay and position was a state college graduate. This other student had taken time for his personal life. He dated regularly, for example. He took plenty of weekends off.

The elite college graduate wondered if he had sacrificed too much personal time of those youthful years. Will the extra knowledge help him advance? In the future, will he insist on more personal time away from work, or keep working late?

How much does one succumb to a workaholic ethic at any college? You'll need to make similar decisions for your college choices and life.

The Mental Fortitude to Not Be Perfect

Students will have to honestly examine their mental attitudes about perceptions of failure and success.

I suggest you develop the fortitude to mentally survive going to college and getting a C, a D, or worse, if we may entertain such bad scenarios, even withdrawing from a class before failing it.

It can happen and the world, and your prospects in it, won't end when it does.

Ever hear the story about the student calling home to announce that the car was totaled, the bank reported a large shortfall and might call the police, and the student had married a freshman in Las Vegas last weekend? After the parent took a deep breath, the student said:

"No, not really, but I had to drop calculus. I'll have to retake it."

Have Confidence in Yourself, Whatever Your Personality Type

Inner fortitude and confidence are important anywhere, and by confidence, I don't mean an outgoing personality. I mean the quiet grit to get the work done when no one is patting you on the back; the grit to continue after you make mistakes; and the grit to ignore the jerks who treat you as if you don't belong.

If you are from a foster family, from the working class, from the poor side of town, yet you know you are smart and diligent, then you can end up in a selective college, or in an honors program at your state university. Realize that you deserve to have that inner confidence to build up your high school record and try for several options.

Apply. Try. If you get in, you can make it.

What if I Get In? Then What?

Suppose you get into your state university honors program or a private selective college?

If you don't know all that the highly-tutored rich kids know, so what? You'll pick things up as you go along. To start, just pass the classes.

So what, if another student started trigonometry in 9th grade and another kid has been reading Plato since 7th grade? Big deal. That's their problem. They, not you, will have to turn that into something useful. What else can they do or cannot do?

- Can they get along with people?
- Can they supervise people?
- Can they be creative and collaborative?
- Can they sell a product, present an idea or persuade someone?

Or just recite trig or Plato until everyone is sick of them?

196

Whatever someone else is doing, it doesn't mean that you can't get something done, in your way, in a field you like. If you have the quiet confidence to talk to professors, to other students, and to collaborate, you will be fine.

Are you more reserved? Fine. You can succeed with a quiet personality. Is stock investor Warren Buffett successful in his chosen field? Sure, because he's one of the richest individuals in human history. He's also not a whirling dynamo when he speaks or gives an interview. Yet, he is very charismatic in his down-to-earth sincerity. He may speak quietly, but when he does, everyone listens very closely.

Wherever You Go, Ignore the Jerks

If some people are arrogant jerks at a fancy college, then you should ignore them and find the students who are not.

Arrogant jerks in college will get what's coming to them in the work world, in the business world and in personal life soon enough, which is usually to be bypassed.

And when money comes up and you don't have much money, either quietly decline to do something, or be unapologetically forthright about it and say, "I can't do it. I don't have the money."

The Choices Among Different Colleges

Students and parents should give these ups and downs in different college settings serious consideration. There is a lot more to know about the advantages and disadvantages of selective colleges, regular colleges, small colleges, large colleges, narrow specialized majors and broad liberal arts majors. Read articles, books and blogs. To be better-informed, read the three guide books from Ch. 8 (listed again) and two more books:

The Other College Guide: A Road Map to the Right School for You, By Jane Sweetland, Paul Glastris and the Staff of the Washington Monthly, 2015, The New Press, New York.

Ms. Sweetland, Mr. Glastris and the Washington Monthly staff cover every subject with tons of information, including "Best- Bang-for-the-

Buck" data about hundreds of colleges. Detailed profiles of 50 great colleges are included. It shows you how to sort college databases to find good college fits for you.

Where You Go Is Not Who You'll Be: An Antidote to the College Admissions Mania, By Frank Bruni, 2016, Grand Central Publishing, New York.

Mr. Bruni warns families about the overly inflated perceptions of the worth of elite colleges, and backs it up with facts and true stories about great lives and success achieved without such colleges. See the minuses of elite colleges that others skip over, such as entitled students stuck in pre-set career paths who settle for play-it-safe mindsets, who get by, once they get in.

Colleges That Change Lives: 40 Schools That Will Change the Way You Think About Colleges by Loren Pope, 2012, Penguin Group, New York.

Mr. Pope's book, revised by Hilary Masell Oswald, gets beyond the hype and confronts college myths. The book details colleges that may or may not be highly ranked, but where scholars thrive. Most aren't excessively hard to get into, but some aren't cheap either. Do you know about Birmingham-Southern College, Hendrix College, Knox College or Willamette University? You ought to.

The Graduate Survival Guide: 5 Mistakes You Can't Afford to Make In College, by Anthony ONeal with Rachel Cruze, 2017, Ramsey Press, The Lampo Group, LLC, Brentwood, Tennessee.

Mr. ONeal and Ms. Cruze write about finances, a subject many of us avoid, but shouldn't. Good financial decisions lead to happier lives for years to come. Don't know much? Not sure? Think you know it all? This readable, short book fits smart finances into your college choices, and everywhere else, with life-changing potential.

Cool Colleges for the Hyper-Intelligent, Self-Directed, Late Blooming and Just Plain Different, by Donald Asher, 2007, Ten Speed Press, Berkeley, California.

Mr. Asher highlights distinctive colleges for all fields and types of students, along with detailed, insightful discussions about selecting a college. The last edition was 2007, but this remains a valuable book.

Chapter 20

Selective Admissions:
The Hows & Whys

The Admissions Pool for One College
The National Admissions Pool
Application Overlap

Before you can decide later whether to go to a selective college, you first have to be in the running to get in, so let's move on to that subject.

The basics of selective admissions are in this book. Even this basic discussion is detailed and if you are serious, there is much more to read about the nuts and bolts.

I recommend the books listed next. You may find these books in libraries. These books contain important facts, down to some of the smallest details about selective college admissions.

A is For Admission: The Insider's Guide to Getting Into The Ivy League and Other Top Colleges, by Michele A. Hernandez, 2009, Grand Central Publishing, New York.

> Ms. Hernandez was an Ivy League college admissions official. She explains how things work and provides her own advice to students.

What College's Don't Tell You (and Other Parents Don't Want You to Know): 272 Secrets for Getting Your Kid into the *Top Schools,* by Elizabeth Wissner-Gross, 2007, Plume, New York.

> Ms. Wissner-Gross has left no stone unturned. She's examined every possible angle. She's seen it all. I think she's thought of nearly everything students and parents can do to try for a better college, and she seems to know everything that won't work.

The Gatekeepers: Inside the Admissions Process of a Premier College, by Jacques Steinberg, 2003, Penguin Books, New York.

> Mr. Steinberg had full year's access to the admissions process of an elite college, a rare thing. From staff travels to the personal lives of applicants, the good and the bad, down to the final cut, it's all on the record. For admissions, it's a page-turner to see who gets in, and where, and who doesn't and why.

The Price of Admission: How America's Ruling Class Buys Its Way into Elite College – and Who Gets Left Outside the Gates, by Daniel Golden, 2007, Crown Publishing Group, New York.

> Mr. Golden isn't a fan of admissions preferences for wealthy donors and influential families. As Golden takes aim at such preferences, the reader learns a lot about admissions. Good at polo? (Not water polo.) That will help at one selective college.

What it Really Takes to Get Into the Ivy League & Other Highly Selective Colleges, by Chuck Hughes, 2003, McGraw – Hill, New York.

> Mr. Hughes worked inside Harvard admissions and knows what he's talking about. If you have made up your mind to try for the very selective colleges, read this book. Though the book is several years old, I read it for the first time in 2017 and found it more valuable than many recent writings. It's thorough, helpful and, at times, blunt.

Selective University Standards: See Where You Fit In

This discussion involves three main categories:

1. academic requirements
2. other admissions fits
3. your finances and the college's finances

Selective Means from 10% to 35% Acceptance Rates

It is fair to say that colleges with a 50% admittance rate are also selective, because half of applicants cannot get in. Only a few colleges are as low as 5%, 6% or 7%.

For general purposes, let's use the range of 10% to 35%.

Colleges at 35% and under are often in the private category. Some public, tax-payer-funded state colleges are hard to get into as well, with acceptance rates from 18% to 35%. An acceptance rate from 10% to 35% means a high majority of applicants are not accepted.

Basically, 10 to 35 out of 100 applicants get accepted.

Conversely, from 90% to 65% of people who apply are rejected. That's a lot.

Most certainly, anyone with a chance should proceed, but should do so with their eyes wide open.

The Appendix (p. 315) has detailed admissions data.

Here's the Right Attitude to Have

Sure, if you try, you can be turned down and disappointed. Let's just get that out of the way up front. Students, make peace with yourselves that you will be disappointed if you are turned down and that it might happen.

Parents, accept the fact right now that your children could be turned down by some of the top colleges.

Visualize that moment when the college says no.

After completing this mental experiment, then your proper attitude is that you accept that you may not make it in and if you do not, it will still be great wherever you end up, but that it was worth the try.

A proper perspective may enhance the applications and the interaction with admissions staff as the student won't come across as pestering and desperate and the parents won't be overly pushy.

Still, Here Are the Reasons to Hope and Go Forward

Still, if students and parents or guardians are serious, there are reasons to hope.

Here's one: When you apply to just one selective college, 99% of the rest of America is *not* applying to that one college.

Who Applies
To Just ONE Selective College,
Out of the Whole United States?

Answer: 99% <u>Do Not</u> Apply
To That ONE College

Total U.S. Freshmen Entering Four-Year Colleges in One Year	2,000,000[29]
Total Applicants to One Typical Elite College	20,000
Percent of Total U.S. Freshmen Who Do Not Apply to One Typical Elite College	99%

(20,000 ÷ 2,000,000 = .01 which is 1%)

An Example of Percentages:

10% = 10 people out of 100
35% = 35 people out of 100

<u>For A Winning Mega-Lottery Ticket,</u>

If   35   Winning Tickets Were Absolutely
            Guaranteed To Be Given Away
            In a Room Of
     100   People,

Would You Try To Be In The Room?

If   10   Winning Tickets Were Absolutely
            Guaranteed To Be Given Away
            In a Room Of
     100   People,

Would You Try To Be In the Room?

Are 10% to 35% Odds Worth Being in the Room?
Those are Selective College Acceptance Rates.
Sending in a Good Application Puts You in the Room.

APPLICATIONS to ONE COLLEGE

From all 2,000,000 freshmen, it is encouraging to see that the number of applicants drops down dramatically for one college. It's still tough, but, really, there is ray of hope, as 98% to 99% of U.S. students entering full-time for bachelor's degrees don't apply to each college below.

Approximate 2016 total applicants (per College Navigator, Undergraduate, Fall 2016):

39,000 applicants - Harvard - So, 39,000 kids (2% of the U.S. freshmen) had the nerve to apply for Harvard? Why not? It's Harvard, after all.

32,000 applicants – Vanderbilt – A private selective college in Nashville, Tennessee.

20,000 applicants – Dartmouth – The smallest Ivy League college, in Hanover, New Hampshire.

19,000 applicants – Notre Dame – A selective private college in South Bend, Indiana.

14,000 applicants - College of William and Mary - A public college with great credentials and history (President George Washington went there.)

7,000 applicants - Bowdoin College – A premier small private college, with still fewer applicants.

6,400 applicants - Occidental College - A private college with one U.S. President as an alum.

6,000 applicants – Macalester – A small private college in St. Paul, Minnesota.

3,700 applicants - Whitman College - A small private college in the beautiful countryside of Washington State.

You should consider applying to any college you care about for which you are generally in the running, such as if your scores and grades are in the bottom quartile or higher.

Each college has a different pool of applicants, though there is overlap, as many students apply to multiple colleges. If you make a serious effort at several of them, chances for success may increase.

U.S. Totals for a National Selective College Pool

Small and large colleges are grouped together (*Public colleges in italics & underlined*)

50 Top Selective Colleges/Universities (in order of % of accepted students who enrolled)

Stanford	82%	Cornell	52%	Williams	45%	Washington & Lee	39%
Harvard	79%	Barnard	51%	*U.C.-Berkeley*	44%	Johns Hopkins	38%
M.I.T.	73%	Dartmouth	51%	Middlebury	43%	*Virginia*	38%
Yale	69%	Bowdoin	50%	Wellesley	43%	*Georgia Tech*	37%
Penn	68%	Duke	50%	Cal. Tech.	42%	*UCLA*	37%
Princeton	68%	*Florida*	49%	Colorado Coll.	42%	Washington Univ.	37%
U. Chicago	64%	Georgetown	47%	*Michigan*	42%	Lehigh	36%
Columbia	62%	Pitzer	47%	Swarthmore	42%	Wesleyan Univ.	36%
Brown	56%	Tufts	46%	Amherst	41%	Hamilton	35%
Notre Dame	56%	Vanderbilt	46%	Bates	40%	Rice	35%
Claremont McKenna	54%	Davidson	45%	Harvey Mudd	40%	Carnegie Mellon	34%
Pomona	54%	*North Carolina*	45%	Haverford	40%		
Northwestern	53%	*Texas*	45%	Carleton	39%		

Totals for 50 above 1,179,602 applications

199,707 acceptance letters sent (17% admissions rate)

108,458 acceptance letters tossed, 91,249 enrolled (46% of the accepted)

+ 50 More Top Selective Colleges/Universities (listed alphabetically)

50 colleges with 17% to 51% acceptance rates (35% average acceptance rate) and admissions yield rates are 34% or less (% of accepted students who enroll)

Babson	Emory	Occidental	Tulsa
Baruch-CUNY	Franklin & Marshall	Pepperdine	*U.C.-San Diego*
Baylor	George Washington	Reed	*U.C.-Santa Barbara*
Binghamton-SUNY	Grinnell	Rensselaer Poly.	*U.C.-Davis*
Boston College	Kenyon	Richmond	*U.C.-Irvine*
Boston Univ.	Lafayette	Rochester	Union College
Brandeis	Macalester	Scripps	Vassar
Bucknell	*Maryland*	Skidmore	Villanova
Case Western Reserve	Univ. of Miami	Southern Methodist	Wake Forest
Clemson	*Minnesota*	Southern Cal.	*William & Mary*
Colby	New York Univ.	Stevens Inst.	Worcester Polytechnic
Colgate	Northeastern	Trinity	
Colorado School of Mines	Oberlin	Tulane	

Totals for 100 above 2,353,378 applications

614,205 acceptance letters sent (26% admissions rate)

426,232 acceptance letters tossed, 187,971 enrolled (31% of the accepted)

+20 More Top Public State Universities (Average ACT mid-range is 25-30)

Colorado	*Illinois*	*Penn State*	*Stony Brook-SUNY*
Connecticut	*Indiana Univ.*	*Pittsburgh*	*Texas A & M*
Delaware	*Massachusetts*	*Purdue*	*U.C-Santa Cruz*
Florida State	*North Carolina State*	*Rutgers*	*Washington*
Georgia	*Ohio State*	*South Carolina*	*Wisconsin*

Totals for All 120 3,072,645 applications

1,030,158 acceptance letters sent (34% admissions rate)

721,737 acceptance letters tossed, 308,419 enrolled (30% of the accepted)

At the other 2,158 four-year U.S. colleges, about 1,700,000 other freshmen enrolled[30]

Discourse and tables for the statistics above are in the appendix (p. 315).

National Totals: 120 Top Colleges
See page 204 for statistics.

3,000,000 applications are received

500,000 incoming freshmen are potential candidates

1,000,000 acceptance letters are sent by these 120 colleges

700,000 acceptance letters to these 120 colleges are tossed **out, 70% of all sent**

300,000 freshmen enroll at 120 top colleges, private and public, small and large

Are **1,000,000** openings out there at 120 colleges? No. Only **300,000** students enrolled.

Why were **1,000,000** acceptance letters sent out?

Yes, a distinct, single letter of acceptance from the 120 colleges listed on page 204 was sent out in 2016 exactly 1,030,158 times. But a whole lot of students got multiple letters. About 700,000 acceptance letters are turned down each year to these colleges. "Yes letters tossed", is my statistical term. That's a whole lot of yes letters being tossed. Which tells us that a whole lot of overlap is occurring.

Many students each send 5 to 10 applications. That's how the application total gets jacked up to almost 3 million. Then some of those same students each get 3 to 5 or more acceptance letters, which is why the acceptance letters total gets jacked up to one million. When one student gets 6 acceptance letters, he or she is taking up 5 times his or her actual availability. But when he or she turns down 5 colleges, it opens spots for others. It shows that good students have something to aim for.

What Should You Do?

Compile a great application and apply to multiple colleges. Then you might get one of those 1 million acceptance letters from one of those 120 top colleges, or others like them.

2,000,000 (2 million) Total U.S. Freshmen at 4-year Colleges

About two million U.S. students start college full time at four-year colleges, which is one government count in a recent year.[31]

The 75th percentile and above is about 500,000 students who meet a general minimum, per test scores. In addition, the top colleges accept some applicants from the 65th percentile to the 79th percentile, as shown below. * Not all students have the right combination of scores, GPA, and activities to apply, and they don't. Many great students have a local or other college in mind and don't apply elsewhere. So, a group of 500,000 kids is a ballpark estimate, but we can't tell, with all the duplicate applications.

An Example of a National Selective College Pool

The 120 colleges on page 204 provide ballpark statistical estimates for a national selective college admissions pool.

For 50 top colleges, I selected colleges (small, medium and large) with low admissions rates and the highest yield rates, which means the fewest people turn them down, for a smaller, elite national admissions pool.

For 100 top colleges, I added 50 more colleges with admissions acceptance rates of 49% or less in a mixture in sizes with high test scores. Seventeen public colleges are in the top 100.

For 120 top colleges, I added 20 more top public colleges for an expanded pool for high achievers. These colleges have a combined acceptance rate of 58%, which isn't highly exclusive, yet their test scores are very high, mid-ranges are around 80th percentile to 96th and the top quartiles at 97th percentiles and up, so you'll find serious students and honors program, along with lower in-state rates. (Some colleges aren't in the 120 total, yet have high enrollment rates due to special appeal to applicants and/or are highly selective, such as military academies, arts academies, and religious colleges. These are excellent colleges worthy of attention, but they don't fit this general national pool.)

---

*Selective Colleges Do Take Some Lower Scores and GPAs (p. 325.)

For 79th percentile SAT test 599 reading scores:

- Ivy League colleges had from 3% to 8% of freshmen with a 599, about 30 to 55 students per college. Cornell had 7.7% for about 175 freshmen with 599.
- M.I.T. had 4.5% of freshmen with a 599, which is about 40 students.
- UC Berkeley had 14% of freshmen with a 599 which is about 682 students.
- New York University had 15% of freshmen with a 599, which is 606 students.
- Georgetown had 9% of freshmen with a 599, which is 114 students.

For Middle-Class on up to Wealthy Families

Now, if your family is wealthy or solid middle-class and you are in a strong school district or in a private high school, then those are good circumstances. But bear with me, as I address readers who are from working-class and lower-income households and schools, until the bottom of this page.

I'm From a Regular High School, From the Poor Side of Town, So There's No Room at the Best Colleges for Me.
That's the Real Story, Right?
No. That is Wrong. Wrong. Wrong.   Really Wrong.
There is Room for You

The perception of a student from the poor side of town, from a rough neighborhood in the city, from a small town out in the sticks, is that the spots in the great colleges are all spoken for. "Students from *here* don't go *there*."

A student in these situations may not see many others, or any others, trying for the Fanciest Universities In The World, so why should he or she? One of those colleges? Yeah, right. The chances are slim to none. Why do all that extra work? It's a pipe dream, a long shot, a waste of time. That is how it might feel.

What if I could prove to you that this perception is wrong? Give me your careful attention for just the next few pages of reading.

Rich Kids Aren't More Qualified, They Just Apply, While Working-Class Kids Haven't Yet

For the top 100 colleges, working-class kids can get the same scores and grades as wealthy kids are getting. It won't be easy, but you can do it. But when the wealthy kids usually apply and working-class kids usually don't, it's one of the reasons more of the wealthy students end up going to the top 100. For working-class students, get going and you can get those good grades and good test scores. For wealthier students, you too will need good academics, so get to it as well.

Too many students conclude that is not worth it to try because of the premise that nothing is open for them. Both the conclusion and the premise are wrong, based on general assumptions from incomplete information. Here is the complete information: Due to massive overlap in the process, a lot fewer students are applying than it looks on the surface, which means that you can compete for these spots. If you understand that right now then, you can skip the statistical details, and jump ahead to the sections on how to get ready. If you need the proof, it is in the next pages.

Overlapping, Multiple Applications and Acceptance Letters

For 300 students,
100 students with 4 applications each =   400 applications, and
100 students with 6 applications each =   600 applications, and
100 students with 10 applications each = 1,000 applications,
thus,   300 students   generate   2,000 applications.

Good grief, 2,000 applications from only 300 students? So, how many from 300,000 students? At those rates, about 2,000,000. That many are sent to the top 100 colleges (2,353,378). Overlapping applications affect the process. These are inflated numbers, sort of, due to the overlap, but with real documents flowing back and forth between colleges and applicants about real open spots. How does it shake out?

Let's look at the 50 colleges listed first, which are among the hardest to get into. They report an exact total of 1,179,602 applications. There are not 1 million students applying to these 50 colleges, but 1 million applications from perhaps 300,000 students, as an estimate, although there is currently no way to tell that I have found.

Most People Turn the Best Colleges Down. Is This True?

Next look at this fact: The top 50 colleges *get turned down most of the time*. At first, it doesn't sound logical. Yet only 18 of 50 colleges have an enrollment rate of 50% or higher. (Remember, this list of 50 excludes special colleges like West Point.) Thus, 32 of the 50 are told no by more than half of accepted applicants. That is, by the standard definition,
208

getting turned down most of the time. A lot of the time 55%, 60% or 65% of accepted applicants tell a top 50 college no. This includes colleges with acceptance rates of only 8%, 11% or 14%, for example, with an average acceptance rate of 21%, some of the hardest colleges to get into. Sounds nuts, but it is true (p. 210 and p. 315).

At 50 Top Colleges, 1 of 2 yes letters are tossed.
At 100 Top Colleges, 3 of 4 yes letters are tossed!

Thus, 200,000 acceptance letters are sent by the 50 most "to die for" colleges, but 54%, of acceptance letters are tossed out, more than 1 out of 2. For 100 top colleges, 7 out of 10 yes letters are tossed!

Why are so many acceptance letters getting tossed out? Because that one student tosses 5 or 6 to select 1 yes letter, many likely from among colleges the group of the 50. This shows a huge amount of overlap.

What's Comes Out of The Overlap? Here's Some Good News

Knowing about overlap, is this good news? Yes, it is. I don't mean that it's good news that everyone involved will have to keep up this pace. I agree that applications are already enough of a pain in the neck. The good news is that the odds are better for applicants than it seems at first.

Here's why. Without a coordinated tally of individual applicants among a group of colleges (which I couldn't find), one can't calculate a net enrollment rate for a group of applicants to a group of colleges. Yes, each college reports an admissions and enrollment rate, but no *group* of undergraduate colleges does while at the same time accounting for duplicate applications within the group.

For a pool of applicants to a pool of colleges, a higher percentage of applicants is likely enrolled somewhere within the pool, as overlap shakes out, than is shown by the regular low acceptance rate of the single applicant to the single college.

Though this sounds like statistical hair-splitting, it is important for students, parents and counselors to know that if one qualified student sends extra applications within a group, his or her odds of a yes letter somewhere in the group are better than the odds to just to each college.

Table C, 50 Selective Colleges 2016 - In order of Yield Rate (% of accepted students who enrolled) *Public colleges are in italics.*	Yes Letters Tossed	Yield Rate	College	Yes Letters Tossed	Yield Rate
Stanford University (CA)	396	82%	*Georgia Inst. of Technology.*	5,000	37%
Harvard College (MA)	410	79%	*University of California-LA*	11,013	37%
Massachusetts Inst. of Tech.	411	73%	Washington U.-St. Louis (MO)	3,127	37%
Yale University (CT)	585	69%	Lehigh University (PA)	2,230	36%
Princeton University (NJ)	656	68%	Wesleyan University (CT)	1,374	36%
University of Pennsylvania	1,121	68%	Hamilton College (NY)	884	35%
University of Chicago (IL)	907	64%	Rice University (TX)	1,778	35%
Columbia University in NY	984	62%	Carnegie Mellon Univ. (PA)	3,077	34%
Brown University (RI)	1,283	56%			
University of Notre Dame (IN)	1,631	56%	**Total Number of Acceptance Letters Turned Down to all 50 Colleges**	**108,458**	**46%**
Claremont McKenna (CA)	263	54%			
Pomona College (CA)	335	54%			
Northwestern University (IL)	1,815	53%			
Cornell University (NY)	3,022	52%	This is out of 199,707 total acceptance letters sent.		
Barnard College (NY)	589	51 %			
Dartmouth College (NH)	1,114	51 %			
Bowdoin College	510	50%	About 1 out of 2 acceptance letters are turned down in total for this group of 50 colleges.		
Duke University (NC)	1,742	50%			
University of Florida	7,066	49%			
Georgetown University (DC)	1,802	47%			
Pitzer College (CA)	307	47%	Why are half of the acceptance letters from this group of colleges turned down?		
Tufts University (MA)	1,529	46%			
Vanderbilt University (TN)	1,927	46%			
Davidson College (NC)	618	45%			
University of North Carolina	5,181	45%	Because many of the people were accepted to several colleges in this group and except for the one college they want to move up to, they turn down the rest of the colleges in the group.		
University of Texas–Austin	10,452	45%			
Williams College (MA)	692	45%			
Univ. of California-Berkeley	7,860	44%			
Middlebury College (VT)	804	43%			
Wellesley College (MA)	802	43%			
Calif. Inst. of Technology	318	42%			
Colorado College	733	42%			
Swarthmore College (PA)	582	42%	This shows the application overlap.		
Univ. of Michigan-Ann Arbor	9,336	42%			
Amherst College (MA)	694	41 %	See full admissions and enrollment statistics on pages 315 to 332. Source: Admissions, Fall, 2016, (as of 9-2017) College Navigator, U.S. Dept. of Education; calculated from number of applications, acceptance rates and enrollment.		
Bates College (ME)	739	40%			
Harvey Mudd College (CA)	326	40%			
Haverford College (PA)	512	40%			
Carleton College (MN)	910	39%			
Washington & Lee Univ. (VA)	747	39%			
Johns Hopkins University (MD)	2,245	38%			
University of Virginia	6,022	38%			

Here's an important clue with statistical evidence to back up that conclusion. The same overlap situation occurs with medical schools and they do track the overlap. In an internet search for real medical school acceptance rates one will find an enrollment (matriculation) rate of about 40% for all applicants after the overlapping applications shake out, not the very low 2%, 5% or 10% admissions rate at many individual schools. It's really 40%. That's a huge jump. Again, this distinction is a bit confusing, but it's important. Going from thinking that only 5% to 10% of people get in, to knowing that 40% do in fact get in, is important. The ratios are better than advertised, so to speak, for qualified applicants who send out multiple applications.[32]

<u>Within 50 Top Colleges: The Overlap Settles Out</u>

Let's start with one applicant who applied to 10 colleges.
- She got 5 acceptance letters and 5 rejections.
- Then, she turned down 4 colleges and went to 1.
- Who gets those other 4 coveted spots in the top 50?
- Four others, each with a yes letter in hand.
- Then each of those 4 people says yes to 1 and turns down 4 other colleges in the top 50 (4 x 4 = 16).
- The next 16 spots go to someone with a yes letter in hand.
- Thus, from 5 applicants deciding, 20 other spots are affected (4 + 16 = 20). And so on, and so on, through 199,707 yes letters, down to 91,249 who will enroll. (That's 108,458 letters tossed.)

The overlap settles out to the wait lists.

Now let's look at the same situation from the college's viewpoint, as it decides to send out extra acceptance letters.

Colleges Send Out Extra Acceptance Letters

Most colleges get told no by most people. Admissions staff tracks it. It's the yield rate. Because the college is quite often turned down, the admissions office sends more yes letters. It sends extra letters to top-quartile applicants, because some of them will turn the college down, heading elsewhere. Then the college sends extra letters to middle-quartile applicants. Yet those middle students are sending out 12

211

applications, and getting 6 yes letters, so those students must turn down a bunch of yes letters too. Thus, the admissions office sends more letters to the bottom-quartile applicants. Remember, the bottom quartile is not a theoretical admissions equation. Not at all; those bottom-quartile applicants are now freshmen at that college. But if you don't have an application in that college's bag, the staff can't find your nice high-, middle- or lower-quartile application and send you one of the yes letters.

Colleges Expand the Number of Offers

Look at the extra letters yes sent and tossed (p. 210). It's hundreds at some and into the thousands at others, all at prestigious universities.

If you could match up for a selective college, try for one of those letters. Don't sit this out. So what if you're the first in the family to go to college? Get busy now so you can send a bunch of applications later.

A lot of applicants are doing so and a whole lot of them get told no, but they're not shy about trying. Your grades and scores might match up, but if you don't get an application in the bag, you can't get the yes letter. Get in on this. Seriously. What have you got to lose but some goofing off time? Getting into a selective college happens only among those who try. And if you are turned down, it's still better to get some no letters than wonder what might have happened. Now, for you, the future applicant, since we can't know yet, one yes letter could be the result. The best choice is to try. It's going around in a circle logically, certainly, and it requires diligent work, but that's my advice to you.

To Boost Your Odds, Add More Applications

In summary, on this specific point, the situation looks as if there is a much smaller number of competitors than it seems at first. That is, for example, among the whole group of 100 colleges. If you apply to just one college, your odds are exactly what it shows for that one college. To boost your odds, you must apply to more of them with a good application, so you are joining into the overlap party.

Are all 500,000 potentially qualified students in the U.S. jumping in? Probably not. Among the potential applicants, here's why many are *not* in the competition for all those yes letters to the top colleges:

⇒ Many students want to stay close to home, so they apply only to a top college if it is in their area, maybe one or two. The rest of their applications go to other local colleges.

⇒ Many students are uncomfortable with the selective colleges, nervous about the harder work, and the perception of a more upper-class, snooty atmosphere. So, they don't apply.

⇒ Many students do make a serious effort, but to only three or four, leaving 46 or 47 others in the top 50 off their lists.

⇒ Some in the 80th to 90th test-score percentiles don't think they have much of chance, so they plan for the state college. They might apply to two or three of the top 50 colleges on a "Why not? Who knows" basis, but not with a very serious application.

How Serious Are the Other Applicants?

For one example, let's use a college application total of 30,000, which is pretty large, but still common. Let's use a 16.6% acceptance rate to get to 5,000 people accepted. Do you, out of 30,000 applying, have to beat out 25,000 others to get your one spot among the 5,000 accepted? Yes, you do.

Yet, of those 25,000 you must pass up to be one of the 5,000, how many of those 25,000 have sent in a very strong application to that one school? The problem is that you don't know.

At one college, for example, if you have a strong, serious application, you may bypass two thirds, leaving 10,000 left. Sure, you still have very stiff competition, but you may still be in the running. Now you're trying to be in the 5,000, out of 10,000. That's 50%, a one out of two ratio, not that dreaded 16% admissions rate.

Is A One Out of Two Chance Worth Trying For?

You could be in the one-out-of-two basket, but not even realize it. With a small college, the ratios are similar, but the overall numbers are much lower, so maybe something unique you do will stand out more readily. Is a one-out-of-two chance worth getting in gear for? A 50% acceptance rate? Sure, it is.

If you could know that up front, you might get going sooner, with more seriousness. To be honest, the big problem is that you just can't tell up front, so don't give up too soon. That is why I am going on and on about this, trying to get students, parents and counselors to look at the scenarios with more understanding of the factors involved. It might not be a lack of ability, but a lack of foresight and diligence which prevents the student from getting into that basket.

Get advice. Ask at an admissions office, or speak with a friendly teacher or counselor. If your qualifications are lacking right now, you should find that out so you may either improve them or plan on a regular college. The point here is not to pump you up to unreasonable expectations or promote wasted effort under wishful thinking, which is irresponsible.

The point here is to get realistic and if it is realistic, to not give up too soon. If you do have a chance, avoid taking the advice of someone who will not consider your potential to improve or who may not know all the facts as you know them. Especially in a working-class environment, counselors, teachers, friends and family members may not be shooting for the stars on your behalf, at least not at first, but also maybe not later either.

Remember that the parent in our story was told flat-out by the first counselor to only plan for the community college, period. That really happened. Then the kid ended up with an Ivy League scholarship because the student and parents went beyond that person's advice. That really happened too.

With good qualifications, you and the other applicants are all deserving, so you can hold your head just as high as the next person. In the end, the admissions staff must select someone. At that point, it could be you, or not. You just don't know. Unless you try.

Increase Your Odds

Thus, my best advice to serious students who can meet the minimum requirements for the top 50 to the top 100, is to apply to a good mix of colleges. They're all very good after all, so give it a serious effort. But don't just try for two tough ones and then your state college, for three total. That's won't increase your odds a lot. How about five or more harder ones, five mid-range ones and a few for which you are well qualified, and a state college? Or more? That'll boost your odds.

What About Application Fees?

Will the fees cost more? Yes. First, check your status for fee waivers (pp. 182-185). If family income is above that status, then plan for it. This isn't coming out of the blue, hopefully. Skimp on something else. It is responsible to ask that a family spend $500, one time, for a qualified student, to boost the chances for a great college.

If you have paid for every application you possibly can, but you really should apply to more colleges, do not be shy and use the hardship waiver form (pp. 184-185). I am not condoning the sending of ten flaky applications for free which will be marked "No" right away. But the colleges all say they don't want serious students not to apply due to the fee.

Let's Increase the Applications? What Else is the Alternative?

Does this advice increase the number of applications, if a lot of readers heed it? Yes, but after looking into the situation very carefully, if I had to testify under oath as to the truth and nothing but the truth, to you students and parents, that is the advice I would give.

Upper-class and middle-class kids send in multiple applications, so if working-class and lower-income kids do the same, well, tough. The kids did not create this system. If more lower-income kids, more foster-care kids, and more working-class kids work hard to get ready for the top colleges, what is the alternative? Tell those kids that they are gumming up the works and not to apply? Absolutely not.

I say to smart, hard-working students who are the first in their families to attend college, to shoot for top colleges. If they beat out some wealthy kids, that's fair, open-market capitalist competition.

The U.S. is will soon have 40% more people than it had in 1970, about 122 million more people. Yes, in some ways, the enrollment slots for top colleges have grown in number as the NYUs, USCs and top public colleges accept more kids, but a lot of the elite colleges haven't budged much since 1970. More room could be made for a larger number of deserving kids. Excellent professors are available. The colleges' reputations and endowments wouldn't be too worse for wear. In the meantime, should deserving students hold back? No. Not in the least.

State Colleges Have Programs for Top Students

Students, apply as well to your better state colleges and universities, which are outstanding institutions that students worldwide would love to get into. Honors colleges at state universities have students go to the top corporations, graduate schools, law schools and medical schools.

www.PublicUniversityHonors.com has information.

Want to be a Rhodes Scholar? (Only 32 U.S. students are selected.)

One student, Robert Fisher, excelled in the honors program at the University of Tennessee at Chattanooga. Yes, he won a Rhodes Scholarship to Oxford.[33] That's only one example, among many. From Montana State to Florida State, students have been selected as Rhodes Scholars. Public college students also become Churchill scholars, Marshall scholars, and rack up the Fulbrights too.

Don't just look at a college's list of degrees, but search out honors programs, research projects, special offices, special symposiums and laboratories. State universities have a lot going on. You can get involved.

State colleges also send extra admissions letters, because so many people will still turn them down. It can be from 5,000 to 10,000 extra acceptance letters sent out, that are tossed out by students. Within your own state, that may give you get a better chance at a fine college, and the honors college, with lower-cost in-state rates.

We have such a wide range of options in the U.S. that most colleges are turned down by a majority of accepted applicants.

Take advantage of that situation as best you can.

Chapter 21

Selective Admissions: The Quartiles

Let's Better Understand the Selective Admissions Bucket
What About the Lower 25%? The Lower Quartile?

Can You Reach the Lower Quartile, or Better?

You Should Find Out

After offering a bit of encouragement, to be responsible, any college adviser must continue to point out to parents and students that it isn't easy to get into a selective college. Let's go into more detail about the selective admissions process.

With the following analysis, the use of only the test score range is for ease of the discussion. The scores are put into quartiles (i.e. one quarter, or 25%) of admissions.

For any college, check its scores. After taking some practice standardized tests, a student will have an idea of what range he or she might accomplish by senior year. Students with scores in the range of the lower quartile or higher, (along with good grades and activities) do have a legitimate hope for admission, as those 25% of students all got into the college's freshman class. The lower quartile, however, is the starting point, and your chances for admission will increase if you can move into the middle range or better.

Students should know the factors which can help their chances and hurt their chances. So, let's go into it starting with the charts on the next pages.

The Admissions Quartiles: What Is a Quartile?

Remember, All These Students Got In.

Mid-Range Quartiles   Colleges usually list the following range:

2nd Quartile &
3rd Quartile Combined - 25th Percentile to 75th Percentile

Top Quartile   Colleges do not list: (But you can estimate it.)
4th Quartile – 76% to 100% -
The range is all scores above the 75th percentile.

Lower Quartile   Colleges do not list: (But you can estimate it.)
1st Quartile - 1% to 24%

To estimate the lower quartile: The 25th percentile score is published. Scores just below that are at the top of the lower quartile. You can estimate that if your score is just below the 25th percentile score that you are in the lower quartile, and might be admitted, because *one quarter of enrolled freshmen got below that score. That is the lower quartile. They got in.* You might too, but the lower quartile might have a lot of special fits, so read about that starting on page 221. If your score is way below the 25% score, you cannot be sure, but you can compare your score to the lowest score range of actual enrolled students for any college. Each year this is listed in Section C9 of the Common Data Set (p. 83), but not with one specific lowest score. You can also see GPA ranges for all freshmen.

A 599 SAT reading score in the Ivy League?

It happens,
per Sect. C9 in the Common Data Sets.[34]

Yes, folks, the lowest to highest range of test scores and GPA for all freshmen enrolled at any college is there for all to see, in Sect. C9 in the Common Data Set. See page 83 for instructions.

Selective College Admissions Quartiles

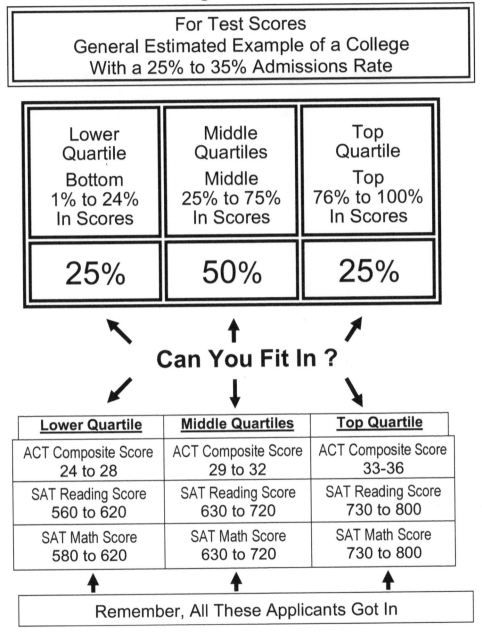

For Test Scores
General Estimated Example of a College
With a 25% to 35% Admissions Rate

Lower Quartile	Middle Quartiles	Top Quartile
Bottom 1% to 24% In Scores	Middle 25% to 75% In Scores	Top 76% to 100% In Scores
25%	50%	25%

Can You Fit In ?

Lower Quartile	Middle Quartiles	Top Quartile
ACT Composite Score 24 to 28	ACT Composite Score 29 to 32	ACT Composite Score 33-36
SAT Reading Score 560 to 620	SAT Reading Score 630 to 720	SAT Reading Score 730 to 800
SAT Math Score 580 to 620	SAT Math Score 630 to 720	SAT Math Score 730 to 800

Remember, All These Applicants Got In

Estimates are based on score reports from the public selective colleges Univ. of California - Berkeley, Georgia Tech, Univ. of Michigan - Ann Arbor, Univ. of Texas - Austin, Univ. of Virginia and the College of William and Mary, which are shown in the Appendix (pp. 330-332).[35]

To Find Mid-Range Admissions Quartiles:

Any of the five methods below can work.

☐ Use College Scorecard (www.CollegeScorecard.ed.gov)
Select a college, select test scores, which are mid-range

☐ Use College Navigator (www.nces.ed.gov/CollegeNavigator)
Select a college, select ADMISSIONS and scroll down
to TEST SCORES

☐ Use a web browser search with:
"College Name" (and) "Common Data Set" *
Find the quartiles in Section C9

☐ Go to the admissions section of a college website
Look for a Freshman Class Profile, test scores

☐ Use a guide to colleges book, or a college ranking website, or college search website
Look for college admissions data, student body profiles, test score data or enrollment data

To Estimate the Bottom Admissions Quartile:

See page 218.

* The Common Data Set (CDS) initiative is a collaborative effort among data providers in the higher education community and publishers as represented by the College Board, Peterson's, and U.S. News & World Report, per www.commondataset.org, Nov. 22, 2016.

Selective Admissions: What the Colleges Want: Admissions Fit Factors

From a College's Point of View: Admissions Fit Factors

Yes, there are students who attend top colleges without perfect test scores and with GPAs closer to 3.0 than 4.0. Part of the story includes college admissions fit factors. Admissions fit factors can work for or against any applicant in any academic quartile.

For the best shot at a selective college, a student should understand the mishmash of factors that make up admissions decisions. These factors help explain why some people are accepted, but others are not.

So, how did the successful applicants get in? They were good admissions fits for the college for one or more reasons, including:

① Academics
　② Special Accomplishments
　　③ Sports
　　　④ Legacies (or Parents Didn't Attend College)
　　　　⑤ Demographics
　　　　⑥ Majors
　　　　　⑦ Income
　　　　　⑧ Demonstrated Interest

Let's go over these eight factors. I aim to be responsible to readers by presenting factors to consider and offering my conclusions as to each factor's importance.

You may read more on the impacts of each of these factors, from admissions staff, education reporters, book authors, and admissions counselors in books, articles and blogs.

Search *college admissions* and other topics on the web and on a bookseller's website.

Admissions staff can provide direct advice if you visit or call colleges, or speak to staff at college events.

This Admissions Fit Benefits the College, *Not* the Student

The admissions fit factors are *not* for a student's benefit, but for a college's benefit.

These fits are not preferences of the student, but rather preferences of the college. This admissions fit is how the colleges select students into the desired makeup for their freshman classes.

This is not what you want. This admissions fit is what the college wants.

These factors can affect all applicants. Even applicants with very high test scores and GPAs (the academic factor), for example, are turned down by some colleges for applicants who have lower grades and scores, but also have other desired attributes.

What does that tell us? Factors other than GPA and scores count.

For applicants who are in the middle of the academic range of a college, additional factors might help them, because their academic indicators are lower than about half of those who will be admitted.

Applicants who rank in the lower 25 percent do meet the minimum requirements (which are still high, let's remember) and thus they should try to get in. The odds are longer, however, for them, because their academic indicators are lower than 75 percent of those who will be admitted. Other factors can help these applicants.

Let's look at how these factors mix together from a college's self-interest and point of view, rather than from that of the applicant.

For selective admissions, these fit factors, in some combination, affect 100% of the spots.

① Academics

The college wants academic achievers, who will contribute in class, in activities, on research and, later, in the world. In the short term, a freshman class with high test scores helps a college compete in rankings.

In the long term, graduates who achieve good works provide prestige and a network for future graduates.

Yes, academics are primary, the essential ingredient, as they show, that you can do the work in that college. Remember, however, the applicants with perfect scores who were told no? They had good academics and not much else.

The college may admit an applicant with somewhat lower academics (which won't tank the college's test score average), because that applicant also adds something else that the college wants.

For the student who has great academics, extra factors help cinch the deal.

Academic achievement is the bedrock of selective admissions, a factor involved in every spot.

② Special Accomplishments and Activities

Some applicants who get in show unique appeal through their activities. As I've attended many, many college forums, I've heard from Deans of Admissions on down to new admissions staff. They all state repeatedly that they look for unique thinking, deep accomplishments, and special contributions to society in the applicant's record, activities and recommendations.

Activities are important to show that a student can and will do more than hole up in a room to study for good grades. An activity can be an individual project, if shaking hands to run for student council isn't your thing.

Activities follow academic achievement in primary importance, and activities are a factor involved in every spot.

③ Sports

For non-athletes, a sport is an admissions-fit factor that excludes them, so non-athletes may jump ahead (or read about how an athlete might just get the spot you want).

Sports can play a role in admissions at colleges which do not offer sports scholarships. Colleges without athletic scholarships may consider admitting a student athlete who meets academic requirements and can improve a team, if a coach gives admissions a nudge, perhaps, so I've heard and read.

Now, do not quote this book to conclude that sports will get anyone admitted to the fancy college of his or her choice. Making any varsity team and getting into any selective college isn't easy, to say the very least. A sports connection will not work out for many individuals.

It, however, will be a positive factor for some. Athletes, and their parents and guardians, should know about the subject. More details are in Selective Admissions: Sports (p. 265).

Financial Aid in Division III or the Ivy League is Based on Family Income or Other Merit Aid, Not on Athletic Ability

The potential sports influence is for admissions only in Division III, not for financial aid at all, in the strictest sense.

Here's how this works:

⌦ Rules do not allow colleges without specific sports scholarships, such as Division III colleges or the Ivy League, to factor sports in any way into financial aid offers; period.

⌦ In Division III and the Ivy League, financial aid staff cannot base aid on sports, and it is checked by auditors.

⌦ In Division III or the Ivies, do not ask the coaches or athletic staff to help on financial aid, which shows that you don't understand the process.

⌦ Division I, non-Ivy, or Division II is another matter.

(Sports continued)

▨ In Division III or the Ivies, if you are not eligible for financial aid in the first place, or merit aid based on academics, playing varsity sports won't change that. Those are the rules.

▨ Sports might help you get a good nudge in the admissions office if the coach wants you on the team, but not in any way in the financial aid office.

▨ Once admitted at fancy colleges, middle- and lower-income students usually get some aid. Low-income students usually get more aid, sometimes a lot.

So, for student athletes with good academics who could make the cut for a college sports team, from Division III on up, this could be a positive admissions factor. Then you should find out more.

Thus, in selective admissions, the sports connections will take up some spots.

④ Legacies (or Parents Didn't Attend College)

A legacy factor applies to an applicant who has a parent who has attended a college. Some colleges take note of an applicant whose brother or sister have attended that college. A further subset is preferential consideration for children of faculty and college staff. (An opposite situation is a student whose parents do not have any college degrees. This status also can be a plus in admissions.)

Legacies

An extended-family connection, such as a grandparent, uncle or aunt may not be officially noted, but it doesn't hurt to mention it somewhere in the application.

While legacies have been criticized as an unfair advantage for family members and faculty, legacies remain important to colleges. Alumni go out of their way to support the college with donations, by volunteering and with career connections for graduates.

(Legacies continued)

Legacies aren't automatic, however, though many of these applicants are highly qualified and well prepared.

When Parents Didn't Attend College

Some applicants have parents who don't have any college degrees. This status definitely should be mentioned in applications. The first to attend college out of a family should mention that. If your older siblings have attended college, you're not the first but it is still viewed positively by admissions for an applicant when the parents don't have degrees.

This status shows that such applicants achieved a great record without the tutoring of parents who have degrees. This isn't to say that such parents aren't involved positively, but the story is clearly different from that of an applicant whose parents are professors, for example. The first in the family to attend college has a good story to tell. The student whose older sibling went to college has a good story to tell too. I've heard directly from admissions staff who viewed the older sibling's success as reassuring to them that the younger sibling has some support and the ability to succeed.

Different Stories and Different Ways to Tell Them

These are two different, competing stories here; the student from the accomplished family and the rooting-for-the-underdog story of a student whose parents didn't attend college. If you aren't a direct legacy at a college but your parents are accomplished, consider how to tell that story. Some admissions advisers warn about being seen as a child of entitled privilege and recommend not mentioning the parent's professions, going for the middle-class look. But on the other hand, accomplished families can be seen as a positive addition to the college's network. It's hard to say. If you include the accomplished parents in the story, include their hard work and sacrifice.

Thus, legacy preferences and preferences for applicants whose parents didn't attend college may take up some spots.

⑤ Demographics

Colleges may have a goal of enrolling students from different demographic backgrounds, thus any demographic factor for any student could matter. These include: rural, suburban, urban, income group, education level of parents, foreign students, minority group, male and female.

Public, tax-payer funded colleges are under some court orders to largely ignore demographics in admissions, though these same court rulings provide leeway. Private colleges may try to match national demographics, if qualified applicants show up. Admissions staffers say that no quotas per se are in place, but they do state that a college may seek a demographic mix for a well-rounded student body within its academic standards. If a college is low in one demographic category, an applicant with that demographic profile may receive extra consideration. Enrollment demographics for each U.S. college are shown on College Navigator.

The Lower-Income Demographic

Lower-income and working-class kids are behind in getting into selective colleges. The demographic category of lower income overlaps with the admissions income factor covered on page 233.

The percentage of lower-income students overall of all races who enroll in selective colleges is much lower than the percentage of those students in proportion to the national population.

▨ A selective college may have a 15% lower and moderate-income enrollment, as indicated by Pell grant figures.

- Perhaps 50% of the U.S. population is low and moderate income. A U.S. median income family income of about $56,000 is eligible on a sliding scale for some amount of a Pell grant. Median means half of U.S. families (50%) are lower, thus eligible.

For some low-income students, selective colleges aren't relevant as the students' abilities match up better with blue-collar work, such as a

(Demographics continued)

person who can make it as a truck driver, but not as a scientist, or as a nurse's assistant, but not as a doctor.

Yes, this happens in all types of families, as not every rich kid is cut out to be a scientist or doctor either.

On the other hand, often a kid from a low-income household is just as smart as anyone else, but social factors keep the student from applying to a selective college. The smart kid doesn't try, because socially it's as if asking questions in class and studying extra is being a traitor to one's social group, being a nerdy teacher's pet. A smart working-class student may not get encouragement from adults, friends and siblings to make a serious effort in school. Speaking English properly is mocked. Reading books isn't encouraged. Rather than forge ahead, the student buckles to peer pressure *to not be well-educated.*

Thus, the student doesn't reach a higher level of college readiness, even though he or she is smart enough to do so. This doesn't happen all the time, but it happens a lot.

And for some students who do get good grades and receive encouraging words, it's just surface-level, and no one provides the detailed, early and sustained guidance that's needed for getting into selective colleges. This book aims to help such students.

These social factors affect the U.S. academic achievement gap for lower-income kids overall of all races.[36]

Are colleges on the look-out for low-income students who can make it in college, including the elite colleges? To some extent, yes.

While there is no rule to include any certain percentage of low-income students, there's an awareness by colleges that enrollment of low-income students is below their ratios of the U.S. population.

Does that necessarily mean much? Maybe not. But, maybe yes. If a qualified, low-income student applies, he or she will receive due attention.

And admissions staff might be rooting for an applicant from a lower-income family whose parents did not attend college.

(Demographics continued)

The Minority Demographic

There are clearly enrollment gaps at some selective colleges in some minority demographics. Students who are Native American, Latino, or black are in shorter supply there than their ratio of the U.S. population. (See College Navigator; select a college, see Enrollment.)

This relates to the academic achievement gaps which are documented for African-American students, Latino students and Native-American students. Studies on this are listed in the endnotes.[37] These gaps include not just low-income kids among these groups, but the gaps are documented among students from middle-class and higher-income households as well. Achievement gaps affect enrollment gaps.

▧ A selective college may have a 7% black enrollment.

- U.S. Black population is at about 13%.

▧ A selective college may have an 11% Latino enrollment.

- U.S. Latino population is at about 18%.

▧ A selective college may have a 0% Native American enrollment.

- U.S. Native American population is at about 1%.

Some Open Spots for Low-Income Students and Minorities?

Do these differences at some colleges present some open spots for lower-income students, for black students, for Latino students, and for Native American students who can meet the requirements?

That may be how admissions offices are looking at it.

If you're from a lower-income family, or are Latino, or are Native American, or are African American and you hit the high academic markers, you are competing fairly, yet a shortage of students such as you are also hitting those high markers.

Is a spot open for you students in these categories? Maybe. Want to find out? You must, first, get the grades and the test scores for whatever level you are aiming for. Then apply to several colleges. That's the only way to find out.

(Demographics continued)

Every applicant has a demographic to understand as a possible fit for a college. It's no exact science, but try to be aware of things.

A college has somewhat of a demographic too, based in part on location, mission, history and temperament, if you will. I've read articles about colleges who purposely seek types of students who don't usually apply to those colleges. You might apply to a place where you wouldn't expect to fit in and see what happens.

Geography comes into play, as the Ivy League colleges, for example, have more than enough qualified applicants to fill their freshman classes just from New York state and Massachusetts. They don't want all their students to be from New York state and Massachusetts. Thus, they clearly give thought to select applicants from other geographic locations, though they don't have quotas, per se.

Perhaps a big city, east coast college would consider more rural-town applicants from the west. Perhaps a western college would consider more big city applicants from back east.

⑥ Majors

Using a certain major as a primary strategy to gain admission to a certain college is a tricky strategy which has no guarantees. It might help and it might backfire.

Some colleges don't let applicants select a major, or allow them to select undecided. Others colleges ask for a major. Here's one selective college that wants different majors, as quoted below.

"We also want a class who studies a variety of disciplines, so the major you put on your application and evidence of your interest in this major is an indicator of how you would fit in the upcoming class. These are examples of institutional priorities, and how factors outside of your GPA and test scores will affect your admission decision."[38]

So, for this selective college, the major will affect the applicant, outside of grades and scores. Thanks for the notice. But what exactly are the institutional priorities this year? That's the tricky catch-22.

(Majors continued)

Let's look at this catch-22. The college wants a mix of majors. The applicant wants in. But the admissions staff can't just post "We are currently short of art majors." Given that many thousands of applicants want to get in, how many extra art students would find out, and how many other applicants would switch to art, digging out their art-class portfolio to attach? It would get ridiculous.

So, even when a college admits, as quoted above from its website, that it considers majors in admissions, it can't tell anyone exactly how that occurs.

There is no sure-fire way to determine if a college needs art majors or zoology majors, for example, in the year you apply. Admissions won't know for sure until after the crush of Dec. 30 to Jan. 1 applications are all in. If you can talk to staff in a department, you might have some insight, but who's to know for sure? Let's say you got a tip. A college has been short on zoology majors.

That could be a legitimate option. But in the past six months, did a lot of others hear about it too? What if that college gets thirty more great zoology applicants? Will they bypass you?

Perhaps your insight is accurate and a real shortage does exist in a certain major at application time, so selecting that major will indeed help, and then you get in. Or, perhaps the college will see through a drummed-up interest for a certain major and turn you down. Maybe. Maybe not.

Do you see the circles you can go around and around in?

Keep to Your Strengths

I recommend sticking with a student's strengths and goals, which can then match up with the record for a strong application. The college quoted earlier asked for "evidence of your interest in this major." Sure, you may find a whole new career while in college as many do, but aim for what you are interested in so your application rings true, even if the major is a common one among applicants. This takes us back to having a record of accomplishment, not busy work.

(Majors continued)

I'm Not Set on A Major

If you are not set on one major, but have varied accomplishments, then it is OK to tell that story as well. Colleges value the overall record of many applicants, and perhaps they leave the majors more to the law of averages. Again, the colleges don't let us know.

MIT and CalTech, two ultra-selective colleges, do not even allow applicants to select a major, although they have varied majors to select from later. (At CalTech one can major in English or Philosophy. At MIT one can major in Theater or French.)

Instead of aiming for a major that you have very little work in, which could weaken your application, your strongest application could rather be as an undecided or undeclared major, which is very often just fine with the admissions office. If that is a possibility for you, ask at each college about the pros and cons of that option.

One Scenario of an Admissions Major Strategy

On the other hand, I know a student who is taking a chance on a targeted major.

This student has not made up her mind at all about her career. She's good in science, but also in art and is an excellent writer who has read 100 novels since 8th grade. As an admissions strategy, she's selecting chemistry, which she estimates will be in shorter supply among the women applicants for her colleges of choice.

She will look at science as a career, but, honestly, it's up in the air. Chemistry seems practical as she has an A in one year of AP Chemistry and an A in one year of IB chemistry. She will take the SAT Chemistry Subject Test. There is some risk.

Every applicant takes some risk in how the major selection, even undecided, affects the admissions fit for each college. Are her math and science credentials good enough? They are pretty good, so she, her parents and her counselor are comfortable with the risk.

(Majors continued)

Yes, undecided would be the most honest description of her mindset, so is undecided the honorable choice to make, when chemistry might help her get in? Life has some gray fuzzy lines between being 100% brutally honest and being practical.

Some college advisers state that students should use a major as way to try to improve the odds of admission, if they are confident of their knowledge of the situation.

Others point out, as I have, the difficulties in determining the odds, regardless of one's motives.

At some colleges, it isn't easy to switch majors, and at other colleges students can change majors more easily.

⑦ Income

This subject involves the income needs of the colleges:
(1) the wealthiest colleges, and (2) not-as-wealthy colleges that need more tuition to pay the bills. Then, the income needs of a college will converge in some way with an applicant's income level.

Colleges Pay the Bills with Tuition

For most colleges, tuition is the main source of money. Even most public colleges, although called tax-payer funded, get much more money from tuition, than from tax-payers (or endowments).

At a selective college, much of this revenue need is met by market conditions, as a lot of the qualified applicants are from upper-middle-class and wealthy families which will pay full price. Might we conclude that the ability of some applicants to pay full price is a factor? Certainly.

Need-Blind Admissions

One situation exists with need-blind colleges, basically very wealthy ones. The need-blind colleges have enough money to pay more for lower-income to middle-class admits.

(Income continued)

Need-blind colleges promise to decide by the merit, while purposely being blind to the financial need (or financial excess?) of an applicant. That is need-blind admissions.

If their applications match up, low-income applicants won't be bumped out by applicants who can pay full price. That's the first part of the idea, which, it seems to me, admits that the opposite is true otherwise in admissions: that most colleges must look at financial need or financial excess of applicants when making admissions decisions, or why even bring it up and announce anything?

Which leads to the second part of the idea of need-blind admissions, the commitment by the college to meet the financial need of lower-income families, not to tell a family with a $50,000 income that yes, the college will admit the student, but expect the family to borrow $150,000 to help cover the $250,000 total cost.

At the wealthiest colleges, the need-blind ones, a lower-income applicant with a good application might have a better chance of admission, than he or she would from a college that needs more tuition, even more so if a college is seeking to increase its percentage of working-class students.

Colleges Which Need More Tuition to Pay the Bills

Some colleges rely more on tuition to cover the bills and then honestly run out of scholarship money. In these cases, can a student who needs a full scholarship get bumped out by a student with an equal record whose family will pay the full price of $250,000? Probably. (Would the college be doing that low-income student a favor to offer a spot with limited aid, even $50,000? Would that family be irresponsible, to sign for a loan for $200,000 when family income is $35,000?)

At state colleges, some slots are given to out-of-state students, and foreign nationals who pay double or triple the in-state price. Among in-state applicants, the college can't give away scholarships to everyone, thus are students whose families can pay full price noticed? Perhaps.

(Income continued)

Those are some spots used up.

Another category regards prospective donors. Could some applicants be noticed because the families are very, very wealthy and could donate substantially later? Maybe. There go a few spots.

Certainly, the situation at top colleges favors wealth. You students who are wealthier should not squander your ability to pay, by studying hard and completing substantive extra work so you can be considered.

But do we say to students from families of average means that you might as well give up now, goof off and remain only moderately educated? No. What is fair to working-class students is that the combined pool of the top 50 colleges and the top 100 colleges has a large number of openings. As endowments rise, more costs are being covered by more colleges. If accepted, and the costs remain prohibitive, go elsewhere to put your good academic start to good use.

⑧ Demonstrated Interest

If two applicants are completely even in all categories, for example, but only one opening is left, will the applicant who has demonstrated a much clearer interest in a college get the yes letter? One would think so.

The admissions factor of demonstrated interest is hard to judge, but for selective colleges, my advice is that students should demonstrate interest in a specific selective college by doing more than just sending in the application.

Let me explain the term "demonstrated interest." Some colleges want a higher rate of enrollment from students who are admitted, which shows that they are desirable places to attend, helping rankings. This is the admissions yield rate. One way to increase the yield rate is to offer openings to applicants who have shown a realistic interest in attending that college, versus applicants with a "maybe, but maybe not" attitude, who are perhaps just as likely to turn the opening down. If all else is even, a student who has demonstrated a sincere interest may be noticed. That is demonstrated interest.

(Demonstrated Interest continued)

So, on the one hand, if you show sincere interest, it may help.

On the other hand, if the admissions office stated that "Applicants who call and email the college a lot to prove they are very interested will get extra consideration for admission," the office would be inundated with contacts, above the huge volume it already receives. Thus, many admissions offices state that they do not keep track of contacts with applicants (visits, calls and emails) nor do they factor in such contacts for admission decisions.

But we outside of the admissions office don't know for sure what they notice.

Early Applications Show Interest

The ultimate in demonstrated interest is a binding early-decision application. If accepted, the applicant agrees to enroll at that college, unless the cost would create severe financial hardship.

Colleges clearly state that early decision applicants are treated to the same standards for admissions as regular decision.

Generally, a slightly higher percentage of students who apply for early decision are accepted compared to those who apply using regular decision. I've heard admissions staff explain this statistic with the logic that early applicants are usually well qualified and well prepared, and being such good candidates, they are accepted at higher rates than regular decision applicants. That sounds plausible.

Another theory would include cases whereby the college wants to lock in some applicants who must attend, but no one's published any statistics on that subject that I've found.

Many advisers strongly advise students to plan for, and apply early on a binding basis to one college. This means having a great application ready two months earlier. Perhaps working-class applicants and those whose parents didn't attend college can stand out more in an early decision pool, as most applicants in these categories apply with the regular decision group. That sounds plausible.

(Demonstrated Interest continued)

Any applicant stills need a strong application to stand out. If a student has a very high preference for one college, has strong qualifications and is ready with a well-prepared application, then an early decision application might make a lot of sense. The student should also select a college that will offer enough financial aid.

For a student with means to pay, an early application makes you appealing to the admissions office as you won't be a drain on scholarship funds and you must accept if admitted. Benefits to students include:

- Those who are accepted can make plans sooner.
- Those who are denied will find that out earlier, to concentrate on other applications for regular decision.
- Some early applicants aren't accepted or rejected but are placed into the regular decision pool, so they still have a chance for their first-choice college, (and certainly have already demonstrated a lot of interest) and can apply elsewhere as well for regular decision.

If considering an early application, prepare for all aspects, including studying earlier for standardized tests and subject tests. You'll have to take tests earlier, get good scores and have a robust application. With an early application, you can still prepare for other applications and even file applications for other colleges, just not any others that are binding.

The Risk of a Rushed Early Application

A risk is that if you rush the early application and you aren't ready, you might be turned down outright for that college, whereas if you use a regular application with better test scores from extra preparation, and with an added internship, for example, you might get in.

John, the student in our story, had a good application, except that his first and only test score in October was low for some of the colleges he was applying to. He skipped an early application because a better score wasn't available at that time. Later he got great scores for the regular applications and did get accepted to several top colleges.

Remember, having demonstrated interest might get you a better

(Demonstrated Interest continued)

look-see, but have you done the work? Showing a sincere commitment is one thing, but do not badger colleges, in an annoying, pestering way, which could backfire. Every single college application is read with serious effort by admissions staff.

To Show Interest, Do So

Take these steps: Register for more information and respond to college emails, click on the links and reading the material to show that you did indeed review the information. Attend a forum in your area. Visit the campus. Register for a tour. Attend a class. Make an overnight stay. Attend another forum in your area. Then another. Meet the area rep. Showing definite interest may not officially help, per admissions rules, but who's to know for sure if it might not help a little, or more?

Overall, Regarding Admissions Fit Factors
Increase Your Own Pool of Colleges

Overall, the best advice that I can give is to apply to a larger pool of colleges, aiming for several tough ones, several middle-of-the-road ones and several easy ones, based on your qualifications

I recommend sending 10 to 15 applications or more.

With 200 great colleges, for example, to aim for, applying to 20 leaves 180 that won't hear from you, so don't feel as if you are bothering those 20.

Can you get your test scores up?

And your grades? To the levels needed?

For a college that would be great for you? Can you mix in some extra-curricular activities and a special project which show accomplishment?

A lot of you students reading this can very well do so.

Any sustained effort to get better grades and try new activities will leave you a better educated person, a more determined person and a more accomplished person.

Chapter 23

Selective College Costs & Finances

Let's go into some specifics regarding paying for selective colleges. The selective colleges fall into two categories:

(b) private (large and small)

(a) public (tax-payer funded)

At Selective Colleges:

Lower Income

+ Higher Academics

= College Money

Both public and private selective colleges might offer significant assistance to low- and moderate-income students.

Students may still pay a lot compared to a community college, for example, but not full price. And from families in the lowest income brackets, such as $30,000 to $60,000, if the student gets in, the college could be very affordable, at least at the wealthier private colleges.

A student whose single parent or guardian, for example, makes $15 an hour, i.e. $30,000 a year, could go to the Ivy League for $7,000 a year, including housing and food (p. 325).

Both public and private colleges attempt to attract the highest academic achievers through merit scholarships, which are in addition to federal Pell grants and standard state aid.

Private Selective Schools

Examples of larger private selective colleges include those such as the eight of the Ivy League[O], the University of Chicago, Duke, Emory, Georgetown, Johns Hopkins, MIT, Northwestern, Notre Dame, Rice, University of Southern California, Stanford, Tufts, Vanderbilt, Wake Forest, and Washington University in St. Louis, to name only a few.

Small private selective colleges include those such as Amherst, Bowdoin, Claremont McKenna, CalTech, Colorado College, Davidson, Grinnell, Harvey Mudd, Haverford, Macalester, Pomona, Reed, Sewanee, Swarthmore, Washington and Lee, Wesleyan, Wellesley and Williams, to name only a few.

Consult the college guides, available at libraries, booksellers and online, which list hundreds of colleges with profiles and statistical information. Recommended college guides are listed on page 78.

Selective Private (Wealthy) Colleges: Some Good News

Private colleges get their income nationally and internationally, and not from tax-payers in their state, so they treat in-state and out-of-state students the same. Everyone's full-price tuition is equal; very, very high.

So, what's the good news? Well, if your family is wealthy, the good news is that you can afford it. And if your family is not wealthy, the good news is that a fair number of very selective private colleges will chip in a decent amount of money.

But, Here's Some Bad News: Average Private Colleges Also Cost a Lot and They Offer Less Financial Aid

The good news cited above doesn't apply to the average private college in the U.S.

An average private college will still charge a lot, and will not chip in as much money, as its resources can't match the larger endowments.

[O] The Ivy League consists of Brown, Columbia, Cornell, Dartmouth, Harvard, Pennsylvania, Princeton and Yale.

Need-Blind Admissions
at Private Colleges

It Means They Might Pay for Some of It,

If You Can Get In

Need-blind admissions are when applicants are admitted whether they can pay for it or not, and with the college making up any shortfall. Need-blind admissions policies are usually from wealthy private colleges.

Most private colleges cannot promise this, which means most private colleges do keep an eye out for full-paying students, or offer less aid money. (Some public colleges do increase aid for low-income students, but still can't offer as much aid money.)

Aid from the need-blind colleges is on a sliding scale, so a student from a family with only $30,000 of income might pay perhaps $5,000 to $10,000 a year with room and board included. A student from a family with $70,000 income might pay $15,000 to $25,000 a year with room and board included, for example.

The colleges with a need-blind admissions policy usually clearly state it on their websites. You may ask. Search for lists of need-blind colleges on the web. Such a list is not provided in this book.

At the average private college, it will cost you something, perhaps a lot. A lot of people make the choice to pay more for a private college, concluding that the private colleges give them their money's worth, a reasonable rate of return. That's the subject of the rate of return on investment in college spending.

The Rate of Return on Investment in College

So, if the offer still requires too much debt, then you should probably go back to lower-cost options such as a community college followed by in-state tuition at State U.

Even with some discount, is a high-priced degree still an over-priced degree? Here's one way to look at it: So what, if a college drops the price from $200,000 to $100,000. Is that like buying a luxury car for $100,000 and concluding you got a good deal, just because the dealer didn't charge you the inflated sticker price of $200,000? All the while, a solid car or truck is available for $25,000, which is like a community-college/state-college degree, which will get you to your job at a good company. Books on this topic are listed on page 31.

Why and How the Selective Colleges Can and Will Help You

The large selective private colleges are multi-billion-dollar operations, even though they are classified as non-profit entities. Some of the small selective colleges are quite wealthy too. They do not return a profit to owners or shareholders the same way for-profit universities do. The large selective private non-profit universities have large endowments. Some small-enrollment private universities have endowments of more than $1 billion, and many have hundreds of millions, which provide investment income to run the school and provide scholarships. They have donations from alumni. The many wealthier enrollees, including foreign nationals, pay the very expensive full price. Thus, these universities can offer aid to some of the lower-income students who are admitted to their courtyards of ivy.

Private colleges are privately-held entities which do get some tax-payer funds such as Pell grants and research money, but they are

242

primarily funded by tuition of full-paying customers. The non-profit private colleges are not funded by stock sold to the public, so their operations are not open to as much public scrutiny. These private entities have more freedom of action. Here's an example:

State Colleges and Private Colleges - Who Can Do What?

State colleges are accountable to the public at large. Private colleges are not so much.

State College

Let's suppose, at a tax-payer funded college, State College, a wealthy parent makes a huge donation to State College's endowment, which is legal and allowed. Let's suppose the parent's daughter applies to State College, barely meeting the minimum requirements. The daughter could be accepted, but is just as likely to be denied, not considering the parent's donation.

Can State College let that student in with few questions asked? Perhaps not. State College is a tax-payer owned entity, run by public officials accountable to elected officials, accountable under state laws to the public that pays the taxes. At State College, if admissions staff blatantly uses the parent's huge donation as the main reason to admit the daughter while turning down other equally qualified applicants, that might raise questions.

Private College

Further, let's suppose that at nearby Private College, the same wealthy parent makes a huge donation to the college. The daughter applies, barely meeting the minimum requirements. The daughter could be accepted, but is just as likely to be denied, not considering the parent's donation. Can Private College let that student in with few questions asked? Probably yes. Private College is a private entity, not accountable to the public at large, but to its own board of directors, alumni, donors and faculty. The huge donation will help Private College, which can consider the donation as one of the main reasons to admit the student, who is eligible, even if barely.

The Freedoms of Private Entities

Overall, for private entities, as the saying goes, it's a free country. Except for criminal behavior and violations of a person's constitutional protections, private entities have leeway to conduct their own matters.

Responding to public opinion, private colleges may try to match national demographics to have a diverse campus, and offer more working-class students a chance. But they don't have to match society.

A luxury car dealership sells $250,000 cars. That's its right. If you cannot buy one, the dealership hasn't violated your rights. A private college sells $250,000 degrees. That's its right. If you cannot buy one or the college doesn't buy one for you (also known as "award a scholarship"), the college has not violated your rights.

Unfair Discrimination? You Be the Judge

Private colleges let in different types of students based on different missions and mandates from their founders and the goals of those who currently run the college. Here are some examples.

What About CalTech?

Private CalTech, the California Institute of Technology, has decided to admit only 250 elite science and math applicants each year. It could add more, but that's CalTech's choice not to. Is that stingy, or elitist? That's for CalTech to decide. Due to exacting math and science standards perhaps, CalTech has about a 40% Asian enrollment, compared to the 5% Asian U.S. population ratio. Is that unfair discrimination against non-Asians? Or should the rest of American students catch up to the Asian students in science and math in unbiased, open competition?

What About Berea College?

Private Berea College of Kentucky has a mission to help lower-income Appalachian students with reduced tuition. Berea's donors and endowment pay for a lot of the costs. Students must work at jobs to chip in. But the program is limited to 1,700 students, so it's selective (only

37% of applicants get in). When Berea reserves openings for students from its region, is that detrimental to deserving students from other regions? Maybe. Is Berea's policy detrimental to an upper-income student who could benefit from the college's special character, but will never be admitted based on high income alone? Could be. Berea helps those it can, and thus must make those decisions. It can't help everyone.

What About Cooper Union?

In 1859, Mr. Peter Cooper started to help poor students at his college, sponsoring tuition. Private Cooper Union in New York City still gives many students significant aid towards tuition. Spots are limited and a lot of people apply, so it is super selective, even more so because only art, architecture and engineering students are eligible. Is that detrimental to deserving students with other skills? Maybe. It is unfair? No. A private college can target its spending however it likes. An art college can restrict admissions to only art students.

What About Wellesley College?

When private, highly regarded Wellesley College admits only women, is that unfair discrimination based on gender bias? That's not how Wellesley sees it, and Wellesley pays the bills.

Nationally, What's Fair About All of This?

U.S. college policy is to fund public colleges and universities largely from tuition and fees. That's what the voters, through their representatives in the states and in Congress have selected.

Tax-payer supported education free of charge only extends to high school. Tuition and fees often pay the highest portion of budgets for public colleges, with smaller amounts from taxes, and a relatively small amount from endowments.

Everyone chips in, though for low-income-families that's much harder to do, but there is the community college. Wealthy families pay full price. Some states are lowering net costs at public colleges.

At private colleges, someone has to keep the doors open, pay the bills and pay top-notch professors to show up. Thus, most families pay a lot of tuition.

Selectivity is Everywhere, Even at the Community College

There is selectivity and exclusion at tax-payer funded colleges. A community college requires that applicants meet college-level English and math standards, which is not unfair discrimination.

Further, more-selective public colleges, such as the University of California, the University of Michigan and the University of Virginia are tax-payer owned and funded, yet they exclude the majority of applicants by requiring high academic levels.

Some public colleges are for students in health careers only, excluding others. Thus, with public colleges also, factors of missions and requirements vary and exclude many people.

At private colleges, admissions officials must meet the selection standards to match college missions and goals. That may be to enroll a few science whizzes at CalTech or to enroll low-income kids from Appalachia at Berea.

That's not unfair discrimination.

That's private free choice.

Here's Some Good News

At both private and public colleges, federal Pell grants help low-income to median-income households pay the bill.

There is no easy chart to refer to, as Pell grants are on a sliding scale, so to speak, depending on all the factors, which vary at each college, such as cost compared to income, which determines the Expected Family Contribution (EFC). Roughly, when a household makes around $20,000 to $23,000 (one parent making $10 to $11.50 an hour) or less, a family can get up to around $5,900 in Pell grants. Pell grants of $1,000 to $3,000, for example, also can go to households with incomes up to $50,000. Even up to $70,000 households may get something, depending on the EFC. There is no set income cutoff. Two or more students in the same household can get full Pell grants, in the same year, with no penalty or reduction in benefits.

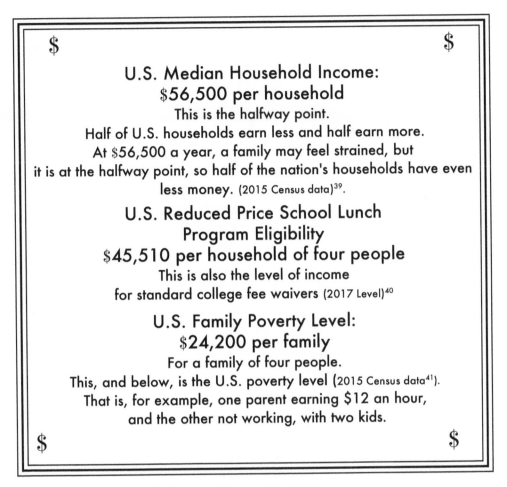

$ $

U.S. Median Household Income:
$56,500 per household
This is the halfway point.
Half of U.S. households earn less and half earn more.
At $56,500 a year, a family may feel strained, but
it is at the halfway point, so half of the nation's households have even
less money. (2015 Census data)[39].

U.S. Reduced Price School Lunch
Program Eligibility
$45,510 per household of four people
This is also the level of income
for standard college fee waivers (2017 Level)[40]

U.S. Family Poverty Level:
$24,200 per family
For a family of four people.
This, and below, is the U.S. poverty level (2015 Census data[41]).
That is, for example, one parent earning $12 an hour,
and the other not working, with two kids.

$ $

Selective Private Colleges: Financial Aid Factors

Here are some factors regarding finances, which are true also for regular colleges and are repeated from the regular college chapter:

☐ A Student Work Contribution up to $5,000 is standard: Most colleges require a student work contribution from $3,000 to $5,000 a year, from a summer job and a part-time job during school. This could include a work-study program. (A student can choose to use money from a loan to meet the work contribution.) A student will have a bill for at least $3,000 to $5,000 based on this student work contribution.

☐ Family Contribution: Next comes the parental contribution or a combined student/parental contribution, based on annual income and assets. Let's call this the family contribution. Some forms refer to this as the EFC, the Expected Family Contribution, which can be in addition to the student work contribution.

☐ Typical assets are OK: Typical assets are not treated as a source of funds to pay for college, unless assess are very high. The idea is that parents do not have to tap home equity or retirement accounts, or drain the savings accounts to pay for college. Families can still get financial aid with typical assets of $500,000 or more.

☐ Formulas vary by college. Home equity value, which can be substantial for many families, might be capped at $125,000, for example, at some colleges, but be calculated at a higher level at other colleges. The cost differences between colleges affect the formulas as do the availability of scholarship funds so net prices could be similar, or much different.

Net Price Calculators Give You an Estimate for Your Family

Get an estimate. Net price calculators on college websites list costs and aid based on income information you enter.

You can do so anonymously by using a generic name, approximate figures and the "Don't Save" option.

One easy online estimate of private college financial aid is anonymous yet still uses your specific income level. This is MyInTuition (www.MyInTuition.org). MyInTuition is a free service for 15 private colleges. (Not all private colleges will be equally generous.)

You can get an estimate without entering data by using College Navigator, which has net prices for every college, listed by different income ranges.

Not all net price calculators work the same. See page 116 for more details.

$30,000 or less Annual Household Income
(For a $15-an-Hour Single-Income Household)
Lower Net Prices per Year (including room and board)
(From U.S. IES College Navigator, for 2015-16[42])

Total Net Annual Cost	Private College
$ 920	Washington and Lee
$ 1,630	Stanford
$ 1,910	Williams
$ 2,469	Princeton
$ 2,551	UChicago
$ 3,294	Harvard
$ 3,482	Vanderbilt
$ 4,728	Duke
$ 4,939	University of Pennsylvania
$ 5,171	Yale
$ 5,398	Rice
$ 5,647	Wesleyan University
$ 5,739	Pomona
$ 5,788	Middlebury
$ 5,849	Brown
$ 6,228	Amherst
$ 6,481	Colby
$ 6,822	Bowdoin
$ 7,236	Haverford
$ 7,847	Dartmouth
$ 8,038	Swarthmore
$ 8,163	Davidson
$ 8,357	Wellesley
$ 8,631	Hamilton
$ 9,038	Smith
$ 9,481	Columbia Univ. in NY
$ 10,518	Washington Univ. in St. Louis
$ 10,929	St. Olaf
$ 11,499	Claremont McKenna
$ 12,207	Carleton
$ 13,812	Emory

For low-income households, above and on the next page are some generous private colleges, with costs comparable to, or lower than: (a) in-state public college costs, (b)out-of-state public college costs and (c) average private college costs.

$30,001 to $48,000 Household Income
Lower Net Prices (including room and board)

(From U.S. IES College Navigator, for 2015-16[43])

Total Net Annual Cost	Private College
$ 1,302	Duke
$ 1,665	Harvard
$ 1,789	Washington and Lee
$ 2,665	UChicago
$ 2,705	Princeton
$ 3,432	Pomona
$ 3,871	Williams
$ 4,035	Stanford
$ 4,750	Vanderbilt
$ 4,764	Amherst
$ 5,251	Columbia Univ. in NY
$ 5,263	University of Pennsylvania
$ 6,165	Swarthmore
$ 6,293	Rice
$ 6,468	Dartmouth
$ 6,985	Middlebury
$ 7,164	Brown
$ 7,929	Yale
$ 8,525	Bowdoin
$ 9,010	Davidson
$ 9,025	Washington Univ. in St. Louis
$ 9,228	Wellesley
$ 9,805	Wesleyan University
$ 10,012	St. Olaf
$ 10,124	Hamilton
$ 10,277	Smith
$ 10,160	Grinnell
$ 12,861	Haverford
$ 13,406	Emory
$ 13,473	Carleton
$ 13,658	Brwn Mawr
$ 14,378	Macalester
$ 15,007	Colby
$ 15,553	Babson
$ 15,875	Sewanee

$48,001 to $75,000 Household Income
Lower to Medium Net Prices (including room and board)

(From U.S. IES College Navigator, for 2015-16[44])

Total Net Annual Cost	Private College
$ 4,061	Stanford
$ 4,536	UChicago
$ 4,557	Princeton
$ 6,551	Yale
$ 6,577	Harvard
$ 6,592	Columbia Univ. in NY
$ 6,975	Pomona
$ 7,880	Duke
$ 8,451	Vanderbilt
$ 8,962	Washington and Lee
$ 9,788	Hamilton
$ 10,048	Dartmouth
$ 10,080	Rice
$ 10,448	Williams
$ 11,057	Bowdoin
$ 11,982	Davidson
$ 11,996	Wesleyan University
$ 12,110	Haverford
$ 12,322	University of Pennsylvania
$ 12,581	Wellesley
$ 12,638	Swarthmore
$ 12,697	Brown
$ 13,208	Washington Univ. in St. Louis
$ 13,268	Amherst
$ 13,966	Middlebury
$ 14,682	Carleton
$ 15,816	St. Olaf
$ 17,088	Colby
$ 17,423	Macalester
$ 17,563	Grinnell
$ 17,814	Smith
$ 17,877	Occidental
$ 18,096	Claremont McKenna
$ 19,348	Emory
$ 20,042	Sewanee

$75,001 to 110,000 Household Income
Lower, Medium & Higher Net Prices
(including room and board) (From U.S. IES College Navigator, for 2015-16[45])

Total Net Annual Cost	Private College
$ 10,346	Pomona
$ 11,222	Harvard
$ 12,069	UChicago
$ 12,228	Stanford
$ 12,614	Princeton
$ 13,934	Yale
$ 14,262	Columbia Univ. in NY
$ 14,577	Vanderbilt
$ 16,240	Dartmouth
$ 17,330	Swarthmore
$ 18,436	Washington and Lee
$ 18,528	Middlebury
$ 19,245	Williams
$ 20,290	Amherst
$ 20,398	University of Pennsylvania
$ 20,451	Colby
$ 20,976	Bowdoin
$ 20,977	Davidson
$ 21,029	Hamilton
$ 21,260	Haverford
$ 22,049	Duke
$ 22,308	Brown
$ 22,396	Carleton
$ 22,435	Rice
$ 22,736	Bryn Mawr
$ 23,158	Washington Univ. in St. Louis
$ 23,161	Macalester
$ 23,218	Wellesley
$ 24,324	Emory
$ 24,553	Smith
$ 24,601	St. Olaf
$ 24,776	Grinnell
$ 25,494	Occidental
$ 25,533	Sewanee
$ 26,759	Howard

Public (Tax-Payer Funded) Selective Colleges

Examples of public selective colleges include: Georgia Tech, Michigan, North Carolina, Texas, UC Berkeley, UC Irvine, UCLA, Virginia, Virginia Military Institute and William and Mary to name a few. Such schools have acceptance rates from about 20% to 35%. UCLA's 2016 acceptance rate was 18%. Texas admitted 40% of 47,511 applicants, admitting 19,004, with 8,552 accepting the offer.

Public (Tax Payer-Funded): It's Best If You Are In-State

With public selective colleges, the in-state students pay significantly less than out-of-state students.

Some colleges may increase aid offers to out-of-state students, so you might still try for a selective public college in another state and see what happens. I've found one public college that offsets this differential, and perhaps others are doing so. It doesn't hurt to check. The University of Michigan has boosted aid to some out-of-state students. Out-of-state applicants to Michigan, however, should note that Michigan admits only about 28 percent of applicants, that most openings are for Michigan residents and that its freshman class has very high academics.

Whereas a lower-income student may get aid that makes in-state costs more reasonable, that is usually not true if the same student must pay out-of-state rates.

That low-income student might pay $5,000 to $10,000 a year or more in-state, not including room and board, but must pay $25,000 to $30,000 or more, not including room and board, a year to a public college out-of-state. The more prestigious image is probably not worth the higher price.

Paying high out-of-state net costs is usually a bad idea, unless your family has the high income to afford the cost. Even then, can that $120,000 in extra tuition be better invested elsewhere? That goes to the return on investment discussion of more expensive degrees, which some analysts say can be worth it (p. 31). Perhaps a Cal-Berkeley, Texas, North Carolina, Virginia or Wisconsin degree will generate career success that pays you back for the higher out-of-state cost. But your state has a good flagship university, with a good honors program, at lower in-state rates. Paying out-of-state tuition is generally a bad idea, unless your family can easily afford it.

For Selective Public Colleges, Regional Discounts Don't Apply

Within every region some colleges offer reduced or in-state equivalency rates (p. 103) to students from other states, but they aren't offered at the more selective public colleges, such as University of California - Berkeley, or the University of Michigan, for example. Some state flagship universities offer discounts to students from other states, but many do not.

Transfers to a Selective Public College Can Save Money

Trying for a transfer to a selective public college in one's own state in the third year of college works for some students. The net cost for a bachelor's degree is much lower by transferring after two years of community college.

This is easier said than done as often there are not a lot of transfer openings and one still needs a great record to be accepted for transfer to a selective college.

You can take additional SAT tests or ACT tests to show improvement before you apply.

A second scenario is a transfer after establishing residency in another state, which is also easier said than done.

Changing Residency May or May Not Work for In-State Tuition

A student may change residency by moving to another state, but this is not guaranteed to get a student in-state tuition.

Many colleges have strict requirements to meet before they will grant in-state rates. One scenario is having to work full time for a year in a new state, thus delaying a year of college. Or proving that you did not move "only for educational purposes." Then after that, will you be accepted to that selective college in the new state? Maybe not.

Be certain about the rules for in-state tuition for each college specifically. See Transfers, Moving to Another State & Study Abroad (p. 101).

Merit Aid for Selective Public Colleges

Merit aid (i.e. a scholarship based on academic merit) is a whole other subject.

Public colleges use merit aid to attract students with strong academics.

Merit awards are available at most major four-year state colleges, not just among the more selective ones. The merit scholarship may or may not be included in cost estimators. You may not find out about specific estimates for this *extra* merit aid until after acceptance.

If, however, you diligently inquire, you might get more information and some idea of how much merit aid you might expect with your grades and scores. Visit, write or call the financial aid office with your specific questions based on your specific qualifications.

Financial Aid Tips

See financial aid tips on pages 123-124. These aren't that special, because hidden, little known tips that save you really big money really don't exist. If one reads financial aid articles, guides and books, the things to know are covered. If you just start the forms and follow the directions, you will get through them just fine.

☞ **Chapter 24** ✍

Selective Admissions: Extra-Curricular Activities

Clubs
Community Service
Internships
Summer Seminars

College Classes
Family Responsibilities
Jobs
Volunteering

For selective admissions, students should find activities beyond classwork, while not neglecting grades and test scores.

Good grades are vital for selective college admissions.

Good test scores are also important, because high scores prove one's knowledge, and thus are trusted by admissions staff.

So yes, test scores and grades come first, but for selective colleges, the crucial third factor is substantial achievement in an extra activity, which helps one stand out from the many students who have high GPAs and high test scores.

The selective colleges expect activities. You can keep it reasonable to still get good grades, good scores and enjoy your high school years. The people do not expect you to go without proper sleep, exercise and relaxation. That's not sustainable or healthy. Don't do that.

The Subjects of Passion, Deep Accomplishment, Being Well Rounded, Resume Building and Resume Padding

Are your activities passions of yours or are they resume padding?

Should you be well rounded, or spend more time focused on gaining expertise in one area?

Whether it is in several activities, or focused on one specialty, showing sustained achievement in your record is a must. A list of only superficial busy work won't help much.

For students with a certain passion, show connected, year-by-year interest and achievement. If you now have or can find such a focus, then you should highlight work in that area in your studies, activities, resume and essays.

What if You Have Tried Different Things?

For students who try different things, that's good too. If you liked one thing freshman year, but in junior year you have moved on to something else, explain that. The key is to show enthusiasm for your explorations, along with above-average achievements.

Meeting your responsibilities, even mundane ones, is very important. Do you work at a job or a family business to help make ends meet? Do you watch over siblings, cousins or an elderly family member? These things show character and diligence so add a Family Responsibilities line to your activity list. I've heard admissions staff specifically recommend that all these activities should be included on a college application. Show what you do with your time

Find Activities; They Are Out There; Create Your Own

With an activity, aim for advanced work. You can conduct research on a project of your own that interests you to achieve something notable. It would be very decent of you to sit at the front desk for many hours at a food bank doing basic stuff, but it's doesn't stand out and you need to stand out for selective colleges. At the food bank, can you help expand the operation, recruit new people, or improve efficiency? Can you run a fund-raiser? Can you set up an extra distribution location on some Saturdays?

Many places have not had a high school intern before, but people will listen if you have the nerve to walk in, even without an appointment, and ask. Sometimes, calling first for an appointment will get you told no right away, so it is better to just walk in.

If they are not sure at first, politely insist on checking back later. Say, "Since we are just exploring options now, I'll check back later. Think it over. I'm sure we can find something I can help with."

"You Are the First High School Student to Do This."

Here's an example I witnessed. A student, my niece, wanted an internship at a university to add to her resume. She had already attended one college summer seminar. She looked through the websites, through the journalism school, the law school, the science departments, etc. She saw an ongoing project that college students were working on. She had no assurances, but decided to go and see about it. I volunteered to go along. She walked into that office with no appointment. She had to wait. She had to explain several times that she just wanted to help for free on a regular basis. She got to see the project manager.

"You are the first high school student to do this. But you can help out," the manager, Ms. Smith, let's say, told her. She had Official Approval. Because this was not a pre-set internship, the student had to see the regular summer seminar coordinator to sign a liability waiver.

"How may I help you?" the summer coordinator asked.

"Ms. Smith sent me here about interning."

"I'm sorry, but we don't have anything available at this time. The summer internships are over. You'll have to apply for next summer," the coordinator said. The student explained that she had approval from Ms. Smith and would be starting the next week. She just needed a form.

"Oh. Well, if they'll let you work there, I guess it's OK with me," said the coordinator, who had just been telling the student how nothing was available. It was sweet, seeing her walk in with nothing, overcome the run-around, and walk out with a very respectable internship.

If you are in a smaller town, local firms and agencies may be very helpful. Find out. If you are in or near a large city you will find charities, think tanks, legal aid offices, literacy programs, advocacy groups, non-profit foundations, chambers of commerce, community projects, labor unions, colleges and universities.

Part of the process is hitting dead ends. When you hit one, go to something else.

Math and Science

For math or science, university labs, scientific businesses, or tech companies may let you help in research labs or on projects. If so, you are a research intern. Consider entering competitions such as the USA Biology Olympiad, the National Science Bowl and the Intel Science competition.

Finance, Business or Law

For finance, business or law, legal or financial firms can have you type and proofread documents, spreadsheets or financial data to start. Ask to help on law-firm's pro-bono (charity) work. Law schools have international law offices and human rights offices. Business schools have start-up incubators with students and others writing business plans, doing research and starting fledgling companies. They'll put you to work for free, if you'll keep showing up.

Humanities, Health and Social Work

For humanities, try health care agencies, hospitals, foundations, university projects, schools, charities, churches, social agencies or political campaigns to do research, outreach, surveys, or tutoring. Universities may have offices or special projects with a special focus on a certain issue. Because these are outside of regular college courses, they may find some work for you to do. The school of social work might have a project.

Writing, Radio, TV and Journalism

Local newspapers, media, or publications may have options. You might assist a reporter or conduct research. You may write an essay, opinion article, a letter-to-the-editor or a news report about your high school, a local event, and submit it to a local newspaper, which may (smaller ones, especially) run the item. Try a local or college radio station, newspaper or magazine.

260

The Concord Review publishes high school essays on history from high school students four times a year. The Claremont Review publishes young writers and artists, aged 13-19. Your work, even unpublished, can comprise a portfolio to attach to your application. Admissions may not go though it thoroughly, but they may regard it favorably.

Religious Faith and Activities

For colleges with an explicit religious mission, statements of faith are acceptable. But for most colleges, only if you have put in a very significant amount of extra time in a substantial manner might faith-based activities be relevant. Regular activities for a faith are part of many people's lives, and can be mentioned, but they should not be counted as special activities, even if they are personally very important to you, as they are to many of us. As well, do not use the application as an extended statement of faith or an invitation to readers to join your faith, church, mosque, synagogue or atheist meeting.

Political Work

Political activity with a decent amount of work shows accomplishment, but describe the work, not the political arguments. Keep political opinions out of the application.

College Programs for High School Students

Using the school breaks to enhance your ongoing activities and for test prep is always good to do and can be better than chasing after something new to do. That said, there are beneficial new things out there, if you also keep up your academics.

Colleges offer programs for high school students during breaks, most in summer. Some programs are free, some offer scholarships and some have a reasonable cost, from $100 to $300. Any of those, even ones for a few days only, look nice on an activity list, but they are not needed for a college application. If you can't afford it, you can skip it.

What about summer seminars for $300, $600 or $1,200? Some, at elite colleges, are $8,000. They are not necessary. Attend a program only if your family can easily afford it or you get a scholarship. Such programs may, or may not, help you in admissions. Evaluate the impact before spending the time or money. You may be on a mailing list, which is marketing something as a so-called "selective" or "competitive" program, but it is open to anyone who pays the fee. If anyone who pays the fee gets in, how selective or prestigious is it? Perhaps not at all.

With that time, you might do better on test prep, using free or low-cost sources. That would be worth it. If you have the money to spend on something, you could pay for advanced test prep. You could take a regular college course (p. 264), intern or get a job. Remember that how an activity looks on a selective application depends in part on the context of the family's situation. A student could enhance the application by helping to pay expenses with a job, even at fast food, and finding a low-cost or free project to work on, more so than going to a paid program that is a strain on the family.

Overall, paid summer programs are not needed to compile a good college application, although some are beneficial and should be considered if time and money is available. Search for colleges by name and "Programs for high school students."

Two sources for extra activities are:

✋ Imagine Magazine from Johns Hopkins Center for Talented Youth has very good national listings of programs and resources on its website, www.cty.jhu.edu - Select: Resources, Imagine Magazine, Opportunities and Resources for Gifted Students.

✍ MIT admissions also has a list on its website: www.mitadmisssions.org. Search for "summer programs."

National Competitions and Leadership Roles in Regular Clubs

It will get some notice if you enter a national or international competition, because doing so requires work. You don't have to win the grand prize to add it to your activity list. The Intel International Science and Engineering Fair, for example, recognizes 1,700 students worldwide, starting at local levels. Ask teachers and counselors for listings.

Obtaining leadership roles in any of the clubs or activities which are already at your school or in your town also gets notice. These include in scouts, being the yearbook editor, the newspaper editor, a leader in FFA, being president of your National Honor Society, going further in Model United Nations, the debate team, and other such endeavors.

Sports are a respected activity, even if you can't make a college team later. If you can make a college team, see p. 265.

You Can Start Something New

Start something at your high school. Admissions staffers state that new projects often stand out. Most national and international charities and issue groups will let you set up a high school chapter.

Try a one-time project: a research project, a survey, a forum, a publication, a website, a blog, a video production, a symposium, a fundraiser or an information fair. If something doesn't take off, that's OK, just don't exaggerate it.

Do not puff up your activities. Exaggeration will backfire when people check. Be honest. That's all people want, some honest effort.

Keep Up Your Grades; Study for the Tests

Yet, remember, activities are important, but secondary. Devoting too many hours on something, resulting in lower grades and lower scores, will seriously harm, not improve, your college application.

If an activity is seriously hurting your grades and test prep, and you are very serious about selective colleges, then switch to a less time-intensive activity so you can keep up your grades and test prep.

Whatever you end up with, however, still apply and see what happens.

Prices for One College Course

For High School Students
Start at $248 + fees and books

A **high school student can attend college** as a non-degree student. A regular class (late afternoon, evening, or in summer) in person on campus looks the best, but completing an online class is a good accomplishment as well.

Here are some approximate public college, in-state tuition-only costs for one class on campus. Books and fees are extra.

A common, standard class is 3 credits.

College	3 credits tuition (2016)
Miami - Dade (FL) College	$ 248
South Georgia State College	$ 272
Seattle Central College	$ 309
Pasadena (CA) City College	$ 346
Chicago (IL) City Colleges	$ 599
Manhattan (NY) Community College	$ 630
California State University Los Angeles	$ 744
State University of New York – New Paltz	$ 810
Louisiana State University	$ 842
University of Texas Permian Basin	$ 846
University of Missouri – St Louis	$ 1,005
Hunter College of New York City	$ 1,200
Cleveland State University (OH)	$ 1,204
University of Massachusetts at Boston	$ 1,638
University of Texas	$ 1,750

☞ Chapter 25 ✍

Selective Admissions & Sports

Sports have a role in college admissions and scholarships. Sports scholarships are awarded at junior colleges and large universities. Sports can influence admissions decisions, even when there is no sports scholarship. The factors may intertwine.

Students who can use sports to their advantage fall into two main categories, with a third smaller subset of students who overlap.

① A Sports Scholarship

An elite athlete can get a sports scholarship. With high academics, additional factors apply.

② Sports Helps with Admissions at a Selective College

Students who are very good varsity athletes with high academics can use sports to help their admission fit to a college that has varsity sports teams, but does not offer sports scholarships. This is for students for all income levels, including well-off families. A sports admission fit may help a wealthy applicant get accepted, just as well as an applicant who will later seek financial aid.

① and ② Combined

Students who are elite athletes who can get a sports scholarship and who also meet the higher academic standards of a selective college have to pick category 1 or category 2, or combine them.

For Average-Income and Low-Income Families, Money for College from Sports (Sort of), Without a Sports Scholarship:

Is your family middle class, moderate income, or low income?
For a student athlete:

Can you play varsity sports very well?

Could you get As in harder classes if you study?

Will you practice for tests to score higher?

If so, one option might be financial aid at a selective college.

With good grades and scores, helped by a sports coach who wants you on the team, you could be accepted.

Let's say a student may not get a regular sports scholarship, but could still play college sports for a Division III team. That can help his or her admissions fit for a college, if a college coach knows about the applicant, and requests that the student be considered.

Thus, at selective colleges, which do not offer athletic scholarships, athletics can play a role in admissions.

Can You Help the Team?

At every selective college, every year, the various athletic teams for both women and men may need some new players. Beating the detested rival in sports, it seems, can be just as irrationally important for small private colleges as it is for major colleges. (As an Arizona alumnus, I'll admit I notice when Arizona's upstanding Wildcats beat those questionable Arizona State Sun Devils, as usual.)

Did you know, for example, that Amherst and Williams first squared off in 1859 in the U.S.'s first college baseball game, which is still a rivalry more than 150 years later.[P] Thus, it's important to the Amherst

---

[P] Amherst beat Williams 72-32 in 1859 (foul balls were fair then). Amherst leads the series. The last contest in 2017 was closer, Amherst 8, Williams 5.

coach and to the Williams coach, who both want some good players next year, if anyone's interested who can also keep up in classes at Williams or Amherst. So, at a selective college with varsity teams, athletes might get an extra special admissions look-see.

The Two Cuts

In this scenario, there is a harder academic cut to Fancy U., combined with an athletic cut, but it is a less demanding athletic cut at Div. III Fancy U. than at Div. I or II Athletic U. Can you make both those cuts at Fancy U? Can you get the grades, the scores, and help a Division III team?

Good athletes from average-income families hear all about working at athletic camps and promoting themselves for sports scholarships to pay for college.

Athletes, however, should look further to category 2. If you take your studies seriously to meet those academic requirements for Fancy U, you can promote yourself to that college's sports coaches to help your admissions fit.

If you're academically strong, and a proven athlete, you ought to check into this. This is not only for the top 50 colleges on various lists, but to colleges with varsity athletic teams further on down the lists. Sports can help with admissions to any of them. Division III is about 80 percent private colleges.

Perhaps, a sport helps you get in. Then, non-athletic financial aid follows regular formulas based on family income. If you get the financial aid based on your family's income level, you still get money, even if it is not a regular sports scholarship.

One More Time, The Financial Aid is Not Based on Sports, But Only on Family Income

To be clear, an admissions office might consider sports if an applicant is academically qualified, but a financial aid office cannot consider sports in any way whatsoever (other than those sports scholarships in category 1, which is _not_ what we're going over here).

College regulations are clear that a Division III or Ivy League college coach cannot contact the financial aid office, so do not even bring it up. What you should bring up to the coach is that you can meet academic standards and help the team. The coach can then mention you to the admissions office. That is allowed, as it does not involve the financial aid office.

If you are entitled to financial aid, you will get whatever that college would regularly offer. If your family can pay, you will be asked to pay. Either way, sports can help you get in.

Private College Offers May Vary

Realize too that some private colleges would be happy to have you on the team, but they cannot pay as much of the bill as the wealthier colleges.

This subject of sports is not raised to offer false hope for some unrealistic pie-in-the-sky dreamers. Students and parents, please realize that it is a lot of work to get into a selective, wealthy college that will pay a lot of your costs.

The point is that many working-class kids who are very good at sports and who can also produce strong academics are unaware of this option, which is real. They may be too uncertain of themselves to try.

Now that you are aware of the option, talk to your coach about playing in Division III.

The Smart Athlete:

① A Sports Scholarship or ② A Selective College Either One, or Both?

Only some students fit this category, but to be thorough, let's go over it for those students.

If you can get a sports scholarship, and you can qualify for a selective college, you should have some good choices. During high school, your harder choices may be about your use of time.

Do you spend more time improving your athletics, or your academics, or split it down the middle?

One factor will be your family's income level.

If Your Family is Well Off

For a middle-class and higher income families, colleges pay less of the bill. Thus, these families' choices are between saving money with a sports scholarship at a regular college compared to paying more at any selective college that accepts you. If your family has the money, what's better? The fancy degree? Or saving $150,00 to $250,000?

So, for example, do you go to Emory (and commit to play sports to help you get admitted) and pay the $250,000 price, but have the fancy degree?

Or play sports at the University of Wyoming, for example, get the degree for free (which is a great degree to have) and invest the $250,000?

A third option is getting into a selective college that also offers sports scholarships and making that team's sports scholarship cut. Now, that's much easier said than done. Such colleges include Cal, Duke, North Carolina, Rice, Stanford, USC, Vanderbilt and Wake Forest, among others. Then you would have the fancier degree and save that $250,000 for investing.

If Your Family Qualifies for Financial Aid at a Selective College

A regular financial aid package at a selective college could match or exceed what a sports scholarship offers at a State U. or a junior college. Some working-class families may not realize this and then concentrate only on the sports scholarship.

So, for example, do you play sports at Wyoming and enjoy playing major-conference sports, while you get a great degree for free due to the sports scholarship?

Or play sports for Emory (which admitted you in part so you could help the team) on a Division III squad which isn't as glamorous as a

Division I team? Then you get the fancy degree, still at a decent price because Emory covers a lot of the cost for working-class students such as you.

So, do not just think only about the sports scholarship, but also think about Elite U. for the income-based financial aid, with sports helping you get in

Chapter 26

Selective Admissions Essays & Recommendation Letters

For selective colleges, essays and recommendation letters need special attention from you, the student.

Recommendation Letters

Admissions officers state that these recommendations are very important. Students, do take steps to have very positive statements in these letters.

For selective admissions, it's best if the recommendation would state, for example, that:

> Rachel is one of the best students I've had in my career.
> rather than
> Rachel is one of the best students in our high school.
> rather than
> Rachel is one of the best students in my current class.

Politely encourage this by explaining to people which colleges you are applying to, and clearly asking for their highest recommendation.

Help People Help You

Students, ask early. People submitting recommendation letters will prefer plenty of notice. Other students may ask the same person as well.

Make a file for your recommendation. An email file may do, but a physical manila file is good too. I recommend both. Start with a short letter or note thanking the person for helping you.

It is appropriate and helpful to the person to give them a file with your resume and suggestions from you about how to describe your accomplishments and personality. As people are busy, that is all right to do. I know teachers and counselors who request the resume-style information. They can't remember everything about you, unless reminded.

In providing the suggested language, use strong words to describe yourself, such as independent, thorough, inventive, leading, thoughtful, meticulous and considerate. Describe your work and conduct to be of the highest caliber, above and beyond, original and insightful. Go ahead and put such words into your own descriptions of your accomplishments to encourage their use. When you speak to or write to the person, be honest that for selective colleges you hope they will use very positive language. Seriously, this is not the time to be humble.

Essays

The essays should be started well before the application deadline, so others can read them to offer advice. Rewrite them, and then repeat the process.

With essays, realize that it is an exaggeration that the essays alone win people their spots. Sure, in the essay-writing books they will highlight such cases, but don't believe too much hype that the essay is a deciding factor.

Without a solid record, the essay can't be a deciding factor. The essay confirms that you are a level-headed person with a good command of written English.

That said, write an essay that enhances your qualifications with solid writing that tells your story. What the essay can do is explain your qualities, personality and qualifications in a way that a list of activities cannot. Review the advice in books and blogs on admissions essay writing. Do not wing it on the essay.

Write mostly about yourself. It's OK. That's what you are supposed to do. Don't, for example, use up too much of the essay describing all the details of the life of someone you admire. Tell why you admire the person, but most of the details should be about you.

The essay reader wants to learn all about you, your personality, and your life. You are the one applying to that college.

One technique is to answer the question, "Why?"

Tell *why* you did things, and *why* you want things in the future, not just *what* you did and *what* you want. Let the reader get to know you.

Don't Be Lazy with an Essay

Certainly, a lazy essay with errors hurts your chances. Take your time. Put some effort into. Most writing improves with rewrites.

If special or trying circumstances are part of your story, include them, but without going overboard. Don't lead off with your problems, but rather lead off with positive goals and your hopes for the future. Then you can include the circumstances you overcame.

If your parents didn't attend college, mention that. If you are a foster child, for example, you can bring that up. Whatever's relevant can be mentioned.

Overcoming adversity is important, but avoid a long list of problems. Avoid deep dark secrets. Write mostly about the positive future you are building.

Many of us have had fairly-routine, regular lives in regular towns in regular schools with regular friends. The U.S. is often a pretty regular place. If that's you, that's OK too. Worked at a fast-food joint or a car wash, not the National Laboratory? So have a lot of Americans. [Q] Working shows character. Put it in.

Write about your hopes and dreams. We all have a few of those. Being honest about hopes and dreams is fine. Let it fly. Write in your

---

[Q] Dwight Eisenhower worked nights in a creamery for college money. Lyndon Johnson worked as a substitute teacher. Martin Luther King, Jr. worked a summer on a tobacco farm for college money on his way to a PhD, and Ronald Reagan's summer job during college was as a lifeguard.

voice, but use formal English, not slang. Don't let your parents change everything. The reader should know that a 17- or 18-year-old student wrote the essay, not two 45-year-old parents in combination with an admissions adviser and a college English major who also helped. People other than the student should check for errors and give advice, but the writing should be that of the student.

☞ Chapter 27 ✍

Selective Admissions Visits & Forums

With selective colleges, interaction with staff can be very important. Treat it seriously. Be prepared.

Can we go overboard with admissions staff? Yes, and that's a mistake. But students and parents should use interaction with college staff to their advantage, which is often possible.

If you don't interact with staff at all, your worthy application will still be read seriously by the staff. I recommend, however, using college visits and college events to try to make a connection with admission staff, in a polite, good way.

If a selective college is in driving distance, then visit. Meeting staff and students from a selective college knocks down the unattainable image of these colleges. Sitting in on a class, for example, a student can see that it is doable. Use virtual online tours too.

Consider trips to colleges as a good investment, compared to spending on other things that are optional. It could be well worth it, if a student and parents see the light that a selective college is possible. Can college visits be combined with or replace other travel plans? You can still have fun, but seeing the college and meeting the admissions rep is more important than seeing some vacation spot during high school years.

College Admissions Area Reps and You

Admissions offices assign one staff person to know about a state or about an area of a state. The area rep will often be the first to read applications from the area, including yours.

Sign up for more information on an admissions website to get admissions event notices. Some events may be in your area. But from experience, I can report that for some events, notices are sent and for other events, notices are not sent. To be on top of these events, you'll still need to check every few months on the college websites.

You will find these events by looking in the admissions portion of college websites, though they are not always easily found in the admissions screens. Search for "College XYZ in your area" or "College XYZ in your town." Bookmark those web pages, so you can regularly check them.

To find admissions events see pages 86-88. Try to meet the area rep at events. When visiting colleges, ask for your area rep. If you can't meet the area rep, leave a message for that person that you stopped by, with a resume, business card and a note. Get the name of everyone you meet. Put the names in your notes. After a visit, check your email regularly and if contacted, promptly reply. If you are serious about a certain college, send a thank you note or letter to anyone you met, including the front desk staff.

For an Event, Methods for Better Interaction

If possible, research the college before you go to an event, but if you don't have time, still go, get the information and talk to the people. The first time I went to one of the forums, I learned about need-blind admissions. It was a revelation. You mean they'll pay, if a lower-income kid can get an acceptance letter? I had no idea.

When speaking with admissions staff, don't ask any basic questions that you can look up yourself or call the front desk to ask about. (Such as, can I have a car when living in the dorms?) Ask about a finer point about an option, a program, a regulation, or about a department, which shows you care enough to know some details.

If you don't have any such questions about fine points, then tell the person about what you hope to do and ask for the person's opinion about something at their college that connects to your story and accomplishments.

Your overarching goal *at this stage is to get in,* not find out where to park your car. Use this very valuable time to make a connection with your college rep about your story and with you as a person.

One student I know explained a vital point regarding her application. (The name is not her real name.)

Girl: "Hi, I'm Sarah Smith. We met at an event last year."

Staff: "Yes, I remember. Your brother is at UCLA, isn't that right?"

At an earlier admissions forum, the student got out parts of her story; that the student's parents had not attended college, but her brother got into a good college and that she was aiming high. This time the student decided to use the time to address a problem, get needed advice, and add to her story. Usually, avoid problems, but this one was going to come up, so it was important that the admissions staff understood it.

Girl: "Yes, that's right. Thank you. I need your advice. For the early application, I won't know my November ACT score, but I think it will be good. Here's my problem: In 8th grade, my Algebra I class wasn't the correct curriculum, but my high school and I didn't know this. We found out much later. I have As in math, but my first math scores have been lower, not having had the proper Algebra I. The schools admitted the error and I have been redoing Algebra I on my own. Should I wait until regular decision so I can include the December score?"

In less than a minute, the student let the rep know why the early math scores were low, and how she was doing work on her own to improve.

Staff: The staffer then offered advice specific to that college.

Remember, this example is about how to talk to admissions staff to make the best impression and convey even more details about the student's story. If you need vital advice, then ask, just as the girl did in the example above. But remember that your goal is to make a good impression, conveying important, memorable details about your story.

The student above didn't ask mundane questions, but interacted with the rep with specifics about her story. The rep got to know even more about her.

Be Bold and Get Their Attention, But in A Good Way

Get their attention, but don't brag annoyingly. Many times, I have seen students try to impress the college reps in a blatantly obvious manner, and this backfires. Here's an example that occurred at a college forum I attended. I didn't write down the exchange verbatim, but it went something like this:

Oxford, Oxford, Oxford. Did I Mention Oxford?

Main group Session Q & A

Girl: I have a question. I went to Oxford for a summer program. Would Oxford receive any notice by your college?

Staff: Everything is evaluated. It depends on the work.

Girl: Well, traveling to Oxford was so fun and Oxford was so intriguing.

Staff: It certainly sounds great. We welcome any extra activities.

Girl: OK. Thank you.

The girl didn't say it with an arrogant tone and she seemed likeable, but I recommend a different style. Of course, she wanted the area rep to remember a major accomplishment. Let's suppose she had a better, planned-out approach instead.

Main Group Session Q & A

Girl: Are summer programs at a college good to list, even though it wasn't for regular credit?

Staff: Yes. Everything is evaluated. It matters what work was involved.

Girl: OK. Thank you.

In this case, she would not have blurted out the accomplishment in the group session in front of everyone, but, she did get up, ask a question and got noticed. Thinking ahead, she left a tie-in to the accomplishment for later. This works if, one-on-one, or in the Q & A for the smaller groups later, she will continue with her next planned question:

Girl: I'm wondering how extra activities help and what to highlight.

278

I'm a band section leader, so I'll highlight that.

Staff: Yes, that's good. What helps is to show accomplishments.

Girl: Earlier, you said that summer programs were OK. If I change majors, though, it's less relevant, but because it took a lot to get in, I'd like to highlight it. I got to attend a program at Oxford, which was very inspiring.

After two questions, and after waiting for two answers, then she mixes in Oxford, The Big Accomplishment, and only says it once, not four times right away, as in the earlier example. This way, it was without bragging about it outright the first time or the second time she opened her mouth or repeating it too many times. This technique works for any big accomplishment. Don't blurt it out right away. Start with your background. Lead up to it.

Describe accomplishments in terms of the work it took and with gratitude for the opportunity. Yes, absolutely, you must bring up your accomplishments, as no one else will do it for you, but it's how you bring it up. You can show that you are above the crowd in potential and ability, without being boastful; best yet, by being humble. To be honest, this is pre-planned modesty.

Staff: Oh, that's wonderful you could go. We'd like to hear about Oxford, whatever major you choose.

Girl: Thank you. Do you have a card? Are you the rep for this area?

Staff: Yes, I am. Here's my card.

Girl: Thank you. I'm Rebecca Jones. I go to Smallville High School. I'm hoping to be our first graduate at your college. You'll be hearing from me. (Nice smile. Firm handshake.)

Staff: That would be great.

In the first case, the staff person could be annoyed, thinking, "Oxford, Oxford, I got it already. You went to something at Oxford." In the second case, the person will think, "Wow, she went to something at Oxford." Either way, Oxford will be remembered, but how will the student be remembered?

Perhaps, the student sends a thank-you letter, mentioning that she was the one who hopes to be the first from Smallville High to attend that college, and listing accomplishments, purposely mixing Oxford in the middle, not placing it first.

9th Grade:	Science Club
10th Grade:	Band, Section Leader
	Art Fair Honorable Mention
	Summer Program, Oxford University, England
11th Grade:	Band, Section Leader

The student is proactive, meeting staff, letting them know about her and presenting a mature image. This way, after getting the letter, perhaps the person thinks: "That was the nice girl from Smallville who went to Oxford. I'll keep an eye out for her application."

Now, when meeting people, will it go just like that, as planned? Maybe not, but when you've thought through the conversation, it might, and if things change, thinking on your feet for new ways to get your points across may be easier.

How you make people feel about you is equally important, or even more important, than what you've done. Whatever your accomplishment, someone else out there usually has done it too, or exceeded it, so it's also about being a likeable person. Be someone that people want to help. Be someone that people can root for.

Be Firm. Get Your Point Across

Avoiding arrogance does not mean that you don't speak up. Accomplishments should be firmly stated. Do not be shy. If you are a quiet person, fine, but speak up and get your point out.

High school students, most adults want to help you, so there's no reason to be intimidated. Look adults in the eye when you talk to them, not looking up at the ceiling, off to the side or down at the floor.

Impress with Grace

Learn to impress with grace, carefully bringing out your accomplishments throughout a conversation. Ask a well-researched question about something that relates to you. Ask how to go further in an area, explaining your accomplishments in a context of wanting to excel, not just pointing out what you did.

Long, rambling introductions and questions make a bad impression. Others deserve a chance too and the meeting time is limited. Yes, make your point, but get to the point.

Use Your Name. Get the Other Person's Name.

A selective college interaction, even a short conversation in a hallway, at the front desk or at an event, should be treated by you as a formal type of interaction to make the best impression. This includes using names and using handshakes.

As you meet someone, say, "Hello, I'm John Smith," or "Hello, I'm Jane Smith." Sometimes that's optional, but it's usually good to do.

Always let a college representative know who you are, where you are from and find out who they are. Write down the name. Every time.

Using your name at the introduction is appropriate. First, you want to be remembered, not just one of the crowd. The other person often gives you his or her name. Be ready to recall the name and use it again. Thus, get their card or write down the name. Thus, always have a folder, notepad or address book and a pen. I have been to a lot of college events, and <u>most people do not do this.</u>

If you don't use names at the beginning, use them at the end, as you part ways, such as "You've been very helpful. Thank you. I'm, John Smith, (or Jane Smith) and you are?" as you extend your hand.

Proper Handshakes

Regarding handshakes, this is going to be more detail than some people need, but I get a lot of bad handshakes. Many young people don't readily use a proper handshake when they should. So, here is some belaboring of the point.

Include a handshake in the introductions, especially for an interview or a formal meeting before you sit down. At some point, a handshake should occur, certainly after the conclusion of the conversation, just before you part ways. If the other person does not offer a handshake, you should do so. Go ahead and put out your hand. Smile. Look them in the eye. This shows respect. It says that you don't regard them as run-of-the-mill and that you're not run-of-the-mill.

With the handshake, be a little firm, but not too firm. Do not fail to squeeze the other person's hand at all, with your hand completely limp. I think that's nuts. Unless your hand is disabled, have a bit of squeeze in the handshake. Some people squeeze too hard. I've had people squeeze like it was a combat drill at a Marine Corp boot camp. That's nuts. Firm is fine.

Overall, by my mental tally, limp handshakes are the most common mistake. Do not act as if your hand is paralyzed. Give a modest, short squeeze with your fingers and thumb for a proper business-style handshake.

If you are concerned about germs, wash your hands later.

As far as the style of the hand shake, the standard business-style handshake is usually expected. This is with one's fingers forward and one's thumb on top. I know that in many neighborhoods, families, and amongst friends, the grip is with your fingers on top and the thumb on the side or with a fist bump. If the other person starts with one of those, OK, but most college representatives will use the standard style. Expect it and use it.

Do You Want to Get In?

Act in a professional manner with names, introductions, handshakes, clothing and language. You are trying to enter a better college, after all, not your cousin's backyard barbecue.

How You Dress is Important.
Dress Respectfully.

This is about going to selective college events, visits and interviews. Selective college events should be taken seriously with business casual attire or business attire.

You want the selective college staff to take you seriously for their highly valuable admission. Your earnestness is your most vital attribute and respectful clothing will make an even better impression. Business attire and business casual attire can still be inexpensive, from a resale shop or the discount store.

What's your message with how you dress? That you're a valuable contributor to society? Or that, you must show off your physique? We all like to look good, but derive your self-worth primarily through the diligence of your mind, not primarily from your physique.

Full business attire guidelines for interviews and one-on-one meetings are on pages 290-291. **Business casual guidelines are:**

- Young men, wear a shirt with a collar. A button-down one with long sleeves is more formal. A suit jacket? Sure. You'll look great.
- Young ladies, wear a blouse or shirt with sleeves, perhaps with a collar, or a business style dress. You'll look great.
- Do not wear a t-shirt. (Mark Zuckerberg likes to, since he's already left Harvard and made a few billion, but he puts on a suit and tie to meet the U.S. President or China's President.)
- Guys, no wrinkled, baggy jeans. Girls, no torn jeans.
- Casual dress shoes (even from Payless) are better than gym shoes.

If you can't buy or borrow something, wear whatever you have, **but still go to the event, no matter what.**

Chapter 28

Selective Admissions Interviews

Students, if available, make the effort to do interviews, even by phone, but be ready for them. Look up tips on interviews in articles and in books on selective admissions. Getting an interview and doing well can be a great addition to an application.

Interviewing skills are learned and practiced, even for outgoing people. So, practice! If you are reserved, or not practiced in public speaking, which is what an interview is, then practice even more. Public speaking, without rambling, is not easy. (Renowned British Prime Minister Winston Churchill practiced his speeches out loud in front of a mirror, even after decades of public speaking.)

Try this. What would you say, right now, if you were asked: "So, what can you say about yourself?" Can you give a good, full, well rounded, intelligent two-minute presentation to start things off? Or not? Try it, out loud, timed, for two minutes.

Be Prepared, But Let Your Personality Show

I will give advice on being prepared, doing research and practicing. Mainly, do not end up reciting the college's facts and figures, while not showing that you are a relatable, interesting person who is ready to get things done. Tell some stories about yourself.

Before the Interview, Practice

If you do not practice, what sounds easy and great in your head may get jumbled and sound disjointed when you speak. Later in this chapter is a list of ways improve to your interactions with people.

It's fine and normal to be nervous. Expect to stumble at times, yet still end up telling your story and coming across well. Offer information. Give your opinion. Ask thoughtful questions (have a list).

Phone Interviews

A lot of young people clam up on the phone, when they are normally pretty talkative in person. It is vital to get into the swing of things. Keep the conversation going. Be outgoing. Tell stories about yourself. Ask questions.

Be Informed, Not Unprepared or Uninterested

Know a lot about the college and use the knowledge. Avoid being perceived as unprepared or uninterested. If you have gotten an interview, you are taking up the valuable time and attention of people from this college, which many other applicants would gladly have. Do you want to go to this college, or not? If not, do not schedule an interview. Thoroughly read up about the college.

Things to look up (Make notes. Have the notes with you to refer to):

1) Know the admissions procedures very well.
2) Read the news and announcements on the college website. Look up the college in media and the local newspaper. Mention recent coverage, even if it is controversial, to show that you are paying attention.
3) Learn about someone who attended the college that did something notable, but isn't the most famous alum. That would be great to mention. "I liked what I read about so-and-so, who went to your college."
4) Know about all the college's reputed strong majors.
5) Know the college's history, like who founded it and why. Which college presidents were important? For sure, know who the current college president is and about his or her career. Write down the name. Use it.
6) If undecided on a major, know about the college's accomplishments to discuss various options. You must know what is available.
7) If you know your major, then know about that department's research, accomplishments and staff, and mention it.
   a) Know the history of your major's department at that college, perhaps

scholars from the past.

   b) Know the department chair and his or her professional history. Look for a book. Read a review or some of the book and mention it.

8) Know about the college's special programs and research projects. For study abroad, explain why you are interested in specific locations.

9) Know something about the local area. Mention where you might like to go for a weekend trip. Ask where they went to relax on weekends.

☎ **DO YOU KNOW HOW** ☎
TO ANSWER THE PHONE?

Answer a phone call correctly as follows:

You: "Hello."

Caller: "Hello. Is Rebecca Jones there?"

You: "This is Rebecca Jones."   or

              "Speaking."   or

              "This is she."

These are all grammatically correct. While this isn't the most pressing issue in the world, you should be aware of the correct grammar.

While "This is her" or "This is him" are commonly used and sound OK to the ear, they are grammatically incorrect. "This is he" or "This is she" may sound old-fashioned, but the grammar is correct and many people will notice that your grammar is wrong if you use the incorrect "This is him" or "This is her."

Now after you do all that, do not recite a bunch of facts by rote, or without any context, desperate to show off. Remember that the interviewer knows all about the place.

Still, be sure to say enough, even a lot, so the person knows you did the research and so you get credit for it. Deftly mix in your knowledge. Let them know that you care about going there and you have taken time to learn about the college.

Be ready for that age-old tricky question: Why?

    Why are you going to college?

    Why do you want to go to this college?

Checklist: A Folder with Notes, Questions, Resume and a Pen

☐ Folder. It can be a dollar-store manila-paper folder or a classroom folder. A neutral color, such as brown or white, not bright orange, is best, but use what you have. Any folder works, as long as you have one.

☐ Resume. Microsoft Word, Mac Pages and Google Docs have resume templates. You can print a resume at the library with a document attached to an email to yourself or use Google Docs. (Retype it there if you have to.) Pick up a few sheets of resume paper at a copy shop for less than $1, or use regular paper, which is fine. Do not, however, have *any* errors.

☐ Get business cards if you can afford the $15. A no-frills business card on a first-time order online with regular shipping is about $15.

☐ Have paper to make notes on and two pens (one may quit writing).

☐ Have a list of topics and questions for discussion.

"Do you have any questions?" "Let me check my notes."

Have a list of a few topics and questions for discussion, which shows that you are prepared and that you care. Often in such a setting, a good topic or question for discussion will slip our mind if we haven't written it down. Seriously, it looks best to have some questions written out. Even if it is just two notations to ask about study abroad and weekend trips, write them out and have it in a folder. Also, include a general question as explained next. When asked, "Do you have any questions?" Say "Let me check my notes."

• Get out your folder, and check the notes for your specific questions.
• After specific questions are covered, always as a general question as a tool to interact with the interviewer, such as, " I would like to ask about your experience at the college to get your advice. How did the college help you the most?" or "What was most important for you?" or "What do you think will be important for me at this college based on your experience?"

What Is Everyone's Favorite Topic?
Himself or Herself
What is Everyone's Second Favorite Topic?
His Opinion or Her Opinion

Ask questions about the other person's experiences. Ask questions about the other person's opinion about something. Then listen. Carefully.

After they respond, ask another related question, if possible. Research shows that people consider you more friendly and they like you more after you ask questions about them and their experiences and listen.

Overall and at the End

Set the right tone. Be respectful, but not fawning. Be confident, not boastful. In any interview, that college must be your top choice, at least for that day.

You want to show a lot of interest without being annoying. Think about a closing statement.

Here's are examples of general complimentary sentences (you would use the college name.):

"I really love this college. So many colleges have a lot to offer, but this college is unique. In case I'm not accepted here, I'll have to apply to other places but I am extremely excited about the opportunities here. I have found out so much that interests me about the college. I'm grateful and excited to be considered."

And that, my friends, is the truth. Going to a selective college in the U.S. is a great opportunity. Show that you care, or you won't get in.

Interaction with People, Public Speaking, Avoiding Mistakes

Recognize your own speech habits for ways to improve. Some people jump into other people's sentences, not letting others finish. If that's you, work on being more patient.

Some people are too brief in conversation, not elaborating enough. If that's you, then add more details. After stating a conclusion, explain *how* you came to that conclusion. Use a story to elaborate a point. Tell a few stories about yourself.

Using correct English will distinguish you as a better educated person. See Ch. 32, English Grammar and Use (p. 303).

You Should Dress in Business Attire at Interviews

For a sit-down interview for a selective college, the applicant should dress in business attire as a sign of respect for the institution. If you have no money for purchases, then yes, of course, wear what you have available and hold your head high. You could borrow an outfit, a tie, some shoes. If you buy something, you do not need to spend much. Use a resale shop, the bargain bin, markdowns, Goodwill, or discount stores. The outfit only needs to fit well enough, not be designer wear. Wear modest dress shoes, not athletic shoes if possible.

The other person could be dressed casually, but they will expect and appreciate that you are in business attire. They may even say don't dress up over the phone, but ignore that. Dress up. It shows that that you are serious. College admissions advisers and interview advisers regularly state this and they repeat it. So will I.

Business attire is a long-sleeve, button-down shirt with a collar. Add a suit jacket if you can for both young ladies and young men.

For young men, wear a tie.

Young ladies should wear a shirt, blouse or dress with sleeves. For dress length, knee length or longer is universally professional, not super short or tight. Young ladies, a sleeveless shirt or dress, or high heels are not recommended.

Both young men and young women should be modest, not overly highlighting their physiques.

"But the other person won't be dressed that way," is the most common rebuttal I hear from young people. Yes, the interviewer may be in more casual attire, but you shouldn't be.

The applicant is showing with business attire that he or she is taking this once-in-a-lifetime opportunity seriously. The interviewer will respect that, not feel out of place. The interviewer has the power to help get you in, or to keep you out, so he or she won't feel timid because you dressed up.

Dressing casually on your part, honestly, leaves it open to question as how serious you are, no matter what the other person wears.

Some friends or family members may say it doesn't take all that. Ignore them. Let them diminish their own interview, not yours. Get something more formal, even if inexpensive or borrowed, to wear.

Dressing up shows seriousness.

This college is serious. The other applicants are serious.

You need to be serious.

They may say, "You look nice in that." Accept the compliment with "Thank you," and move to the next topic.

Do not be self-deprecating, such as "I hope I didn't overdress," or "I never dress like this, but I thought I'd better do it this time," which blows the whole idea that you are a professional type of person.

Whatever you wear, once you are seated, sincerity, drive, enthusiasm and curiosity will be your best attributes, not what you're wearing.

Interviews in Restaurants or Coffee Shops

Have money to pay, and make one offer to pay, but expect the interviewer to pay and allow them to do so. Eat before you go, so you can order something simple, like a bowl of soup. Thus, you are spending your time impressing the person, not spending your time wolfing down a Caesar salad, then lasagna, then pie and then ice cream because you are so hungry and they're paying. That's not impressive.

Methods for Better Interaction

See pages 276-282 for more information about:

◻ discussing accomplishments without bragging,

◻ proper interaction with people, and

◻ proper introductions and handshakes.

Parents Should Stay Away from Interviews

If parents drop off and pick up the student, they should stay in the car, not meet the interviewer, nor hang out nearby. Parents should return after the interviewer has left. Parents, don't meet the interviewer if you can avoid it. Put the attention on the student, emphasizing the independent, mature person that he or she is.

☞ Chapter 29 ✍

Selective College Applications: Final Steps

For Selective College Applications: Do Not Have Errors

If you decide to apply to a top college, do not have errors on your application. Errors stand out, especially for a selective college. I've heard admissions staff report many bloopers on applications. After completing any application, wait to hit the send button. A waiting period between edits gives you fresh eyes. With a selective college, errors stand out. At times, we all miss errors in plain sight.

To make this point, did you notice the redundant sentence in the above paragraph from a copy and paste error? Let's say I copied a sentence, pasted it lower in the paragraph, changed it a bit, and then the phone rang. I talked for ten minutes. Now, where was I? Looking at the curser, the sentence is OK, so I continued, not remembering to delete the redundant sentence above it. Autocorrect or spell check won't find it. If you just skim, looking for autocorrect highlights, you may miss errors, maybe some serious ones.

Do You Care Enough to Triple Check? Then Again?

Application readers state that such errors give them a moment's pause, a bit of doubt about the thoroughness of the person, and doubt about whether the person cares about the college. You don't want that.

Watch out when pasting sentences into an essay to match up information specific to one place, such as the college name, the college town, a street name, the weather, etc. Admissions staff report a lot of errors with this. The essay has a sentence about seeking warm weather at Christmas for an application to a college in snowy Vermont, because the essay was copied from the previous application to the University of Florida. It happens. A lot.

After completion, do not look at it for a while. Have a second person and a third person thoroughly read the application. Then do so yourself. Re-check everything. Do not have *any* errors. Sounds picky? Fine, go to the regular college.

The High School Transcript

Check your high school transcript for errors and omissions. What you see online with your school account may differ from what will be sent. This is worth a trip to the registrar's office to review a printout.

Some tests can be cancelled; thus, the score can be removed from a transcript.

One student cancelled an AP subject test in sophomore year, after a bad score. Per the test agency, the score didn't exist anymore for the student who cancelled it, but she had to double check for her transcript.

Some selective colleges require all test scores, so score choice does not apply for those colleges. Request a transcript for those colleges with all scores. For others, if you think it might help, you can request a transcript for those colleges that show only the scores you want to report. Yes, this is extra work for you and the registrar, but selective colleges require extra attention, so you can insist.

Be Responsible on Your Social Accounts

Clear your internet social accounts of any sketchy posts and photos or links to others with sketchy posts or photos.

Finish Well

Be diligent at the end. You've worked four years to create a great application. Take the time you need at the end to avoid errors and make it as good as you possibly can. Know that you know, that everything is just right. Then, hit that send button and get ready, hopefully, for some good news later.

Chapter 30

Files, Forms
& Keeping Track

Succeeding in high school is demanding enough.

Then add in the mishmash of details of everything else needed for college decisions and applications. If you try to keep it all in your head, mistakes will occur. Organizing things saves effort, reduces stress, and provides extra time to improve your accomplishments and extra time to relax.

Somebody Has to Keep Track of All of This. It Should Be You

Every student should use daily/weekly to-do lists and weekly/monthly planners. The schedule app is only as good as your use of it, however.

Every student should use annual planners to keep track of events and deadlines later in the year, next year and the following year. You can print calendars from free websites, use computer apps, or write them out. You can buy wall calendars, desk planners or a pocket planner, smaller than a phone, for $6.98, a little black book (see endnote).[46]

Get a System *and Use It*

If you can keep a lot in your head, great, but you still limit your effectiveness by failing to use a system. A system saves you time, which you can use to accomplish even more.

Successful people treat their lives seriously enough to be organized about everything. Each one thing in life is simple, but the volume of the details is why organization is important. You can be as quirky and cool as you want, and still keep track of each item.

Einstein may not have combed his hair, but I'm guessing he kept notes on what to do next for his work, kept information where he could efficiently find it, and wrote down the dates for the Solvay conferences, saving him the time he needed to figure out that $E=MC^2$.

Here's an example. In freshman year, a student and I found a prestigious summer program with a scholarship. He had to apply junior year. We rechecked each year, several times, to be ready. But he didn't put the Feb. 1 deadline on any calendar, nor did I. He was busy with school and sports, but again remembered to check. On Feb. 5th. He missed it by only a few days. I forgot too. Even with two years of notice, we blew it. We thought that it was so important that we wouldn't forget the date, but we did.

Organization Promotes Relaxation

For procrastinators and people with junky rooms, desks and inboxes, here's some incentive: Being organized helps you relax more and goof off better. Being organized isn't more work, it's less work!

When you write down all things you have to do tomorrow, you can relax and be all set the next morning. Or, the next morning, when you have no list, you must recreate the list again in your head, which is a waste of time and mental effort. You could be thinking about what's after $E=MC^2$ or, more importantly, who's all going to the movies, but no. You must repeatedly try to remember, that last thing to do, a waste of even more time and mental effort.

> "Get the library book that's overdue from dad's car, get the pencil leads from the kitchen junk drawer, get lunch cash from mom before she leaves early, get the colored markers from under the bed for art and, now, what was that last thing?"

Why do this over and over and over your whole life? It wastes time, your most valuable commodity. Avoid that. Make a list.

With future events and tasks, you can forget all about it for a time, even for months or a year, because you made notes on what you have found out so far and you have lists of what to do later. Why look up stuff multiple times? Put information in the proper file the first time.

Students, parents and guardians, let's recognize that a teenager should not be expected to do everything for college without any help. Work together to get it done correctly.

Along with electronic files on phones, from email and on computers, paper checklists and notes in paper folders are also efficient and portable, sometimes more so than scrolling or searching electronically.

"But, I'm Just Disorganized." That's Easy to Fix

Organize Your Papers

Take the pile of papers, mail, slips of paper and do this: Get some folders. If you can't afford folders, use old large envelopes from junk mail. Or you can paper clip papers together with a label and stack them alphabetically. Take the first thing in the pile. Toss it, keep it, or note the information on a list. Then, label a folder and drop the item, or the list, into the folder.

The point is to quickly find that piece of paper or notation later. Use a box or stack the folders somewhere. Regularly with a new item, place it in a file, or make a new file. Every single item.

There, the stack of papers has disappeared into a filing system.

Organize Your Emails

Go through the emails. Delete the excess. To keep one, label a folder and put it in the folder. Make as many folders as you have subjects and colleges. Continue until every single one is either deleted or in a folder. When new ones come in, delete or file them. Emails with something to do soon, or to be read soon, or for your schedule can go into one of three folders with an "a" in front so these will be at the top of your folder list:

a - To Do

a - To Read

a - Schedule   There, your emails are organized.

Organize Your Schedule, Events and Deadlines

With an item with a date involved, promptly place it on your calendar. If you can't place it onto a calendar right away, make a paper note, send a text or put an email in the schedule folder for later. Put events and deadlines in the right spot, right away, each time.

There, your schedule is organized.

Suggested Paper Checklists

For longer, overall to-do lists, full sheets of paper with notes may help supplement your phone apps or computer apps. Sample forms (pp. 187-190) are for you to photocopy with the publisher's permission. Look for larger 8½ x 11 forms on the book's website at www.StarterGuide.org.

Make It Easier on Yourself

What may not be so easy is to change your bad habits of not writing things down right away or entering them into apps immediately and letting things pile up. Being organized is easy, after you set up a system and use it faithfully.

Chapter 31

Master's Degrees, Law Degrees, Medical Degrees & PhDs

As a student starts an associate's or bachelor's degree, he or she may consider looking ahead to a master's degree, law degree, medical degree or PhD.

People with advanced degrees generally earn more money over a lifetime, the statistics show. Still, beware of extra college costs and debt. A lot depends on majors, specialties, the type of job and business conditions. During college seek advice as to if an advanced degree will be worth it. After getting an associate's or bachelor's, or after working for a while, people in your field can advise you.

For Low-Income Students, There is Aid for Advanced Degrees

Financial aid for advanced degrees is calculated the same way it is calculated for bachelor's degrees, with low-income to moderate-income families getting more aid from wealthier private colleges. Otherwise, prices are high. But, you have to be accepted to these more generous colleges by meeting their higher academic requirements.

Otherwise, advanced degrees are quite expensive at many private and state colleges, and many colleges can't give much financial aid.

Early on, consult with a university about your specific situation to obtain estimates of costs and aid.

You will never know for sure until you make your best effort in creating a good record, applying, and seeking financial aid.

Regions offer Discounts on Master's Degrees

Regional agreements offer tuition discounts for a master's degree at some public universities for students within those regions. These graduate degree discounts are listed on the websites on page 103. So, an Ohio resident, for example, can get in-state rates or a similar discount at a Missouri master's program and vice versa.

By agreeing to teaching duties, a master's degree student might also obtain discounts or in-state rates.

Still Want to Try for the Top 50? It's Possible for a Master's, for Law School, for Medical School or for a PhD.

With great grades and extra accomplishments, a student might get into a selective university's advanced degree program. Many students go on to get a master's degree or attend law school, for example, at a top 50 university, even if they didn't get into one for a bachelor's. You won't know, if you don't apply.

Know About Feeder Colleges

For each advanced specialty degree, some colleges are very successful in preparing students to be accepted to master's programs, law schools and medical schools. The term for such colleges is feeder colleges, as they feed students into the advanced programs. With some research, students can find feeder colleges for their specialties.

Law Degrees

After getting a bachelor's degree, law school takes three years. The application usually requires the Law School Aptitude Test (LSAT), although some law schools accept the Graduate Record Examination (GRE) instead of the LSAT, including Harvard. Both the GRE and the LSAT require serious preparation for high scores, such as starting two years in advance.

Another format is to take a 3 + 3 law program which combines three years of undergraduate classwork with three years of law school classwork, with the result of a bachelor's degree and a law degree in six years instead of seven. The bachelor's degree is awarded after the first year of the law school program.

An accelerated two-year law program is also available at some law schools. The U.S. has about 200 law schools, ranging in selectivity from about 20 percent of applicants accepted up to about 80 percent of applicants accepted.

Medical Degrees (M.D.)

Advanced medical jobs requiring an M.D. degree include being a doctor, a biomedical scientist or a research physician. A physician's assistant job also pays very well, more than a technician job, yet has fewer requirements than that of a doctor, taking fewer years.

If you are not accepted to medical school, you can use the credits toward certification for other medical jobs. These include being a technician, nurse or physician's assistant, for example. If you change your mind along the way, you can also use the science-related credits towards another type of degree.

The M.D. degree is the abbreviation for a doctor of medicine degree. The M.D. degree starts with four years for a bachelor's degree. Plus, there are four years in medical school and then three more years, or more, for a residency or fellowship.

After that, one must pass the licensing exam and meet requirements for board certification. That's eleven years of study, plus the exam and other requirements.

The Medical School Enrollment Rate Nationally Is About 40%

The U.S. has about 145 medical schools. Each year about 4 people enroll out of 10 applicants nationally among this whole group of applicants and schools. One can find information on this with an internet search for the real medical school acceptance rate.

Be warned that you may see 5,000 to 10,000 applicants for one medical school with 100 to 200 openings, which looks nearly impossible, but it isn't what it seems.

If you, like most students, apply to about 10, 15 or 20 medical schools, your chances increase, as about 40% of applicants end up enrolling somewhere.

Now, that's still 60% turned down, so you'll need strong accomplishments to be approved for medical school. Some medical schools have many fewer applicants.

PhD Anyone?

The PhD is also called a doctorate degree, from its official title, the Doctor of Philosophy degree. It is not, however, a philosophy degree, unless one gets a PhD in philosophy. It applies to science and humanities majors.

PhD requirements vary as the programs offer some flexibility. After obtaining a bachelor's and a master's degree, students complete two years of classes, research and examinations in a specialized field. Then the student writes a long research paper, the thesis, of a few hundred pages or more, under the supervision of professors, completed over two or three years.

You do not have to be a genius to get a PhD, but you will have to be diligent. The PhD degree gives the holder the title Doctor, but not as a medical doctor. That is why some people ask to be referred to as 'Dr. Smith', for example, though they are not medical doctors. They are referring to their PhDs.

Chapter 32

English Grammar & Use

Interviews
Meetings with College Staff
Essays

For conversations with college staff and for interviews, please note these suggestions regarding English use. For essays, see pages 307-308.

Um, Um, Well, Hmm, Uh, Uh, Um. . .

In conversation, when pausing to think for several seconds about an answer, do so, but remain silent. Do not say "Um, Um, Well, let me think about that. Um. Hmm. Ummm." Practice this: Just pause, (without saying anything) think for a bit, then answer. This looks thoughtful and dignified.

Don't Repeat Yourself Too Much

Do you use the same phrases and words repeatedly, to the point of annoying overuse? Some examples are:
"Actually, ..."
"You know what I mean?"
"You know what I'm saying?"
"Like, ..."
"What you need to understand is ...."
No one phrase is wrong a few times. But over and over and over? For an hour? If you have that habit, force yourself to stop using the one phrase after several times. Add to your inventory of phrases, with "Certainly," "Very well," and others. Mix it up. Limit the dramatic "Absolutely" to a few times only; "Yes" will do in most cases.

"Between You and Me" is Correct

The correct grammar is: "Between you and me, he's silly."
not

"Between you and I, he's silly" which is incorrect.
"I" is a subject of a sentence. The word "between" makes a pronoun an object, thus "me" is correct, not "I".

Here is a way to remember this:

Between you and me, it is wrong to say "Between you and I."

Other variations of this mistake are:

"You and me should go" is wrong.
"You and I should go" is correct.

To check it, make it singular. Thus, "Me should go" is wrong.

"He gave my sister and I the tickets" is wrong.
"He gave my sister and me the tickets" is correct.

To check it, make it singular. Thus, "He gave I the tickets" is wrong.

Thank you   You're welcome

When someone says the correct response is	"Thank you"; "You're welcome."
When someone says it is incorrect to say	"Thank you"; "Thank you" back to them.

You are not properly acknowledging their expression of thanks, which you do with "You're welcome" not "Thank you." This is a very common error, but if you don't commit the same error, you sound more refined. Use "You're welcome." To express thanks in return, first acknowledge their thanks with "You're certainly welcome." Then thank them with "Thank you for your time as well."

Yes   and   No

Say - "Yes." or "Yes. That would be fine."

NOT - "Yeah." "OK." "Sure." "Sure thing." "No worries."
"No problem." "You bet." "You got it." or "Uh huh."

Say - "No." or "No, thank you,"

NOT - "Nah." "Nope." "No Way." or "Not a chance."

I Don't Know

If you don't know something, look straight at the person and say: "I don't know," in a firm, steady, dignified tone. And that's it.

Not knowing something *is not an error*, it is a fact, to be conveyed authoritatively without any apology. When you don't know something, do not stammer, or say you are sorry or have an apologetic tone. Do not add multiple qualifiers such as: "I'm not sure about that. I didn't think to find that out earlier," et cetera, which wastes time. Don't speculate about the correct answer ("Maybe it's this, but it could be...."), which wastes time.

You may add "I can check further, if needed." Then stop talking. Let the other person move the conversation forward. No one knows every fact, so say in a direct tone, "I don't know." You then sound authoritative even when you don't know something.

Have You Done That Yet?   No, I Haven't

The same concept applies to the question, "Have you done that yet?" Whatever it's about, if you haven't done it yet, just say "No," or "No, I haven't," or "No. I will get to that," and leave it at that.

If it is not an error on your part, but something that you will finish later within a proper deadline or timetable, then do not say, "I'm sorry," and go on and on in an apologetic tone about how and when you will get to it as soon as you can. Rather, say firmly, "No, not yet." Then let the person move to the next topic. You will sound like you are on top of things, which you are.

Do Not Say "Sorry" When You Have Not Made an Error or Omission, Or When Someone Doesn't Need Any Sympathy

In an effort to be polite, many people overuse "I'm sorry."

The use of "sorry" is appropriate in two types of human interaction. First, to express sympathy. If he or she totaled the car, it works to say "I'm sorry to hear that." Secondly, for an apology when you have made an error. Many people, however, overuse "sorry" beyond these two cases.

People create an image that they are bumbling and error prone when they say sorry but have not made one single error. They apologize when the *other* person is walking on the wrong side of the hallway. They apologize for things that are out of their control, for things unrelated to them. They apologize if the *other* person is late. Don't say "I'm so sorry your plane was late," which had nothing to do with you. Instead, say "I'm glad you made it," then get to the subject at hand.

May I?

Use "May I?" as a main phrase with interaction with others. "May I?" asks for permission on equal footing with others, showing that you respect them, while at the same time, you are not unduly subservient to them. When, for example, you step into an elevator that has several people in it, say, "May I?" to get them to move over, not "Sorry." It is not your error that some people are in the elevator, so don't apologize.

When you reach near someone to get a pen in a meeting room, say "May I?" not "Sorry." You are not in error when you reach for something that has been provided for you, and the person who sees you reach over doesn't require sympathy, so do not say "Sorry," when getting the pen.

Here are two people, who are overly polite and sound like, well, wimps.

"Oh, the coffee counter doesn't have stevia."
"I'm sorry."
"Oh, don't be sorry. That's not your fault."
"Oh, maybe, but sorry about that."
"No, really, I'm sorry."
"OK, sorry."
"OK, sorry."

Knock it off with all the apologies. Get "sorry, sorry, sorry" out of your speech patterns, if that's you. Project an image that you are on top of things, by not being sorry for every rain drop that falls.

Finally, you are not really being polite. Politeness is at its root a two-way street, whereby each party shows respect to the other. When you say you are sorry for things that are not errors on your part, or when the other person doesn't need sympathy (like someone on the elevator) you waste the other person's time, which is not polite.

Know About Words that are Often Misused

For essays and for spoken English, look up lists of common grammar mistakes and commonly misused words. One source, The Glossary of Troublesome Expressions in The Chicago Manual of Style has about 25 pages of proper uses to learn, hundreds of them, all helpful, and fun. Often, the common use differs from traditional use or meaning. Some people prefer the traditional use. Here's why students should know about these cases:

People who prefer (and notice) the traditional use may include:

1. people who read your college essay,
2. college staff you meet at events or in an interview,
3. teachers who will grade your work in high school,
4. professors who will grade your work in college, and
5. hiring managers.

In addition, many times the original meaning and use will be intended in articles, books and in lectures, so you should understand both the original use and the common misuse. Use the original meaning and use to avoid being viewed as one who uses incorrect English (written or spoken), or avoid the word or phrase to play it safe.

Here are few examples to get you started.

bring or **take**   You *take* the thing there, but *bring* it here.

connect and **disconnect**   These are traditionally verbs, not nouns. The noun *disconnection* is commonly now shortened to *disconnect*, which many people have adopted as being cleverly edgy, but it isn't correct (or that clever). Do you have a *connection* to a friend, or a *connect* to a friend? The noun *connection* is correct. Likewise, a *disconnect* from a friend isn't regular English. Use *disconnection*, the correct form of the noun.

data   *Data* (multiple pieces of information) is the plural of a datum (a piece of information). *Data* is now used often in singular form, and accepted by dictionaries as allowable, while still meaning multiple pieces of information, such as "The data is overwhelming." English traditionalists will use *data* as a plural word, such as "The data are overwhelming," which is correct.

disinterested   A common misuse of *disinterested* is to be "not interested in" or "not paying attention" to a topic, i.e. uninterested. Some dictionaries now accept this as a definition. The word, however, by traditional English is supposed to mean fair, objective, and unbiased, i.e., based on fact, not opinion. The word is *not* to mean uninterested, as if one did not care. For a professor, use the original meaning, but for a general audience, some readers will think you mean uninterested, and they will not understand the sentence correctly. To avoid confusion, use unbiased or uninterested, as is appropriate.

lay or **lie**   Did this get covered in class? If not, look it up.

myriad   This is in common use as a noun as in "a myriad (large number) of reasons," but the original use was only as a descriptive word, as in, "there are myriad (many) reasons." To be safe, don't use myriad as a noun.

since or **because**   *Since* is sometimes used incorrectly as if it <u>only</u> means *because* or *thus*, but *since* should have a time element to the cause-and-effect. "Since the last storm, he stored sandbags" is correct as it has a time element. "Since he is careful, he stored sandbags" is not correct, as there is no time element. "Because he is careful, he stored sandbags" is correct.

whom   *Whom* gets a little tricky, so look it up. It is noticeable when *whom* is skipped for a lazier *who*. It's also noticeable when it's used in the wrong spot. For example, "Give water to whomever wants some" is incorrect. If unsure, rework the sentence. It's great to use *whom* when you get it right, including in conversation. Here's one correct use I like: "Whom should I call?" I mean, doesn't it irk you too, when someone says, "Who should I call?" Yes, students, *whom* is still often used, so get on board.

Chapter 33

50 States, D.C. & 5 U.S. Territories: Application & Information Websites

Websites were compiled in 2017
and are subject to change.

State College Systems:

The state systems are listed for application links to four-year state colleges, general college planning, financial aid and community colleges. Some sites have links to private colleges in that state. For state financial aid programs, a site that links to all 50 states and 5 territories is:

www.nasfaa.org - on the top, select Students, Parents and Counselors, then on the left, select Financial Aid in Your State.

State Systems with Shared Applications

Nine state college systems have their own type of joint application online. You may apply to multiple colleges without repeating the data entry each time. These include:

Alaska	California	Texas	Maine	Minnesota
New York	Pennsylvania	South Carolina	Wisconsin	

Alaska

University of Alaska System (3 colleges)

    www.alaska.edu/alaska   Select: Campuses

California

California State University System (23 colleges)

    www.calstate.edu

University of California System (10 colleges)

    www.UniversityOfCalifornia.edu

Texas

University of Texas System (8 colleges)

Texas A & M System (8 colleges)

University of Houston System (4 colleges)

   All use: www.ApplyTexas.org

An additional 41 public and private four-year colleges use www.ApplyTexas.org; including Baylor, University of Dallas, Southern Methodist University and Texas Tech University, and an additional 74 community colleges.

   See also www.CollegeForAllTexans.com

Maine

University of Maine System (7 colleges)   www.maine.edu

Minnesota

Minnesota State Colleges and Universities (7 colleges)   www.mnscu.edu
   Does not include University of Minnesota. 24 state community colleges and technical colleges also use the same application account.

New York

State University of New York (37 colleges)   www.suny.edu
   In addition, has 27 community colleges.

City University of New York (11 colleges)   www2.cuny.edu
   CUNY allows up to 6 applications. Also, has 7 community colleges.

Pennsylvania

Pennsylvania's State System of Higher Education (14 colleges)

   www.passhe.edu

      The application portal does not include public Pennsylvania State University or private University of Pennsylvania.

South Carolina

University of South Carolina System (8 colleges)

   www.southcarolina.edu

Wisconsin

University of Wisconsin System (13 colleges)

   www.wisconsin.edu   Includes 13 community colleges.

State System Websites with Links but with Separate Applications

Some states and territories provide a website with links to colleges, but each college still has its own separate application. Some colleges link to the Black College App, Common App, Universal App or Coalition App. These states, the District of Columbia and territories include:

Alabama
The University of Alabama System (3 colleges) www.uasystem.ua.edu

American Samoa
American Samoa Community College (1 college)   www.amsamoa.edu

Arizona
Arizona Board of Regents (3 colleges) www.azregents.edu

Arkansas
Arkansas Department of Higher Education (11 colleges)

www.adhe.edu

Select: Students & Parents; Arkansas Colleges & Universities - includes links to 12 private colleges and 22 two-year colleges

Colorado
Colorado Department of Higher Education (13 colleges)

https://highered.colorado.gov   Select: Students & Parents; Colleges & Universities; Public Institutions; Four-Year Institutions

Connecticut
Connecticut State Colleges & Universities (5 colleges)   www.ct.edu/cscu

Delaware
University of Delaware (1 college)   www.udel.edu

Delaware Department of Education's Higher Education Office
www.DelawareGoesToCollege.org
Contains college information and links to area colleges.

Florida
State University System of Florida (12 colleges)   www.flbog.edu

From top of page, select Universities; University Home Page (or) Admissions-Undergraduate.

Georgia
University System of Georgia (29 colleges)   www.usg.edu

https://www.gafutures.org (62 public and private colleges)

Select college planning; explore schools; search for colleges; view schools to reach application links.

Guam
University of Guam (1 college)   www.uog.edu

Hawaii
University of Hawaii System (3 colleges)　　www.hawaii.edu
Idaho
Idaho State Board of Education (4 colleges, 4 community colleges)
　　https://nextsteps.idaho.gov/schools/
　　　or　http://www.idaho.gov/education/colleges-universities/
　　　　Has Idaho Scholarships,
　　　　Public Higher Education
　　　　and Private Higher Education.
Illinois
Illinois Board of Higher Education (12 colleges)　http://www.ibhe.org/
　　Select: Colleges & Universities; Public Universities
Indiana
Indiana Commission for Higher Education (16 colleges)
　　secure.in.gov/che/index.htm　(Make sure screen is wide enough to show links in a left column. Scroll to the bottom, left, and select either College Profiles or College Portraits for links.
Iowa
State of Iowa Board of Regents (3 colleges)　　　www.regents.iowa.gov
Kansas
Kansas Board of Regents (8 colleges)　　　www.KansasRegents.org
Kentucky
Kentucky Council on Postsecondary Education (9 colleges) www.cpe.ky.gov
Louisiana
University of Louisiana System (9 colleges)　　　www.ulsystem.edu
Maryland
University System of Maryland (12 colleges)　　　www.usmd.edu
Massachusetts
University of Massachusetts System (4 colleges)　www.massachusetts.edu
Michigan
For links to 15 public universities, see the Michigan Economic Development Corp. (MEDC) website at: www.MichiganBusiness.org/universities-and-colleges-partners
　　On the MEDC home page, select: About MEDC; Partners; scroll down to the　bottom to Colleges and Universities, to "15 public universities."
Mississippi
Mississippi Public Universities (8 colleges)　　　www.mississippi.edu
Missouri
Missouri Department of Higher Education (13 colleges)https://dhe.mo.gov/
Montana
Montana University System (5 colleges)　　　www.mus.edu

Nebraska
Nebraska State College System (3 colleges)   http://www.nscs.edu/
& University of Nebraska (3 colleges & 1 medical center)
   https://nebraska.edu/

Nevada.
Nevada System of Higher Education (5 colleges)
   system.nevada.edu/Nshe   Select: NHSE Institutions

New Hampshire
University System of New Hampshire (4 colleges)   www.usnh.edu

New Jersey
State of New Jersey Office of the Secretary of Higher Education (11 colleges)
   http://www.state.nj.us/highereducation/
   Select: NJ Colleges and Universities; by Sector; sorts first by public colleges and
universities, then scroll down for private colleges and universities

New Mexico
New Mexico Higher Education Department (7 colleges) www.hed.state.nm.us
   Select: Students & Parents; Find a College or University

North Carolina
University of North Carolina System (16 colleges) www.northcarolina.edu

North Dakota
North Dakota University System (6 colleges)   www.ndus.edu
   Select: Colleges and Universities, see below the map for selections to links.

Northern Marianas
Northern Marianas College (1 college)   www.marianas.edu

Ohio
University System of Ohio/Dept. of Higher Education (14 colleges)
   www.ohiohighered.org (also has 23 community colleges)
   Select: Students; Ohio's Campuses;
   Ohio's Public Institutions - Interactive Campus Map. Scroll down below the
   map to links to 14 public colleges. See 136 private college links from the
   previous page (Ohio's Campuses; Independent Colleges & Universities).

Oklahoma
Oklahoma State Regents for Higher Education   www.okhighered.org
   49 public 2-year & 4-year colleges & 18 private colleges
   See also: www.okcollegestart.org

Oregon
Oregon Higher Education Coordinating Commission (7 colleges)
   www.oregon.gov/highered - Look in the middle for Student Opportunities;
Find Colleges and Programs; has links to 17 community colleges and 49 private
colleges and trade schools

Puerto Rico
University of Puerto Rico (11 colleges)   www.upr.edu

Rhode Island

Rhode Island Board of Governors for Higher Education (2 colleges)
https://www.riopc.edu/ Select: For Students & Families, Exploring URI, RIC, and CCRI

South Dakota

South Dakota Board of Regents (6 colleges)   www.sdbor.edu
On the map, click college name for a link.

Tennessee

University of Tennessee System (3 colleges)   www.tennessee.edu

Utah

Utah System of Higher Education (6 colleges) www.higheredutah.org
Scroll to bottom of page for links.

Vermont

Vermont State Colleges (4 colleges)   www.vsc.edu &

University of Vermont   www.uvm.edu

Virgin Islands (U.S.)

University of the Virgin Islands (2 colleges)   www.uvi.edu

Virginia

State Council of Higher Education for Virginia (15 colleges)
www.schev.edu

Washington

Washington Student Achievement Council (8 colleges)
http://www.wsac.wa.gov/college-admissions
See Community and Technical Colleges or Baccalaureate Institutions and then scroll down to links to public college freshman information (or)
University of Washington Dream Project
www.washington.edu/dreamproject/students/wa-colleges

Washington, District of Columbia

University of the District of Columbia (1 college)   www.udc.edu
The site also, has District of Columbia Community College.

West Virginia

West Virginia Higher Education Policy Commission (13 colleges)
www.wvhepc.edu

Wyoming

Wyoming Department of Education (1 college) www.edu.wyoming.gov
Scroll to the bottom of the page to Wyoming Links and select either University of Wyoming or for 7 community colleges, select Wyoming Community Colleges.

☞ Appendix ✍

A Sample U.S. National Selective College Admissions Pool

A Pool of 120 Colleges
Small and Large Mixed Together
With 81 Private Colleges and 39 Public Colleges

Explanation of Selection of 120 Colleges and Notes on Statistical Tables for Admissions

On page 204,

120 colleges are totaled cumulatively for admissions, with further breakdown totals included for:

50 top colleges (42 private and 8 public) - Table A-1 (pp. 318-319)

50 more colleges (39 private and 11 public) - Table A-2 (pp. 320-321)

20 more public colleges - Table A-3 (p. 322)

Table A-4 - A National Selective Admissions Pool - Totals for 120 Colleges Tables A-1, A-2, A-3 2016 Fall Enrollments	Yield Rate	Number of Applications	Admit Rate	Acceptance Letters Sent	Total Enrolled	Yes Letters Tossed	ACT Composite 25%-75%
50 Colleges - Table A-1	46%	1,179,602	17%	199,707	91,249	108,458	30-34
50 Colleges - Table A-2	23%	1,173,776	35%	414,498	96,722	317,774	28-32
Totals for 100 Colleges	31%	2,353,378	26%	614,205	187,971	426,232	29-33
20 More Public Colleges Table A-3	29%	719,267	58%	415,953	120,448	295,505	25-30
Totals for 120 Colleges	30%	3,072,645	34%	1,030,158	308,419	721,737	29-33*

Source: Admissions, Fall 2016, (as of 9-20-17) College Navigator, U.S. Dept. of Education.

* The ACT average for 120 colleges is the average for all 120 colleges, not an average of the ranges for the three tables. ACT avg. scores for 100 Colleges are 29.28-32.93 - for the 20 More Public are 25.30-33.40 - for Totals for 120 are 28.62-32.51, so we see a drop in the average from the 100 total to the 120 total, (-.66 to -.42) but when rounding as the ACT does, the rounded avg. remains at 29-33 for the 120 colleges. This totaling method does not weight each college's scores by enrollment, which statistician readers are free to submit to www.starterguide.org upon completion.

The percentage averages for yield rate and admit rate are calculated for each group by the totals for the categories to all colleges in each group cumulatively, not as an average of each college's separate rate.

A Pool of 120 Colleges (Small and Large Mixed Together)

The 120 colleges were selected as a broad representation of the national pool of selective colleges and applicants. Some very small colleges and some very large colleges were included in the same national pool on purpose to provide a broad general pool.

This list is not based on any detailed analysis of academic measurements, as is purported to be done by traditional rankings. This is not a compilation of other rankings. The traditional rankings were not consulted to select the colleges, but rather a wide variety of colleges with high academics (as shown by the higher test scores of enrollees), lower admission rates, (generally 50% or less) and higher admissions yield rates were selected. By including many small colleges, some excellent larger colleges were left out of the 120. By including many very large colleges, some excellent smaller colleges were left out of the 120.

The Colleges are Listed in Order of the Yield Rate

The colleges are not ranked in a systematic way, other than being sorted in order of the admissions yield rate, which is an inexact measurement of the desirability, so to speak, of a certain college.

The yield rate is the percentage of how many applicants enrolled out of all who were sent acceptance letters. Thus, a higher yield rate shows that more students do want to attend a certain college, but remember, that's for various reasons, not just aiming for the highest academics.

Colleges are Selected by Applicants for Many Reasons, So High Yield Rates are Also at Other Colleges Not on the List

Some other colleges have very high yield rates due to the motivations of the applicants to attend those colleges and such colleges are not included among the 120 colleges.

These factors include local preferences and in-state tuition, which can increase the yield rate for a state college, such as the University of Alaska at Fairbanks or the University of Nevada at Las Vegas which have high yield rates, but are not on this book's list.

This includes colleges with high yield rates that are desirable for religious reasons of applicants as well as the good academics of a college, such as Brigham Young University, Liberty University, North Central University, and Yeshiva University which are not on the list.

The U.S. military academies have high yield rates, as many applicants to each of them are highly motivated to attend if accepted. Some specialized colleges such as music and art academies have high yield rates. Colleges with a special mission, such as Berea and College of the Ozarks, also have high yield rates.

Thus, some colleges that are very beneficial institutions to attend, with very high yield rates, are not included in this general national pool for a broad audience of readers.

ACT Test Scores Indicate Academic Levels, but Some Colleges Are Test Optional

The listing of ACT test scores is for ease of comparison for readers, and doesn't indicate that ACT scores are recommended or that SAT test scores are not recommended or accepted. The SAT test is also good for all colleges.

Some colleges do not require test scores, thus do not report test scores for the College Navigator site. Those colleges have an Optional notation (Opt.), along with ACT scores, taken from either a college website or the Common Data Set as a comparison point for readers. These colleges, however, do not require a test score to apply and students may note those colleges for this reason.

The 120 colleges in this book's grouping was designed to include the selective small colleges so the mix was national, large and small, but also with 20 additional great public colleges; all in one statistical total.

Other published lists of 50 colleges might include only larger colleges, thus more openings would be available in such a group of only larger colleges.

These 20 public colleges, and others like them, have a huge number of academically strong students, as shown by high test scores. These 20 colleges offer challenging work for those who seek it, along with extra options available at honors colleges. Thus, the additional 20 public colleges show readers an expanded pool of opportunity.

Note that 19 other public colleges are in the first 100 for a total of 39 public colleges that offer lower in-state tuition to students who live in those states.

Table A-1 - 50 Selective Colleges 2016 - In Order of Yield Rate (% of accepted students who enrolled)	Yield Rate	Number of Applications	Admit Rate	Accept -ance Letters Sent	Total Enrolled	Yes Letters Tossed	ACT Comp. 25%-75%
Stanford University (CA)	82%	43,997	5%	2,200	1,804	396	31-35
Harvard College (MA)	79%	39,041	5%	1,952	1,542	410	32-35
Mass. Inst. of Tech.	73%	19,020	8%	1,522	1,111	411	33-35
Yale University (CT)	69%	31,445	6%	1,887	1,302	585	32-35
Princeton University (NJ)	68%	29,303	7%	2,051	1,395	656	32-35
University of Pennsylvania	68%	38,918	9%	3,503	2,382	1,121	32-35
University of Chicago (IL)	64%	31,484	8%	2,519	1,612	907	32-35
Columbia University in NY	62%	37,009	7%	2,591	1,606	984	32-35
Brown University (RI)	56%	32,390	9%	2,915	1,632	1,283	31-34
Univ. of Notre Dame (IN)	56%	19,505	19%	3,706	2,075	1,631	32-35
Claremont McKenna (CA)	54%	6,342	9%	571	308	263	31-33
Pomona College (CA)	54%	8,102	9%	729	394	335	31-34
Northwestern Univ. (IL)	53%	35,100	11%	3,861	2,046	1,815	32-34
Cornell University (NY)	52%	44,965	14%	6,295	3,273	3,022	31-34
Barnard College (NY)	51%	7,071	17%	1,202	613	589	29-33
Dartmouth College (NH)	51%	20,675	11%	2,274	1,160	1,114	30-34
Bowdoin College	50%	6,799	15%	1,020	510	510	Opt. 30-34
Duke University (NC)	50%	31,671	11%	3,484	1,742	1,742	31-34
University of Florida	49%	30,118	46%	13,854	6,789	7,066	27-31
Georgetown Univ. (DC)	47%	19,997	17%	3,399	1,598	1,802	30-34
Pitzer College (CA)	47%	4,142	14%	580	273	307	Opt. 29-32
Tufts University (MA)	46%	20,223	14%	2,831	1,302	1,529	31-34
Vanderbilt University (TN)	46%	32,442	11%	3,569	1,642	1,927	32-35
Davidson College (NC)	45%	5,618	20%	1,124	506	618	28-33
Univ. of North Carolina	45%	34,889	27%	9,420	4,239	5,181	28-33
University of Texas-Austin	45%	47,511	40%	19,004	8,552	10,452	26-32
Williams College (MA)	45%	6,985	18%	1,257	566	692	31-34
Univ. of California-Berkeley	44%	82,561	17%	14,035	6,175	7,860	31-34
Middlebury College (VT)	43%	8,819	16%	1,411	607	804	30-33
Wellesley College (MA)	43%	4,854	29%	1,408	605	802	30-33
Calif. Inst. of Technology	42%	6,855	8%	548	230	318	34-36
Colorado College	42%	7,894	16%	1,263	530	733	Opt. 28-32
Swarthmore College (PA)	42%	7,717	13%	1,003	421	582	30-34
Univ. of Michigan-Ann Arbor	42%	55,504	29%	16,096	6,760	9,336	29-33
Amherst College (MA)	41%	8,396	14%	1,175	482	694	31-34
Bates College (ME)	40%	5,356	23%	1,232	493	739	Opt. 27-32
Harvey Mudd College (CA)	40%	4,180	13%	543	217	326	32-35
Haverford College (PA)	40%	4,066	21%	854	342	512	31-34

Table A-1 - (Continued) 50 Selective Colleges 2016 In Order of Yield Rate (% of accepted students who enrolled)	Yield Rate	Number of Applications	Admit Rate	Accept-ance Letters Sent	Total Enrolled	Yes Letters Tossed	ACT Comp. 25%-75%
Carleton College (MN)	39%	6,485	23%	1,492	582	910	30-33
Washington & Lee Univ. (VA)	39%	5,101	24%	1,224	477	747	30-33
Johns Hopkins Univ. (MD)	38%	27,852	13%	3,621	1,376	2,245	32-34
University of Virginia	38%	32,377	30%	9,713	3,691	6,022	29-33
Georgia Inst. of Technology	37%	30,528	26%	7,937	2,937	5,000	30-34
University of California-LA	37%	97,112	18%	17,480	6,468	11,013	28-33
Washington U.-St. Louis, MO	37%	29,197	17%	4,963	1,836	3,127	32-34
Lehigh University (PA)	36%	13,403	26%	3,485	1,255	2,230	29-32
Wesleyan University (CT)	36%	11,928	18%	2,147	773	1,374	Opt. 29-33
Hamilton College (NY)	35%	5,230	26%	1,360	476	884	31-33
Rice University (TX)	35%	18,236	15%	2,735	957	1,778	32-35
Carnegie Mellon Univ. (PA)	34%	21,189	22%	4,662	1,585	3,077	31-34
Totals for 50 in Table A-1	46%	1,179,602	17%	199,707	91,249	108,458	30-34

Source: Admissions, Fall 2016, (as of 9-20-17)
College Navigator, U.S. Dept. of Education.
Public Colleges are in italics.

The ACT Composite score is the score range of the incoming class of students for the 25th percentile to the 75th percentile.

The notation Opt. (Optional) in the ACT Composite column indicates that test scores may be optional at that college for admissions. For colleges that did not report ACT scores to the U.S. Department of Education, the ACT composite score range came from the Common Data Set or the college website.

Table A-2 50 More Selective Colleges 2016 In order of Yield Rate (% of accepted students who enrolled)	Yield Rate	Number of Applications	Admit Rate	Acceptance Letters Sent	Total Enrolled	Yes Letters Tossed	ACT Comp 25%-75%
Univ. of Southern California	34%	54,280	17%	9,228	3,137	6,090	30-33
Vassar College (NY)	34%	7,306	27%	1,242	422	820	30-33
Colgate University (NY)	32%	8,394	29%	2,434	779	1,655	30-33
New York University	32%	60,724	32%	19,432	6,218	13,214	29-33
Oberlin College (OH)	32%	8,518	28%	2,385	763	1,622	29-33
Babson College (MA)	31%	7,648	25%	1,912	593	1,319	27-31
Clemson University (GA)	31%	23,506	51%	11,988	3,716	8,272	26-31
University of Maryland	31%	30,291	48%	14,540	4,507	10,032	29-33
Wake Forest Univ. (NC)	31%	14,006	30%	4,202	1,303	2,899	Opt. 28-32
Bucknell University (PA)	30%	10,487	30%	3,146	944	2,202	28-32
Scripps College (CA)	30%	3,022	30%	907	272	635	28-32
College of William & Mary (VA)	29%	14,382	37%	5,321	1,543	3,778	28-33
Kenyon College (OH)	29%	6,403	27%	1,729	501	1,227	29-33
Colby College (ME)	28%	9,833	19%	1,868	523	1,345	30-33
Grinnell College (IA)	28%	7,370	20%	1,474	413	1,061	30-33
Lafayette College (PA)	28%	8,123	28%	2,274	637	1,638	27-31
Trinity College (CT)	28%	6,073	34%	2,065	578	1,487	Opt. 28-32
Emory University (GA)	27%	19,924	25%	4,981	1,345	3,636	30-33
Skidmore College (NY)	27%	9,181	29%	2,662	719	1,944	26-30
University of Minnesota	27%	49,129	44%	21,617	5,837	15,780	26-31
Boston College (MA)	26%	28,956	31%	8,976	2,334	6,643	30-33
Baylor University (TX)	25%	34,636	40%	13,854	3,464	10,391	26-30
Franklin & Marshall Coll. (PA)	25%	6,953	36%	2,503	626	1,877	Opt. 28-31
George Washington Univ.	25%	25,488	40%	10,195	2,549	7,646	27-32
Stevens Inst. of Tech. (NJ)	25%	7,409	39%	2,890	722	2,167	29-33
University of Richmond (VA)	24%	10,422	32%	3,335	800	2,535	29-32
University of Rochester (NY)	24%	17,485	36%	6,295	1,511	4,784	Opt. 29-33
University of Tulsa (OK)	24%	8,089	37%	2,993	718	2,275	26-33
Macalester College (MN)	23%	5,946	37%	2,200	506	1,694	29-33
Southern Methodist Univ. (TX)	23%	13,250	49%	6,493	1,493	4,999	28-32
Tulane Univ. of Louisiana	23%	32,006	26%	8,322	1,914	6,408	29-32
Union College (NY)	23%	6,648	37%	2,460	566	1,894	Opt. 28-31
Baruch College - CUNY	22%	20,789	31%	6,445	1,418	5,027	25-29*
Brandeis University (MA)	22%	11,351	33%	3,746	824	2,922	29-33
Villanova University (PA)	22%	17,272	44%	7,600	1,672	5,928	30-32
Worcester Polytechnic (MA)	22%	10,468	48%	5,025	1,105	3,919	Opt. 28-32
Binghamton Univ.- SUNY	21%	32,139	41%	13,177	2,767	10,410	28-31
Boston University (MA)	21%	57,441	29%	16,658	3,498	13,160	28-32

Table A-2 (Continued) 50 More Selective Colleges 2016 In order of Yield Rate (% of accepted students who enrolled)	Yield Rate	Number of Applications	Admit Rate	Accept-ance Letters Sent	Total Enrolled	Yes Letters Tossed	ACT Comp. 25%-75%
Rensselaer Polytechnic (NY)	21%	18,524	44%	8,151	1,712	6,439	28-32
Univ. of California - Irvine	21%	77,816	41%	31,905	6,700	25,205	24-30
Colorado School of Mines	20%	12,284	40%	4,914	983	3,931	29-32
Reed College (OR)	20%	5,705	31%	1,769	354	1,415	29-33
Univ. of California-Davis	20%	68,553	42%	28,792	5,758	23,034	25-31
Univ. of Calif. - San Diego	19%	84,208	36%	30,315	5,760	24,555	27-33
Northeastern Univ. (MA)	18%	51,063	29%	14,808	2,665	12,143	31-34
Pepperdine University	18%	11,111	37%	4,111	740	3,371	26-31
Univ. of Calif.-Santa Barbara	18%	77,112	36%	27,760	4,997	22,763	27-32
Occidental College (CA)	17%	6,409	46%	2,948	501	2,447	28-31
University of Miami (FL)	17%	32,528	38%	12,361	2,101	10,259	28-32
Case Western Reserve (OH)	15%	23,115	35%	8,090	1,214	6,877	30-34
Total 50 in Table A-2	23%	1,173,776	35%	414,498	96,722	317,774	28-32

Source: Admissions, Fall 2016, (as of 9-20-17)
College Navigator, U.S. Dept. of Education.

Public Colleges are in italics.

The ACT Composite score is the score range of the incoming class of
students for the 25th percentile to the 75th percentile.
The notation "Opt." (Optional) in the ACT Composite column indicates
that test scores may be optional at that college for admissions. For colleges that did not report ACT
scores to the U.S. Department of Education, the ACT composite score range came from the Common
Data Set or the college website.

*The ACT test score range for Baruch College –CUNY is an estimate based on the
reported SAT test score range in the Common Data Set, using conversion tables provided
by the test companies on their websites.

Table A-3 20 More Selective Public Colleges 2016 In order of Yield Rate (% of accepted students who enrolled)	Yield Rate	Number of Applications	Admit Rate	Yes Letters Sent	Total Enrolled	Yes Letters Tossed	ACT Composite 25%-75%
University of Georgia	44%	22,694	54%	12,255	5,392	6,863	26-31
Texas A & M University	43%	34,780	67%	23,303	10,020	13,282	24-30
University of Wisconsin	37%	32,839	53%	17,405	6,440	10,965	27-31
Florida State University	37%	29,027	58%	16,836	6,229	10,606	25-29
North Carolina State	35%	26,451	48%	12,696	4,444	8,253	26-31
Ohio State University	33%	44,845	54%	24,216	7,991	16,225	27-31
University of Washington	33%	43,517	45%	19,583	6,462	13,120	26-32
University of Illinois	33%	38,093	60%	22,856	7,542	15,313	26-32
Rutgers University (NJ)	31%	36,677	57%	20,906	6,481	14,425	24-30
University of South Carolina	30%	25,057	68%	17,039	5,112	11,927	25-30
Indiana University	29%	34,646	79%	27,370	7,937	19,433	24-30
Pennsylvania State Univ.	28%	52,974	56%	29,665	8,306	21,359	25-29
Purdue University (IN)	27%	49,007	56%	27,444	7,410	20,034	25-31
University of Delaware	26%	24,456	70%	17,119	4,451	12,668	24-29
University of Colorado	25%	34,047	77%	26,216	6,554	19,662	25-30
University of Pittsburgh	24%	29,175	55%	16,046	3,851	12,195	27-32
University of Connecticut	22%	35,980	49%	17,630	3,879	13,752	26-31
Stony Brook University (NY)	21%	34,999	41%	14,350	3,013	11,336	26-31
University of Mass. - Amherst	19%	40,822	60%	24,493	4,654	19,839	25-30
Univ. of California - Santa Cruz	15%	49,181	58%	28,525	4,279	24,246	25-30
Totals for 20 in Table A-3	**29%**	**719,267**	**58%**	**415,953**	**120,448**	**295,505**	**25-30**

Source: Admissions, Fall 2016, (as of 9-20-17), College Navigator, U.S. Dept. of Education. The ACT Composite score is the score range of the incoming class of students for the 25th percentile to the 75th percentile. These 20 public colleges are those with higher test scores and higher admissions yield rates.

Table B:
What's the National Picture?
Out of _All_ U.S.
Undergraduate Students,
At the Larger Top 40 Colleges,
Who Attends?
3%.

U.S. Total Undergraduate Students
& Selective College Percentage (2015)[47]

Undergraduate College Category	Enrollment	Ratio
All Colleges: 4-Year, 2-Year & Trade	18,600,000	100.0%
All 4-Year Colleges	10,745,000	58.0%
40 Top Larger Selective Colleges	581,000	3.1%
15 Top Larger Selective Colleges	139,000	0.7%
Ivy League (8 Colleges)	62,000	0.3%

Out of all U.S. undergraduates, which includes every student at every trade school, community college, private college and state college (about 2,000 colleges), only about 3% attend 40 of the top colleges. Those in the Ivy League are only 1/3 of 1% of all students who attend any type of college in the United States.

Colleges used in the table above are listed on the next page in Table C (p. 324).

Appendix

Table C -Enrollment 40 Larger Selective Colleges (Alphabetical)	
The author's top 40, top 15 and Ivy League enrollment figures used in Table B came from the U.S. Government College Scorecard undergraduate enrollment figures for each college from the College Scorecard web site (www.collegescorecard.ed.gov) as of 11-7-2016, or from the 2016-17 Common Data Set. Selected subjectively by the author as general examples of selective college enrollments to compare to national totals.	

	Larger Selective Colleges (undergraduate)	Enrollment
1	Boston University	16,457
2	Brown University	6,264
3	Carnegie Mellon University	5,819
4	Columbia University	8,100
5	Cornell University	14,195
6	Dartmouth College	4,815
7	Duke University	6,480
8	Georgetown University	7,211
9	Georgia Institute of Technology	13,996
10	Harvard College	7,236
11	Johns Hopkins University	6,039
12	Lehigh University	5,080
13	Massachusetts Institute of Technology	4,476
14	New York University	24,539
15	Northwestern University	8,725
	15 Larger Selective Colleges Total Enrollment	**139,432**
16	Princeton University	5,258
17	Rice University	3,888
18	Stanford University	7,018
19	Tufts University	5,508
20	University of California at Berkeley	27,126
21	University of California at Davis	27,547
22	University of California at Irvine	24,474
23	University of California at Los Angeles	29,627
24	University of California at San Diego	24,801
25	University of Chicago	5,729
26	University of Illinois	31,875
27	University of Maryland	26,532
28	University of Michigan	28,217
29	University of North Carolina	17,908
30	University of Notre Dame	8,427
31	University of Pennsylvania	10,678
32	University of Southern California	18,392
33	University of Texas	38,914
34	University of Virginia	15,515
35	University of Washington	29,468
36	University of Wisconsin	29,302
37	Vanderbilt University	6,818
38	Washington University in St. Louis	6,913
39	William and Mary	6,276
40	Yale College	5,473
	40 Larger Selective Colleges Total Enrollment	**581,116**

Brown	6,264	Harvard	7,236
Columbia	8,100	Pennsylvania	10,678
Cornell	14,195	Princeton	5,258
Dartmouth	4,815	Yale	5,473
Total Ivy League Undergraduate Enrollment			62,019

Ivy League Admissions Yield Rate From U.S. Dept. Of Education, College Navigator, Undergraduate Admissions, Fall 2016		Ivy League Net Price for Low-Income Applicants from U.S. Dept. Of Education, College Navigator, Undergraduate Admissions, 2015- 2016	
College	Percent admitted who enrolled	College	Average net price family with $0 to $30,000 income
Harvard	79%	Harvard	$ 3,294
Yale	69%	Yale	$ 5,171
Pennsylvania	68%	Pennsylvania	$ 4,939
Princeton	68%	Princeton	$ 2,469
Columbia	62%	Columbia	$ 9,481
Brown	56%	Brown	$ 5,849
Cornell	52%	Cornell	$ 16,751
Dartmouth	51%	Dartmouth	$ 7,847
Ivy League Avg.	63%	Ivy League Avg.	$ 6,975

Lower Test Scores and GPAs in Selective Colleges

For statistics on page 206.

An SAT reading score of 600 is at the 79th percentile; see http://www.collegeboard.com/prod_downloads/highered/ra/sat/SATPercentileRanks.pdf or https://collegereadiness.collegeboard.org/pdf/understanding-sat-scores-2016.pdf (as of 6-2-2017). An ACT composite score of 23 is at the 69th percentile as a cumulative measure for years 2014, 2015, and 2016; see http://www.act.org/content/dam/act/unsecured/documents/NormsChartMCandComposite-Web2016-17.pdf (as of 6-2-2017)

Test scores and GPAs are reported in the Common Data Set (CDS), in Section C9, which most colleges publish. CDSs show GPAs, ACT test scores and SAT test scores, if reported. Because some students submit both, I didn't calculate both tests in case of overlap when looking at one college. Thus, my totals have an undercount of equivalent ACT test scores. College statistics cited on page 206 were from the following years of the CDS; Brown 2016-17; CalTech 2016-17; Cornell 2016-17; Dartmouth 2016-17; Harvard 2014-15; Georgetown 2015-16; MIT 2015-16; New York Univ. 2015-15; Pennsylvania 2015-16; Princeton 2016-17; UC Berkeley 2016-17; and Yale 2015-16. Columbia does not publish a CDS, as of 6-2-2017 and apparently does not publish these scores in any source. If Columbia's admissions are like the rest of the Ivies, Columbia has admitted students with a 599 English score.

And the Highest Scores in the U.S. are at...

CalTech is the only college I found with no 599 scores in a published source showing the full range of scores of admitted students. So CalTech's scores are the U.S.'s highest, perhaps, although I didn't average the overall CDS stats by percentages of students within the ranges.

Grades and Scores: One Example for Success

This is a copy of the actual high school grade and score transcript from the student, John, in the story (p.15). John was from rural Arizona, in a moderate-income high school, which had a strong offering of AP and IB classes, although often only 5 to 10 students were in each class. Note that he took harder classes from freshman year through to senior year, but also took some regular classes as well. He wasn't a straight A student, getting several Bs. Note the strong increase in test scores in a three-month period, due to John's being more attentive to the test.

```
                                           Sex    Male
                                           DOB
PO Box                        AZ           SSN
      AZ                                   Entry Date
Phone: (520)            Parent/Guardian    Exit Date
Fax: (520)              Mr & Mrs           Graduation
```

ACADEMIC HISTORY

DATE	GL	TITLE	MARK	CREDIT	DATE	GL	TITLE	MARK	CREDIT
		High School		**AZ**			**High School**		**AZ**
12/10	09	Algebra I	100	0.500	12/13	12	IB/AP Calculus	98	0.500
		Geometry	98	0.500			IB/AP English 12	97	0.500
		Pre-AP Biology	93	0.500			IB/AP History of the Americas	97	0.500
		Pre-AP English 9	92	0.500			IB/AP Spanish 4	95	0.500
		Pre-AP Wld Hist & Geog	91	0.500			Interscholastic Athletics - Boys	100	0.500
		Spanish 1	89	0.500			Teacher Assistant	P	0.500
05/11	09	Algebra I	93	0.500	05/14	12	IB/AP Calculus	96	0.500
		Pre-AP Biology	91	0.500			IB/AP English 12	98	0.500
		Pre-AP English 9	87	0.500			IB/AP History of the Americas	95	0.500
		Pre-AP Geometry	90	0.500			IB/AP Spanish 4	99	0.500
		Pre-AP Wld Hist & Geog	95	0.500			Intro to Painting	98	0.500
		Spanish 1	83	0.500			Teacher Assistant	P	0.500
12/11	10	Comprehensive Health	91	0.500			**ACT**		
		Pre-AP Algebra II	94	0.500	04/13	11	ACT Composite	24	
		Pre-AP Chemistry	95	0.500			ACT English	25	
		Pre-AP English 10	93	0.500			ACT Math	27	
		Reteach/Enrich	P	0.250			ACT Reading	20	
		Spanish 2	88	0.500			ACT Science Reasoning	23	
		Weight Training	95	0.500					
05/12	10	Art I	96	0.500			**SAT I/II**		
		Pre-AP Algebra II	96	0.500	10/13	12	SAT I Critical Reading	640	
		Pre-AP Chemistry	93	0.500			SAT I Math	620	
		Pre-AP English 10	95	0.500			SAT I Writing	660	
		Reteach/Enrich	P	0.250	11/13		SAT II Amer History/SocStud	640	
		Spanish 2	90	0.500			SAT II Math Level II	660	
		Weight Training	100	0.500	12/13		SAT I Critical Reading	600	
12/12	11	IB/AP English 11	90	0.500			SAT I Math	720	
		IB/AP US/AZ History	91	0.500			SAT I Writing	630	
		Pre-AP Physics	96	0.500	01/14		SAT I Critical Reading	710	
		Pre-AP Pre-Calculus	95	0.500			SAT I Math	740	
		Pre-AP Spanish 3	86	0.500			SAT I Writing	570	
		Reteach/Enrich	P	0.250					
		Teacher Assistant	P	0.500			**SERVICE LEARNING HOURS**		
05/13	11	IB/AP English 11	94	0.500	01/12	10	TOTAL: 53 hours		
		IB/AP US/AZ History	93	0.500					
		Pre-AP Physics	96	0.500			**VACCINATIONS**		
		Pre-AP Pre-Calculus	94	0.500					
		Pre-AP Spanish 3	90	0.500					
		Reteach/Enrich	P	0.250					
		Teacher Assistant	P	0.500					

ACADEMIC STANDING						AUTHORIZATION
As of:	Total Credits	GPA Credits	GPA	Class Rank		X

Title — Registrar
Date — 07/01/14

Tyler Technologies, Inc.
Schoolmaster Student Information Systems

Cancelling SAT Tests and ACT Tests

For the SAT Test

You can skip the test on test day. It will be as if you never registered. You lose your fee. You can cancel the test while still in the test room with the proctor before you leave the test room. A cancellation must be either done at the test on test day, or must arrive at the SAT office before midnight Wednesday by 11:59 p.m. Eastern Time, one minute before midnight, via fax; or by overnight service sent on Tuesday, not email. There is no online or email cancellation.

An SAT test cancellation is permanent and the student never finds out what the score was. With the SAT test, after this Wednesday, midnight deadline passes, you cannot cancel the score. After that, the score is permanent for colleges that request all scores.

A school-given SAT test: A school-paid, district-paid or state-paid SAT test can be cancelled in the same manner, per SAT staff I spoke with on the SAT helpline on 10-1-2017, although this isn't noted on the College Board website.

For the ACT Test

You can skip the test on test day. It will be as if you never registered. You lose your fee. You can cancel the test while still in the test room by informing the proctor before you leave the test room, both for a school-paid test and for a student-paid test.

After a score is cancelled in writing, the ACT removes the record permanently. A student may also request that a school remove a cancelled ACT test from his or her transcript, as it does not exist in ACT records anymore. The option to cancel in writing after test day applies only to ACT tests that a student signs up and pays for.

A school-given ACT test: A school-paid, district-paid or state-paid ACT test cannot be cancelled after a student leaves the test room, as per the instruction booklet. If a college requires all ACT scores, it will be reported.

The Stall on the ACT Score

You can in effect stall your ACT score reports to see how well you did on a test you pay for, but you must skip the free college reports to do so. You first either do not list colleges, or cancel the college reports (but not the test) by Thursday at noon the week after the test. Delete the college codes for that test date on your ACT account. The student still gets the score, but it was not reported to the colleges.

After seeing the ACT score, a student can delete a bad score permanently by contacting the ACT in writing.

If the ACT score is adequate or better than expected, it can then be reported to the colleges for a fee. Some colleges always require all scores to be reported, so you don't have a choice with them anyway, except to cancel the ACT test completely.

All ACT Cancelled Tests & SAT Cancelled Tests Cease to Exist

For either the ACT test or the SAT test, with a full cancellation within the proper deadlines, colleges will not know that a student took that test or that he or she cancelled that test. It is as if the student never took the test. Regarding reporting, test results paid for by the student are the property of the student, not of the high school or a college, thus if you cancel a test completely from the record that is your right and it may be removed from your transcript as well.

For colleges that want all scores, report all scores, perhaps explaining the circumstances of a very bad score.

A cancellation may be proper when:

◆ Two or more test dates, preferably, are still available. If only one more test date is available, then the student is putting all eggs in that next basket, making it riskier to cancel a test.

◆ For whatever reason, such as illness, tragedy, an emergency or a complete lack of preparation, the student did not property finish the test, or left many questions unread, guessing on a lot of the test.

◆ The student will be ready for the next test, as circumstances should change so the student will complete some practice and study.

In such scenarios, perhaps the student might do best to skip or cancel a test. Again, it may be just as well to take the test if you can keep your concentration, as the score may be better than expected and if it is low, it will be overlooked for a higher score on an earlier, or later test. Mention any special circumstances in your college application.

MEMO

To: Middle School & High School counselors, honors
       teachers, principals and administrators:

Important Reasons to Schedule PSAT 8/9 test, PSAT 10 tests
and Pre-ACT tests.

   Working-class kids in your schools deserve as level a playing field as
possible for success, including being able to apply to top colleges with good
test scores. When these scores count for so much, are even your best students
getting shortchanged by taking the tests unprepared? Give them, especially
your star pupils, a heads-up with practice tests in earlier grades and the
customized guidance that's included with the test results. Private schools and
wealthy districts know this and don't hold back.

   Set up these tests. Start in the 8th grade with the PSAT 8/9 exam. The
rules allow any student to take any test in any grade. Even if only a few kids do
so to start, they deserve the option. Boost the numbers by encouraging bright,
serious and promising students to take the tests. Explain that the scores are not
reported to colleges. Pay the fee. (For the benefit, it's cheap.) Make it the norm,
not the exception. These tests inform and prod students (and parents) in the
earlier grades so the students can get higher scores junior and senior year.
Higher scores and more students going to better colleges helps your school's
reputation and your career.

   Concerns about too much emphasis on tests are valid. You may promote
test-optional colleges. For many colleges, like it or not, however, scores matter.
Students can decide for themselves. At the very least, have a procedure to
inform students that they can take these tests in another district. Give students
these benefits. After receiving the acceptance letters, they'll thank you, and
you'll be happy for them.

The following are data noted from Common Data Sets (CDS) for selective public colleges. The data are used for an estimate shown on page 219 of selective college quartiles. (The admission rate is not in the CDS, but is figured for your information.)

Admissions Examples, Enrolled 1ˢᵗ year students		
University of California – Berkeley 2015-2016		
Source of CDS: http://opa.berkeley.edu/sites/ default/files/uc_berkeley_cds_2015-16_8-3-2016.pdf		
(C1) Freshmen: Applied: 78,924 - Admitted: 12,048	Admission Rate:	= 15.26%
(C9) Type of Exam	25ᵗʰ Percentile	75ᵗʰPercentile
SAT® Exam Critical Reading	610	730
SAT® Exam Math	640	770
ACT® Exam Composite	29	34
% of freshmen in each test score range	SAT® Critical Reading	SAT® Math
700-800	40%	58%
600-699	38%	28%
500-599	16%	12%
400-499	4%	3%
300-399	<1%	<1%
% of freshmen in each test score range	ACT® Composite	
30-36	72%	
24-29	21%	
18-23	7%	
12-17	<1%	
Admissions Examples, Enrolled 1ˢᵗ year students		
Georgia Institute of Technology 2015-2016		
Source of CDS: http://www.irp.gatech.edu/common-data-set (Select 2015-2016)		
(C1) Freshmen: Applied: 27,277 - Admitted: 8,775	Admission Rate:	= 32.16%
(C9)Type of Exam	25ᵗʰ Percentile	75ᵗʰPercentile
SAT® Exam Critical Reading	630	730
SAT® Exam Math	680	770
ACT® Exam Composite	30	33
% of freshmen in each test score range	SAT® Critical Reading	SAT® Math
700-800	40.30%	65.94%
600-699	48.31%	29.80%
500-599	10.46%	3.84%
400-499	0.89%	0.38%
300-399	0.04%	0.04%
% of freshmen in each test score range	ACT® Composite	
30-36	80.81%	
24-29	17.89%	
18-23	1.06%	
12-17	0.24%	
Admissions Examples, Enrolled 1ˢᵗ year students		
University of Michigan 2015-2016		
Source of CDS: http://obp.umich.edu/wp-content/uploads/pubdata/cds/cds_2015-2016_umaa.pdf		
(C1) Freshmen: Applied: 51,761 - Admitted: 13,584	Admission Rate:	= 26.24%
(C9) Type of Exam	25ᵗʰ Percentile	75ᵗʰPercentile
SAT® Exam Critical Reading	630	730
SAT® Exam Math	660	770
ACT® Exam Composite	29	33

(Univ. of Michigan continued.) % of freshmen in each test score range	SAT® Critical Reading	SAT® Math
700-800	39%	60%
600-699	47%	31%
500-599	13%	8%
400-499	2%	1%
300-399	0.1%	0.1%
% of freshmen in each test score range	ACT® Composite	
30-36	72%	
24-29	21%	
18-23	7%	
12-17	<1%	
Admissions Examples, Enrolled 1st year students		
University of Texas -Austin 2015-2016		
Source of CDS: https://utexas.app.box.com/v/CDS2015		
(C1) Freshmen: Applied: 43,592/Admitted: 17,006	Admission Rate:	= 39.01%
(C9) Type of Exam	25th Percentile	75thPercentile
SAT® Exam Critical Reading	570	680
SAT® Exam Math	600	710
ACT® Exam Composite	26	31
% of freshmen in each test score range	SAT® Critical Reading	SAT® Math
700-800	23.2%	34.5%
600-699	42.0%	40.7%
500-599	26.8%	20.6%
400-499	7.4%	3.8%
300-399	0.6%	0.4%
% of freshmen in each test score range	ACT® Composite	
30-36	51.1%	
24-29	38.0%	
18-23	9.7%	
12-17	1.2%	
Admissions Examples, Enrolled 1st year students		
University of Virginia 2015-2016		
Source of CDS: http://ias.virginia.edu/cds-2015-16		
(C1) Freshmen: Applied: 30,840/Admitted: 9,186	Admission Rate:	= 29.78%
(C9) Type of Exam	25th Percentile	75thPercentile
SAT® Exam Critical Reading	620	720
SAT® Exam Math	630	740
ACT® Exam Composite	29	33
% of freshmen in each test score range	SAT® Critical Reading	SAT® Math
700-800	36%	45%
600-699	48%	41%
500-599	14%	12%
400-499	2%	2%
300-399	0%	0%
% of freshmen in each test score range	ACT® Composite	
30-36	67%	
24-29	29%	
18-23	4%	
12-17	0%	

Admissions Examples, Enrolled 1st year students		
College of William and Mary (Virginia) 2015-2016		
Source of CDS: http://www.wm.edu/offices/ir/documents/cds/cds_1516_part_c.pdf		
(C1) Freshmen: Applied: 14,952 - Admitted: 5,513	Admission Rate:	= 34.46%
(C9) Type of Exam	25th Percentile	75thPercentile
SAT® Exam Critical Reading	630	730
SAT® Exam Math	630	730
ACT® Exam Composite	28	32
% of freshmen in each test score range	SAT® Critical Reading	SAT® Math
700-800	41.90%	38.70%
600-699	43.80%	46.10%
500-599	13.56%	13.56%
400-499	0.74%	1.64%
300-399	0%	0%
% of freshmen in each test score range	ACT® Composite	
30-36	63.85%	
24-29	34.19%	
18-23	1.96%	
12-17	0%	

☞ Index ✍

☞ Endnotes ✍

[1] U.S. Department of Education, College Score Card (https://collegescorecard.ed.gov/search/?control=public&control=private&control =profit&sort=salary:desc&page=0 as of 10-20-2017) College Scorecard shows income from earnings statements for average types of students, ten years after enrolling, which is further explained on pages 41-42 and below.

In fairness to all colleges, including Helene Fuld College of Nursing, Stevens Institute of Technology and Yale University, the College Scorecard survey leaves out those who used with no federal loans or grants, which likely are wealthier students. Including such students could increase the overall average for each college, perhaps by a lot. The statisticians for College Scorecard say as much on page 23 of the Data Documentation for College Scorecard (Version: September 2017), "... so figures may not be representative of institutions with a low proportion of Title IV - eligible students." see:

https://collegescorecard.ed.gov/assets/FullDataDocumentation.pdf.

But, if income statements were averaged by all enrollees for all colleges, then it can get less representative for comparisons which are helpful to average students. For example, Harvard's average would include the billionaire incomes of Bill Gates, Paul Allen and Mark Zuckerberg, along with the many other billionaires and multi-millionaires who have attended Harvard. Is that a fair comparison? How would billionaire Warren Buffet's income affect the income average at the University of Nebraska, where he attended?

Nationally, of all students, about 70% do use federal loans or aid (see footnote #9). Thus, I conclude that the College Scorecard's income figures based on students who used a federal loan or grant program is a fair comparison of income results between colleges for similar types of students, those of more average means, not those coming from already wealthy families who could pay $250,000 for college with no loan. The College Scorecard estimate has validity for most U.S. students.

[2] "Estimating the Return to College Selectivity over the Career Using Administrative Earning Data," © 2011 by Stacy Dale and Alan B. Krueger. Working Paper 17159, http://www.nber.org/papers/w17159, National Bureau of Economic Research, 1050 Massachusetts Avenue, Cambridge, MA 02138, June 2011.

[3] U.S. Census, Educational Attainment of the Population 25 Years and Over, by Selected Characteristics: 2014 Table 2-01. (https://www.census.gov/data/tables/2014/demo/educational-attainment/cps-detailed-tables.html) Select Table 2 – Both.
2014 only
209,287,000 Population 25 years and over,

42,256,000	Attained bachelor's degree	20%
20,790,000	Attained associates degree	10%
17,960,000	Attained master's degree	9%
3,174,000	Attained professional degree	2%
3,719,000	Attained doctorate degree	2%
	Total	43%

4 By most successful, it means the total worldwide box office that is the highest, which as of 1-29-2017, is reported by Wikipedia as being held by Steven Spielberg at $9,246 billion; https://en.wikipedia.org/wiki/List_of_highest-grossing_directors.

5 From www.collegescorecard.ed.gov. As of 10-4-2017, when one sorts for all colleges and selects Salary After Attending, the salary bar graph indicates about $35,000 for the median earnings on page 83 of that sort. This is compiled as described on the website, Version: September 2017. On the home page, at the bottom, click on College Scorecard Data | v1.10.5. then Data Documentation, Documentation Report, which on p. 24 states: "Earnings are defined as the sum of wages and deferred compensation from all non-duplicate W-2 forms received for each individual, plus positive self-employment earnings from Schedule SE. Data are available for each year starting six years after a student enrolls in college, up to 10 years after the student enrolls; enrollment dates are estimated based on FAFSA self-reporting, as with the completion rate cohort construction described above." I did not find the earnings median figure listed, thus I used of the bar graph on page 83 of the Salary After Attending sort as an approximate median figure.
see https://collegescorecard.ed.gov/assets/FullDataDocumentation.pdf.

6 From Reuters Investigates, July 25, 2017, by Michelle Conlin, "Degrees of Debt: Student loan borrowers, herded into default, face a relentless collector: the U.S." (https://www.reuters.com/investigates/special-report/usa-studentloans/)

7 U.S. Department of Education, College Score Card, https://collegescorecard.ed.gov

8 U.S. Department of Labor, U.S. Bureau of Labor Statistics, Table on Earnings and unemployment rates by educational attainment; Source: Current Population Survey (http://www.bls.gov/emp/ep_table_001.htm on 10-1-2017) Last Modified Date: April 20, 2017. Data is for people age 25 and over. Earnings are for full-time wage and salaried workers.

9 See Footnote #10.

10 From www.collegescorecard.ed.gov and nces.ed.gov/collegenavigator (U.S. Dept. of Education) as of 10-13-17. The College Scorecard salary survey does not include students that didn't use a federal loan or grant, so the wealthiest students who used no federal loan are not included, which could lower a college's salary average. Nationally, about 70% of students used a federal loan or grant per the report of Sept. 2015, (Updated Jan. 2017), "Using Federal Data To Measure And Improve The Performance Of U.S. Institutions Of Higher Education." p. 26, Figure 3-3; (https://collegescorecard.ed.gov/assets/UsingFederalDataToMeasureAndImprove Performance.pdf.). Since 70% of students use federal loans or aid, the Scorecard earnings average is a fair comparison for average-types of students who go to college. Also, see footnote #1.
The College Scorecard, this author concludes, shows results for average students in a valid manner, covering a large sample of students at most colleges, and using figures from actual W-2s, 1099s, etc., for income from the IRS, indicating a broad-based survey with reasonably accurate income information.

11 "Estimating the Return to College Selectivity over the Career Using Administrative Earning Data," © 2011 by Stacy Dale and Alan B. Krueger. Working Paper 17159, http://www.nber.org/papers/w17159, National Bureau of Economic Research, 1050 Massachusetts Avenue, Cambridge, MA 02138, June 2011.
Readers, please note that the report by Dale and Krueger has been quoted in various articles and books, including by me, as making a valid conclusion. Still, other

researchers have raised related questions. As I will explain, these questions, do not, in my conclusion, invalidate Dale and Krueger's conclusions.

To be thorough, I will provide the additional questions and findings of the other researchers and discuss them, as follows. Caroline M. Hoxby writes in "The Changing Selectivity of American Colleges," NBER Working Paper No. 15446, issued in October 2009, National Bureau of Economic Research, 1050 Massachusetts Avenue, Cambridge, MA (www.nber.org/papers/w15446.pfd), on page 21, that Dale and Krueger's comparison "is much less credible" because only 1 out of 10 such students do not choose the fancy college, which she writes is "a very odd choice. These are students who know that they could choose a much more selective college and who have already expressed interest in a much more selective college (they applied). Yet, they choose differently than 9 out of 10 students. Almost certainly, these odd students are characterized by omitted variables that affect both their college decision and their later life outcomes." I conclude that as the 10% had equal earnings as compared to the other 90% who had the benefits of a fancy college then their life outcomes were quite good, whatever the omitted variables they had for their reasons for choosing a state college over an Ivy League college. The reasons might have not been so "odd" whatsoever, perhaps to remain near an ill family member, maintain an important courtship, or to save a lot of money, for example.

Hoxby on page 20 points to researcher Mark Hoekstra, who uses a different type of comparison than that of Dale and Krueger. In "The Effect of Attending the Flagship State University on Earnings: A Discontinuity-Based Approach," August 24, 2009, by Mark Hoekstra, University of Pittsburg, Hoekstra compares earnings of students who just got into a flagship state university to those who were just below the admission curve and not admitted. He found earnings for the flagship university students to be 20% higher.

I conclude that those that are similar types of students, but the earnings difference of 20%, while fairly substantial, is not so drastic as to prove that the flagship university was such of a dramatic game-changing experience for similar students. The 20% salary increase could show that flagship colleges offer good opportunities to students who made the selections cut to a flagship college. It could mean that those who made the cut had shown slightly higher accomplishments and success traits to the admissions officers, and those traits, perhaps combined with the additional resources of the flagship college, translated later into the 20% higher earnings. But a 20 % difference in salary is not so drastic as would be 40% higher earnings, for example, for people who got in, compared to people who were just left out. Are Ivies and flagship colleges good places? Yes, but for similar types of students with successful traits, good qualifications and higher levels of ambition, it's not as if earnings are double for everyone who gets in or doom for everyone who goes elsewhere.

[12] "Estimating the Return to College Selectivity over the Career Using Administrative Earning Data," © 2011 by Stacy Dale and Alan B. Krueger. Working Paper 17159, http://www.nber.org/papers/w17159, National Bureau of Economic Research, 1050 Massachusetts Avenue, Cambridge, MA 02138, June 2011, page 1 and page 24.
[13] Page 24, Ibid.
[14] From ACT, Inc., chart of "National Distributions of Cumulative Percents for ACT Test Scores ACT-Tested High School Graduates from 2013, 2014 and 2015," which lists at the 24th percentile of U.S. students a composite score of 16 and at the 74th percentile of U.S. students lists a composite score of 24.
(http://www.act.org/content/dam/act/unsecured/documents/

NormsChartMCandComposite-Web2015-16.pdf)

[15] Virginia Tech reports SAT test scores (reading mid-range 540-640 and math mid-range 560-680 per College Navigator 11-20-2017), so the ACT test mid-range is an estimate based on the College Board score conversion concordance.

[16] Some 1,300,000 U.S. grade-school and high-school students reside in shared or doubled-up housing, motels or shelters. Source: U.S. Department of Education, National Center for Education Statistics, https://nces.ed.gov/programs/digest/d16/tables/dt16_204.75d.asp, school year 2014-15, (as of 7-25-2017).

[17] From U.S. Census, Percent of the Population 25 Years and Over with a Bachelor's Degree or Higher by Sex, Race, and Hispanic Origin, for the United States: 1940 to 2000 (https://www.census.gov/data/tables/2000/dec/phc-t-41.html) Select Table 4.

1940 only

Race	Percent	
White	4.9	
Black	1.3	
Asian	4.0	
Native	0.8	
Total	11.0	For recent total of 33% for higher degrees see Endnote #3.

[18] Stanford social psychology professor Carol Dweck's research is among studies reported on by David L. Kirp in the New York Times in his articles, "Nudges That Help Struggling Students Succeed," Oct. 29, 2016 online (https://www.nytimes.com/2016/10/30/opinion/nudges-that-help-struggling-students-succeed.html?emc=eta1&_r=0) and "Conquering the Freshman Fear of Failure," Aug. 20. 2016, online, (https://www.nytimes.com/2016/08/21/opinion/sunday/conquering-the-freshman-fear-of-failure.html)

[19] David L. Kirp in the New York Times in his articles, "Nudges That Help Struggling Students Succeed," Oct. 29, 2016 online. (https://www.nytimes.com/2016/10/30/opinion/nudges-that-help-struggling-students-succeed.html?emc=eta1&_r=0)

[20] David L. Kirp reports in the New York Times article "Conquering the Freshman Fear of Failure," Aug. 20, 2016 online, (https://www.nytimes.com/2016/08/21/opinion/sunday/conquering-the-freshman-fear-of-failure.html), on research by Gregory M. Walton and Geoffrey L. Cohen of Stanford that intelligence can grow with work. Kirp also cites Stanford's Carol Dweck conclusions on the growth mindset.

[21] "Estimating the Return to College Selectivity over the Career Using Administrative Earning Data," © 2011 by Stacy Dale and Alan B. Krueger. Working Paper 17159, http://www.nber.org/papers/w17159, National Bureau of Economic Research, 1050 Massachusetts Avenue, Cambridge, MA 02138, June 2011.

[22] In the Wikipedia article, "Academic Ranking of World Universities", https://en.wikipedia.org/wiki/Academic_Ranking_of_World_Universities see the Alternative Ranking from Academic Ranking of World Universities (ARWU). The Shanghai Ranking, is an annual publication of university rankings by Shanghai Ranking Consultancy. https://en.wikipedia.org/wiki/Academic_Ranking_of_World_Universities

[23] Advertisement by Arizona State Univ. in Arizona Daily Star, p. C4, May 7, 2017.

24 College Board website for Trends in Higher Education as of 8-19-2017, for Preliminary 2015-16 figures, Trends in Student Aid: Total Aid, Table 1A, Total Undergraduate Student Aid by Source and Type over Time. (https://trends.collegeboard.org/student-aid/figures-tables/total-undergraduate-student-aid-source-and-type-over-time) The 8th line, Private and Employer Grants (i.e. private scholarships) totaled $11.756 billion out of $184.091 billion, the 9th line, for Total Federal State, Institutional, and Private Aid, which is 6.38%. The total from the financial aid office would include federal tax credits and grants, which are not technically not college funds, but are in the federal aid category, not the private scholarship category.
25 https://collegereadiness.collegeboard.org/sat-subject-tests/taking-the-test/test-taking-tips (7-15-2017)
26 https://khanacademy.zendesk.com/hc/en-us/community/posts/245262167-SAT-Vocabulary (7-15-2017)
27 The 56,000 figure is from the annual National Merit Report for the 2014 test (www.nationalmerit.org as of 10-1-2017) For 50 various top colleges, the 100,000 figure is rounded up from the 91,249 total from Table A-1 on page 368, as Table A-1 includes several small colleges as part of the 50. If one were to replace several of the very small colleges in Table A-1 with large colleges (which would still be a fair list of 50 top colleges) the total of freshmen could go to 150,000. For 100 various top colleges, the 200,000 is rounded up from the 188,220 total of Tables A-1 and Table A-2 on page 370, as Table A-2 also includes many small colleges.
28 One mom took the SAT exam seven times in one year to better assist her son with his test. See Debbie Stier, *The Perfect Score Project: One Mother's Journey to Uncover the Secrets of the SAT,* (New York, Harmony Books, 2014)
From act.org look for the section Why Every Point Matters on the ACT Test. From act.org homepage (1) select ACT Test Overview near the middle of the screen (2) select Scores near top of screen (3) under Content on left of screen select Should I Retest and look for Why Every-Point-Matters on the ACT Test.
29 Approximately 2 million students in the U.S. were incoming full-time freshmen in 2015 at 4-year colleges. Another 600,000 started full time at 2-year colleges. Source: U.S. Department of Education, National Center for Education Statistics, Digest of Education Statistics. 2016 Tables and Figures, Table 303.50 at: https://nces.ed.gov/programs/digest/d16/tables/dt16_303.50.asp
The average number of applicants was about 21,000 per college for fall 2015, for the table of 50 top colleges, those with the highest admissions yield rates per College Navigator as of 7-1-2017. As of 9-8-2017, no update to Table 303.50 was shown on the NCES website. The number of applicants is rising, as from fall 2015 to fall 2016 the total for the 120 colleges tabulated for this book by the author rose by about 143,000 applications, from about 2,930,000 to 3,073,000. Thus, when Table 303.50 is updated and with 2-year students removed, the total of full-time freshmen should increase above two million, but the variation from the percentage estimates in the book should not be highly significant.
30 From the Digest of Education Statistics, U.S. National Center for Education Statistics, Table 105.50, for years 2013-2014 for 4-year colleges; 691 public colleges and 1,587 non-profit colleges total 2,278. For-profit colleges are not included. (https://nces.ed.gov/programs/digest/d15/tables/dt15_105.50.asp) as of 6-5-2017.
31 Ibid.
32 Regarding group of colleges and admissions ratios: The example of one set group of applicants and one set group of colleges having a higher matriculation

(enrollment) rate is valid, as shown by the medical college example. It also applies, I conclude, in a valid way with a group of top colleges, even with one statistical variation from the medical example, as follows. Although a group of 50 selective colleges would have applicants who have duplicate applications to the group of 50, for example, and who receive several yes letters from colleges within the group of 50, some will then choose a college outside of the group of 50. This isn't the case with medical schools, as the matriculation rate includes all applicants and colleges in the group, and none outside the group. So, yes, for any group of top colleges one would select, there is some dispersal to colleges not within the group occurring. This is while the settling-down is occurring within the overlapping applicants and colleges within the group. It still seems logical, that this overlap within a group of top, selective colleges is significant, (thus boosting the matriculation rate for the overlap group of applicants higher than the regular reported admission rates) even with some dispersal. Thus, we can tell students who join into the overlap group with extra valid applications to a group of colleges, that it may increase their odds of matriculation within that group.

33 https://blog.utc.edu/news/2014/11/robert-fisher-named-rhodes-scholar.

34 The Common Data Set (CDS) is a product of the Common Data Set initiative which is a collaborative effort among data providers in the higher education community and publishers as represented by the College Board, Peterson's, and U.S. News & World Report as per www.commondataset.org as of Nov. 22, 2016. The Common Data Set Initiative is not affiliated with, and does not endorse this book. For the Common Data Set for a college, a reader will find standardized test score ranges in Section C9. For example, look at the line in Section C9 for 500-599, which usually has a percentage of students listed for an exam score which is usually in the lower quartile.

35 The general estimate of admissions quartiles on page 169 is a model of a moderately-selective U.S. university which was made subjectively by only the author as a broad and general estimate based on general admissions data. Such   general data are provided by colleges in their publication of the annual Common Data Set (CDS) in Section C1 for applications and admissions and Section C9 for test scores. The data are in tables on pages 330-332. The CDS is a product of the Common Data Set Initiative which is a collaborative effort among data providers in the higher education community and publishers as represented by the College Board, Peterson's, and U.S. News & World Report as per www.commondataset.org as of Nov. 22, 2016.

Each Common Data Set (CDS) for each of the following government universities, was published by each university separately on one of each university's websites, on Nov. 21, 2016, as shown in the tables. Some categories with zero are not included. Data are for first-year enrolled students. The author's general estimate of quartiles on page 169 are not statistical averages, medians or means. The author's subjective model is meant for a broad guideline for readers and is not representative of any one college in the U.S. or of any of the government colleges whose data are listed on pages 330-332.

36 The following books document the U.S. academic achievement gaps between various types of students: John U. Ogbu, *Black American Students in an Affluent Suburb: A Study of Academic Disengagement* (Mahwah, NJ, Lawrence Erlbaum Associates, Inc.,2003), Abigail Thernstrom and Stephan Thernstrom, *No Excuses: Closing the Racial Gap in Learning* (New York, Simon & Shuster, 2003) and Christopher Jencks and Meredith Phillips, *The Black-White Test Score Gap,*

(Washington, DC, Brookings Institution Press, 1998)
37 Ibid.
38 http://admission.gatech.edu/freshman/institutional-fit (as of 7-5-2016)
39 https://www.census.gov/library/publications/2016/demo/p60-256.html (as of 7-4-2016
40 https://www.federalregister.gov/documents/2017/04/10/2017-07043/child-nutrition-programs-income-eligibility-guidelines
41 https://www.census.gov/data/tables/time-series/demo/income-poverty/historical-poverty-thresholds.html (2015, as of 7-4-2016)
42 https://nces.ed.gov/collegenavigator/ which is from the U.S. Government Department of Education, National Center for Education Statistics for 2015-16 as of 10-18-2017. From this site, the user types in a college name, selects the college from the list, selects NET PRICE (the 4th category in the list of information categories) for net price by family income categories.
43 https://nces.ed.gov/collegenavigator/ which is from the U.S. Government Department of Education, National Center for Education Statistics for 2015-16 as of 10-18-2017. From this site, the user types in a college name, selects the college from the list, selects NET PRICE (the 4th category in the list of information categories) for net price by family income categories.
44 https://nces.ed.gov/collegenavigator/ which is from the U.S. Government Department of Education, National Center for Education Statistics for 2015-16 as of 10-18-2017. From this site, the user types in a college name, selects the college from the list, selects NET PRICE (the 4th category in the list of information categories) for net price by family income categories.
45 https://nces.ed.gov/collegenavigator/ which is from the U.S. Government Department of Education, National Center for Education Statistics for 2015-16 as of 10-18-2017. From this site, the user types in a college name, selects the college from the list, selects NET PRICE (the 4th category in the list of information categories) for net price by family income categories.
46 **Get a great pocket calendar:** You too can have a little black book for $6.98 to keep your important schedule all year. See the Walmart website for At-A-Glance Unruled Weekly Pocket Planner #: 552733526 with free pickup. This is the smallest one. The wire binder keeps it from falling apart. Use a paper clip to flip to the current week (and hold your business card). If you don't want to be this cool, fine, use your phone.
47 The sources for the approximate figures are as follows from the U.S. Government Department of Education, National Center for Education Statistics: Approximately 18.6 million total undergraduate students in the U.S. attended some type of college in 2015. These include four-year, two-year and less than two-year (public, non-profit and for-profit) and exclude masters, law and doctorate students. The top 40, top 25 and top 15 selections are general selections made by the author by looking at various ranking lists, to be used for approximate statistical totals, not for college comparisons. These selections of the top 40 exclude most small universities (except Caltech) and include several very large public universities. Thus, the top college enrollments would be even lower if one were to include exclusive small colleges in the top 15 to top 40 lists. The author's top 40, Top 25 and Top 15 enrollment figures came from the U.S. Government College Scorecard undergraduate enrollment figures for each college from the College Scorecard web site as of 11-7-2016 and are listed in the Appendix (p. 324).U.S. Government Department of Education, National Center for Education Statistics All Trade Schools, 2-year, 4 year = 18,600,000 total undergraduate students are a total of 472,000 trade school-students [471,998 students at non-degree-granting institutions from Table 303.20 year 2013 and

column #11) of the Digest of Education Statistics 2014;
http://nces.ed.gov/programs/digest/d14/tables/dt14_303.20.asp?referrer=report]
plus 18,155,000 undergraduate students for 2-year and 4-year colleges from Table
303.70; 2015, Column #2 Total.
https://nces.ed.gov/programs/digest/d13/tables/dt13_303.70.asp,   as   of   11-07-
2016.
All 4-Year colleges student enrollment of 10,745,000 is from the same Table 303.70,
4-year-institutions, 2015, Column #2 Total, as of 11-07-2016.
Percentages: 10,745,000/18,600,000=58% at 4-year colleges
389,125/18,600,000=2.1% at Top 40
135,290/18,600,000=0.7% at Top 15
62,019/18,600,000=0.3% at Ivy League.

CPSIA information can be obtained
at www.ICGtesting.com
Printed in the USA
FSHW011744010319
56033FS